C-1900   CAREER EXAMINATION SERIES

This is your
PASSBOOK for...

Cosmetology Instructor

Test Preparation Study Guide
Questions & Answers

COPYRIGHT NOTICE

This book is SOLELY intended for, is sold ONLY to, and its use is RESTRICTED to individual, bona fide applicants or candidates who qualify by virtue of having seriously filed applications for appropriate license, certificate, professional and/or promotional advancement, higher school matriculation, scholarship, or other legitimate requirements of education and/or governmental authorities.

This book is NOT intended for use, class instruction, tutoring, training, duplication, copying, reprinting, excerption, or adaptation, etc., by:

1) Other publishers
2) Proprietors and/or Instructors of "Coaching" and/or Preparatory Courses
3) Personnel and/or Training Divisions of commercial, industrial, and governmental organizations
4) Schools, colleges, or universities and/or their departments and staffs, including teachers and other personnel
5) Testing Agencies or Bureaus
6) Study groups which seek by the purchase of a single volume to copy and/or duplicate and/or adapt this material for use by the group as a whole without having purchased individual volumes for each of the members of the group
7) Et al.

Such persons would be in violation of appropriate Federal and State statutes.

PROVISION OF LICENSING AGREEMENTS – Recognized educational, commercial, industrial, and governmental institutions and organizations, and others legitimately engaged in educational pursuits, including training, testing, and measurement activities, may address request for a licensing agreement to the copyright owners, who will determine whether, and under what conditions, including fees and charges, the materials in this book may be used them. In other words, a licensing facility exists for the legitimate use of the material in this book on other than an individual basis. However, it is asseverated and affirmed here that the material in this book CANNOT be used without the receipt of the express permission of such a licensing agreement from the Publishers. Inquiries re licensing should be addressed to the company, attention rights and permissions department.

All rights reserved, including the right of reproduction in whole or in part, in any form or by any means, electronic or mechanical, including photocopying, recording, or by any information storage and retrieval system, without permission in writing from the Publisher.

Copyright © 2024 by
National Learning Corporation

212 Michael Drive, Syosset, NY 11791
(516) 921-8888 • www.passbooks.com
E-mail: info@passbooks.com

PUBLISHED IN THE UNITED STATES OF AMERICA

PASSBOOK® SERIES

THE *PASSBOOK® SERIES* has been created to prepare applicants and candidates for the ultimate academic battlefield – the examination room.

At some time in our lives, each and every one of us may be required to take an examination – for validation, matriculation, admission, qualification, registration, certification, or licensure.

Based on the assumption that every applicant or candidate has met the basic formal educational standards, has taken the required number of courses, and read the necessary texts, the *PASSBOOK® SERIES* furnishes the one special preparation which may assure passing with confidence, instead of failing with insecurity. Examination questions – together with answers – are furnished as the basic vehicle for study so that the mysteries of the examination and its compounding difficulties may be eliminated or diminished by a sure method.

This book is meant to help you pass your examination provided that you qualify and are serious in your objective.

The entire field is reviewed through the huge store of content information which is succinctly presented through a provocative and challenging approach – the question-and-answer method.

A climate of success is established by furnishing the correct answers at the end of each test.

You soon learn to recognize types of questions, forms of questions, and patterns of questioning. You may even begin to anticipate expected outcomes.

You perceive that many questions are repeated or adapted so that you can gain acute insights, which may enable you to score many sure points.

You learn how to confront new questions, or types of questions, and to attack them confidently and work out the correct answers.

You note objectives and emphases, and recognize pitfalls and dangers, so that you may make positive educational adjustments.

Moreover, you are kept fully informed in relation to new concepts, methods, practices, and directions in the field.

You discover that you are actually taking the examination all the time: you are preparing for the examination by "taking" an examination, not by reading extraneous and/or supererogatory textbooks.

In short, this PASSBOOK®, used directedly, should be an important factor in helping you to pass your test.

COSMETOLOGY INSTRUCTOR

Cosmetology instructors are responsible for teaching beauty school students the basics of cosmetology, and leading the class through the required coursework that prepares them for board exams and to work professionally in the field. In order for beauty school students to gain full understanding of the art and science of cosmetology, instructors must also be able to explain aspects of physiology and anatomy of the body as they relate to cosmetology. Furthermore, it is the cosmetology teacher's responsibility to ensure their students grasp the importance of safe practices for their clients, themselves and their work environments. This may be accomplished through a variety of teaching techniques and methods. You must supervise students as they learn new skills, and especially closely when they begin taking on real clients in the student salon.

A core responsibility of the cosmetology instructor is to prepare lesson plans and demonstrations for their classes that align with the state's curriculum requirements. The course of study should include objectives for the program and the students, as well as structured daily lesson plans. Cosmetology instructors are often required to prepare and submit program budgets each year, as well as request materials and supplies for the classroom within that budget. Many schools ask their educators to get involved in the community and make connections with salons, representatives from the beauty business, conferences and other relevant people to help students network and learn from real working professionals.

You must ensure the proper equipment, tools, textbooks and supplemental materials are available to students so you can properly prepare their students for cosmetology exams and careers. It is the duty of cosmetology teachers to monitor and track the progress and performance of each of their students. You must be able to identify problem areas for students and provide the necessary support to help their students master their lessons throughout the course of the program. You must be comfortable offering constructive feedback to students to help them improve, and you must be firm in implementing the policies and procedures in place for the school.

Beauty school teachers are expected to prepare students for entry-level employment in the business. As an educator, you must help students develop the skills, knowledge and professional traits to be successful in the trade. Some schools offer job placement services to recent graduates, and educators may be expected to facilitate those connections or provide letters of recommendation for students.

- Knowledge of multiple teaching methods, and education principles, practices and methodologies
- Understanding of competency-based curriculum, evaluation and grading
- Competency in administering tests and recording grades
- Good organizational skills for recording and reporting attendance and performance data
- Proficiency in developing a curriculum and creating daily lesson plans
- Credibility and authority as an expert in the beauty trade you're teaching
- Excellent written and verbal communication skills
- Ability to demonstrate hair, makeup, nails and/or skin care services and walk students through the procedures step-by-step

- Ability to lead class lectures and student discussions, coach and critique hands-on skills, and guide students through book learning and assignments
- Comfort and confidence delivering constructive and critical feedback to students
- Comfort interacting with many personality types, including angry, indifferent, challenging or emotional students or parents.
- Understanding of inventory management and budgeting for required materials
- Ability to recognize when students need more advanced training because they're picking up the material quickly, and alternatively, when students are struggling and need additional help and could benefit from a beauty tutor.

HOW TO TAKE A TEST

I. YOU MUST PASS AN EXAMINATION

A. WHAT EVERY CANDIDATE SHOULD KNOW

Examination applicants often ask us for help in preparing for the written test. What can I study in advance? What kinds of questions will be asked? How will the test be given? How will the papers be graded?

As an applicant for a civil service examination, you may be wondering about some of these things. Our purpose here is to suggest effective methods of advance study and to describe civil service examinations.

Your chances for success on this examination can be increased if you know how to prepare. Those "pre-examination jitters" can be reduced if you know what to expect. You can even experience an adventure in good citizenship if you know why civil service exams are given.

B. WHY ARE CIVIL SERVICE EXAMINATIONS GIVEN?

Civil service examinations are important to you in two ways. As a citizen, you want public jobs filled by employees who know how to do their work. As a job seeker, you want a fair chance to compete for that job on an equal footing with other candidates. The best-known means of accomplishing this two-fold goal is the competitive examination.

Exams are widely publicized throughout the nation. They may be administered for jobs in federal, state, city, municipal, town or village governments or agencies.

Any citizen may apply, with some limitations, such as the age or residence of applicants. Your experience and education may be reviewed to see whether you meet the requirements for the particular examination. When these requirements exist, they are reasonable and applied consistently to all applicants. Thus, a competitive examination may cause you some uneasiness now, but it is your privilege and safeguard.

C. HOW ARE CIVIL SERVICE EXAMS DEVELOPED?

Examinations are carefully written by trained technicians who are specialists in the field known as "psychological measurement," in consultation with recognized authorities in the field of work that the test will cover. These experts recommend the subject matter areas or skills to be tested; only those knowledges or skills important to your success on the job are included. The most reliable books and source materials available are used as references. Together, the experts and technicians judge the difficulty level of the questions.

Test technicians know how to phrase questions so that the problem is clearly stated. Their ethics do not permit "trick" or "catch" questions. Questions may have been tried out on sample groups, or subjected to statistical analysis, to determine their usefulness.

Written tests are often used in combination with performance tests, ratings of training and experience, and oral interviews. All of these measures combine to form the best-known means of finding the right person for the right job.

II. HOW TO PASS THE WRITTEN TEST

A. NATURE OF THE EXAMINATION

To prepare intelligently for civil service examinations, you should know how they differ from school examinations you have taken. In school you were assigned certain definite pages to read or subjects to cover. The examination questions were quite detailed and usually emphasized memory. Civil service exams, on the other hand, try to discover your present ability to perform the duties of a position, plus your potentiality to learn these duties. In other words, a civil service exam attempts to predict how successful you will be. Questions cover such a broad area that they cannot be as minute and detailed as school exam questions.

In the public service similar kinds of work, or positions, are grouped together in one "class." This process is known as *position-classification*. All the positions in a class are paid according to the salary range for that class. One class title covers all of these positions, and they are all tested by the same examination.

B. FOUR BASIC STEPS

1) Study the announcement

How, then, can you know what subjects to study? Our best answer is: "Learn as much as possible about the class of positions for which you've applied." The exam will test the knowledge, skills and abilities needed to do the work.

Your most valuable source of information about the position you want is the official exam announcement. This announcement lists the training and experience qualifications. Check these standards and apply only if you come reasonably close to meeting them.

The brief description of the position in the examination announcement offers some clues to the subjects which will be tested. Think about the job itself. Review the duties in your mind. Can you perform them, or are there some in which you are rusty? Fill in the blank spots in your preparation.

Many jurisdictions preview the written test in the exam announcement by including a section called "Knowledge and Abilities Required," "Scope of the Examination," or some similar heading. Here you will find out specifically what fields will be tested.

2) Review your own background

Once you learn in general what the position is all about, and what you need to know to do the work, ask yourself which subjects you already know fairly well and which need improvement. You may wonder whether to concentrate on improving your strong areas or on building some background in your fields of weakness. When the announcement has specified "some knowledge" or "considerable knowledge," or has used adjectives like "beginning principles of…" or "advanced … methods," you can get a clue as to the number and difficulty of questions to be asked in any given field. More questions, and hence broader coverage, would be included for those subjects which are more important in the work. Now weigh your strengths and weaknesses against the job requirements and prepare accordingly.

3) Determine the level of the position

Another way to tell how intensively you should prepare is to understand the level of the job for which you are applying. Is it the entering level? In other words, is this the position in which beginners in a field of work are hired? Or is it an intermediate or advanced level? Sometimes this is indicated by such words as "Junior" or "Senior" in the class title. Other jurisdictions use Roman numerals to designate the level – Clerk I, Clerk II, for example. The word "Supervisor" sometimes appears in the title. If the level is not indicated by the title, check the description of duties. Will you be working under very close supervision, or will you have responsibility for independent decisions in this work?

4) Choose appropriate study materials

Now that you know the subjects to be examined and the relative amount of each subject to be covered, you can choose suitable study materials. For beginning level jobs, or even advanced ones, if you have a pronounced weakness in some aspect of your training, read a modern, standard textbook in that field. Be sure it is up to date and has general coverage. Such books are normally available at your library, and the librarian will be glad to help you locate one. For entry-level positions, questions of appropriate difficulty are chosen – neither highly advanced questions, nor those too simple. Such questions require careful thought but not advanced training.

If the position for which you are applying is technical or advanced, you will read more advanced, specialized material. If you are already familiar with the basic principles of your field, elementary textbooks would waste your time. Concentrate on advanced textbooks and technical periodicals. Think through the concepts and review difficult problems in your field.

These are all general sources. You can get more ideas on your own initiative, following these leads. For example, training manuals and publications of the government agency which employs workers in your field can be useful, particularly for technical and professional positions. A letter or visit to the government department involved may result in more specific study suggestions, and certainly will provide you with a more definite idea of the exact nature of the position you are seeking.

III. KINDS OF TESTS

Tests are used for purposes other than measuring knowledge and ability to perform specified duties. For some positions, it is equally important to test ability to make adjustments to new situations or to profit from training. In others, basic mental abilities not dependent on information are essential. Questions which test these things may not appear as pertinent to the duties of the position as those which test for knowledge and information. Yet they are often highly important parts of a fair examination. For very general questions, it is almost impossible to help you direct your study efforts. What we can do is to point out some of the more common of these general abilities needed in public service positions and describe some typical questions.

1) General information

Broad, general information has been found useful for predicting job success in some kinds of work. This is tested in a variety of ways, from vocabulary lists to questions about current events. Basic background in some field of work, such as sociology or economics, may be sampled in a group of questions. Often these are principles which have become familiar to most persons through exposure rather than through formal training. It is difficult to advise you how to study for these questions; being alert to the world around you is our best suggestion.

2) Verbal ability

An example of an ability needed in many positions is verbal or language ability. Verbal ability is, in brief, the ability to use and understand words. Vocabulary and grammar tests are typical measures of this ability. Reading comprehension or paragraph interpretation questions are common in many kinds of civil service tests. You are given a paragraph of written material and asked to find its central meaning.

3) Numerical ability

Number skills can be tested by the familiar arithmetic problem, by checking paired lists of numbers to see which are alike and which are different, or by interpreting charts and graphs. In the latter test, a graph may be printed in the test booklet which you are asked to use as the basis for answering questions.

4) Observation

A popular test for law-enforcement positions is the observation test. A picture is shown to you for several minutes, then taken away. Questions about the picture test your ability to observe both details and larger elements.

5) Following directions

In many positions in the public service, the employee must be able to carry out written instructions dependably and accurately. You may be given a chart with several columns, each column listing a variety of information. The questions require you to carry out directions involving the information given in the chart.

6) Skills and aptitudes

Performance tests effectively measure some manual skills and aptitudes. When the skill is one in which you are trained, such as typing or shorthand, you can practice. These tests are often very much like those given in business school or high school courses. For many of the other skills and aptitudes, however, no short-time preparation can be made. Skills and abilities natural to you or that you have developed throughout your lifetime are being tested.

Many of the general questions just described provide all the data needed to answer the questions and ask you to use your reasoning ability to find the answers. Your best preparation for these tests, as well as for tests of facts and ideas, is to be at your physical and mental best. You, no doubt, have your own methods of getting into an exam-taking mood and keeping "in shape." The next section lists some ideas on this subject.

IV. KINDS OF QUESTIONS

Only rarely is the "essay" question, which you answer in narrative form, used in civil service tests. Civil service tests are usually of the short-answer type. Full instructions for answering these questions will be given to you at the examination. But in case this is your first experience with short-answer questions and separate answer sheets, here is what you need to know:

1) **Multiple-choice Questions**

Most popular of the short-answer questions is the "multiple choice" or "best answer" question. It can be used, for example, to test for factual knowledge, ability to solve problems or judgment in meeting situations found at work.

A multiple-choice question is normally one of three types—
- It can begin with an incomplete statement followed by several possible endings. You are to find the one ending which *best* completes the statement, although some of the others may not be entirely wrong.
- It can also be a complete statement in the form of a question which is answered by choosing one of the statements listed.

- It can be in the form of a problem – again you select the best answer.

Here is an example of a multiple-choice question with a discussion which should give you some clues as to the method for choosing the right answer:

When an employee has a complaint about his assignment, the action which will *best* help him overcome his difficulty is to
    A. discuss his difficulty with his coworkers
    B. take the problem to the head of the organization
    C. take the problem to the person who gave him the assignment
    D. say nothing to anyone about his complaint

In answering this question, you should study each of the choices to find which is best. Consider choice "A" – Certainly an employee may discuss his complaint with fellow employees, but no change or improvement can result, and the complaint remains unresolved. Choice "B" is a poor choice since the head of the organization probably does not know what assignment you have been given, and taking your problem to him is known as "going over the head" of the supervisor. The supervisor, or person who made the assignment, is the person who can clarify it or correct any injustice. Choice "C" is, therefore, correct. To say nothing, as in choice "D," is unwise. Supervisors have and interest in knowing the problems employees are facing, and the employee is seeking a solution to his problem.

2) True/False Questions

The "true/false" or "right/wrong" form of question is sometimes used. Here a complete statement is given. Your job is to decide whether the statement is right or wrong.

SAMPLE: A roaming cell-phone call to a nearby city costs less than a non-roaming call to a distant city.

This statement is wrong, or false, since roaming calls are more expensive.

This is not a complete list of all possible question forms, although most of the others are variations of these common types. You will always get complete directions for answering questions. Be sure you understand *how* to mark your answers – ask questions until you do.

V. RECORDING YOUR ANSWERS

Computer terminals are used more and more today for many different kinds of exams.

For an examination with very few applicants, you may be told to record your answers in the test booklet itself. Separate answer sheets are much more common. If this separate answer sheet is to be scored by machine – and this is often the case – it is highly important that you mark your answers correctly in order to get credit.

An electronic scoring machine is often used in civil service offices because of the speed with which papers can be scored. Machine-scored answer sheets must be marked with a pencil, which will be given to you. This pencil has a high graphite content which responds to the electronic scoring machine. As a matter of fact, stray dots may register as answers, so do not let your pencil rest on the answer sheet while you are pondering the correct answer. Also, if your pencil lead breaks or is otherwise defective, ask for another.

Since the answer sheet will be dropped in a slot in the scoring machine, be careful not to bend the corners or get the paper crumpled.

The answer sheet normally has five vertical columns of numbers, with 30 numbers to a column. These numbers correspond to the question numbers in your test booklet. After each number, going across the page are four or five pairs of dotted lines. These short dotted lines have small letters or numbers above them. The first two pairs may also have a "T" or "F" above the letters. This indicates that the first two pairs only are to be used if the questions are of the true-false type. If the questions are multiple choice, disregard the "T" and "F" and pay attention only to the small letters or numbers.

Answer your questions in the manner of the sample that follows:

32. The largest city in the United States is
    A. Washington, D.C.
    B. New York City
    C. Chicago
    D. Detroit
    E. San Francisco

1) Choose the answer you think is best. (New York City is the largest, so "B" is correct.)
2) Find the row of dotted lines numbered the same as the question you are answering. (Find row number 32)
3) Find the pair of dotted lines corresponding to the answer. (Find the pair of lines under the mark "B.")
4) Make a solid black mark between the dotted lines.

VI. BEFORE THE TEST

Common sense will help you find procedures to follow to get ready for an examination. Too many of us, however, overlook these sensible measures. Indeed, nervousness and fatigue have been found to be the most serious reasons why applicants fail to do their best on civil service tests. Here is a list of reminders:

- Begin your preparation early – Don't wait until the last minute to go scurrying around for books and materials or to find out what the position is all about.
- Prepare continuously – An hour a night for a week is better than an all-night cram session. This has been definitely established. What is more, a night a week for a month will return better dividends than crowding your study into a shorter period of time.
- Locate the place of the exam – You have been sent a notice telling you when and where to report for the examination. If the location is in a different town or otherwise unfamiliar to you, it would be well to inquire the best route and learn something about the building.
- Relax the night before the test – Allow your mind to rest. Do not study at all that night. Plan some mild recreation or diversion; then go to bed early and get a good night's sleep.
- Get up early enough to make a leisurely trip to the place for the test – This way unforeseen events, traffic snarls, unfamiliar buildings, etc. will not upset you.
- Dress comfortably – A written test is not a fashion show. You will be known by number and not by name, so wear something comfortable.

- Leave excess paraphernalia at home – Shopping bags and odd bundles will get in your way. You need bring only the items mentioned in the official notice you received; usually everything you need is provided. Do not bring reference books to the exam. They will only confuse those last minutes and be taken away from you when in the test room.
- Arrive somewhat ahead of time – If because of transportation schedules you must get there very early, bring a newspaper or magazine to take your mind off yourself while waiting.
- Locate the examination room – When you have found the proper room, you will be directed to the seat or part of the room where you will sit. Sometimes you are given a sheet of instructions to read while you are waiting. Do not fill out any forms until you are told to do so; just read them and be prepared.
- Relax and prepare to listen to the instructions
- If you have any physical problem that may keep you from doing your best, be sure to tell the test administrator. If you are sick or in poor health, you really cannot do your best on the exam. You can come back and take the test some other time.

VII. AT THE TEST

The day of the test is here and you have the test booklet in your hand. The temptation to get going is very strong. Caution! There is more to success than knowing the right answers. You must know how to identify your papers and understand variations in the type of short-answer question used in this particular examination. Follow these suggestions for maximum results from your efforts:

1) Cooperate with the monitor

The test administrator has a duty to create a situation in which you can be as much at ease as possible. He will give instructions, tell you when to begin, check to see that you are marking your answer sheet correctly, and so on. He is not there to guard you, although he will see that your competitors do not take unfair advantage. He wants to help you do your best.

2) Listen to all instructions

Don't jump the gun! Wait until you understand all directions. In most civil service tests you get more time than you need to answer the questions. So don't be in a hurry. Read each word of instructions until you clearly understand the meaning. Study the examples, listen to all announcements and follow directions. Ask questions if you do not understand what to do.

3) Identify your papers

Civil service exams are usually identified by number only. You will be assigned a number; you must not put your name on your test papers. Be sure to copy your number correctly. Since more than one exam may be given, copy your exact examination title.

4) Plan your time

Unless you are told that a test is a "speed" or "rate of work" test, speed itself is usually not important. Time enough to answer all the questions will be provided, but this does not mean that you have all day. An overall time limit has been set. Divide the total time (in minutes) by the number of questions to determine the approximate time you have for each question.

5) Do not linger over difficult questions

If you come across a difficult question, mark it with a paper clip (useful to have along) and come back to it when you have been through the booklet. One caution if you do this – be sure to skip a number on your answer sheet as well. Check often to be sure that you have not lost your place and that you are marking in the row numbered the same as the question you are answering.

6) Read the questions

Be sure you know what the question asks! Many capable people are unsuccessful because they failed to *read* the questions correctly.

7) Answer all questions

Unless you have been instructed that a penalty will be deducted for incorrect answers, it is better to guess than to omit a question.

8) Speed tests

It is often better NOT to guess on speed tests. It has been found that on timed tests people are tempted to spend the last few seconds before time is called in marking answers at random – without even reading them – in the hope of picking up a few extra points. To discourage this practice, the instructions may warn you that your score will be "corrected" for guessing. That is, a penalty will be applied. The incorrect answers will be deducted from the correct ones, or some other penalty formula will be used.

9) Review your answers

If you finish before time is called, go back to the questions you guessed or omitted to give them further thought. Review other answers if you have time.

10) Return your test materials

If you are ready to leave before others have finished or time is called, take ALL your materials to the monitor and leave quietly. Never take any test material with you. The monitor can discover whose papers are not complete, and taking a test booklet may be grounds for disqualification.

VIII. EXAMINATION TECHNIQUES

1) Read the general instructions carefully. These are usually printed on the first page of the exam booklet. As a rule, these instructions refer to the timing of the examination; the fact that you should not start work until the signal and must stop work at a signal, etc. If there are any *special* instructions, such as a choice of questions to be answered, make sure that you note this instruction carefully.

2) When you are ready to start work on the examination, that is as soon as the signal has been given, read the instructions to each question booklet, underline any key words or phrases, such as *least, best, outline, describe* and the like. In this way you will tend to answer as requested rather than discover on reviewing your paper that you *listed without describing*, that you selected the *worst* choice rather than the *best* choice, etc.

3) If the examination is of the objective or multiple-choice type – that is, each question will also give a series of possible answers: A, B, C or D, and you are called upon to select the best answer and write the letter next to that answer on your answer paper – it is advisable to start answering each question in turn. There may be anywhere from 50 to 100 such questions in the three or four hours allotted and you can see how much time would be taken if you read through all the questions before beginning to answer any. Furthermore, if you come across a question or group of questions which you know would be difficult to answer, it would undoubtedly affect your handling of all the other questions.

4) If the examination is of the essay type and contains but a few questions, it is a moot point as to whether you should read all the questions before starting to answer any one. Of course, if you are given a choice – say five out of seven and the like – then it is essential to read all the questions so you can eliminate the two that are most difficult. If, however, you are asked to answer all the questions, there may be danger in trying to answer the easiest one first because you may find that you will spend too much time on it. The best technique is to answer the first question, then proceed to the second, etc.

5) Time your answers. Before the exam begins, write down the time it started, then add the time allowed for the examination and write down the time it must be completed, then divide the time available somewhat as follows:
   - If 3-1/2 hours are allowed, that would be 210 minutes. If you have 80 objective-type questions, that would be an average of 2-1/2 minutes per question. Allow yourself no more than 2 minutes per question, or a total of 160 minutes, which will permit about 50 minutes to review.
   - If for the time allotment of 210 minutes there are 7 essay questions to answer, that would average about 30 minutes a question. Give yourself only 25 minutes per question so that you have about 35 minutes to review.

6) The most important instruction is to *read each question* and make sure you know what is wanted. The second most important instruction is to *time yourself properly* so that you answer every question. The third most important instruction is to *answer every question*. Guess if you have to but include something for each question. Remember that you will receive no credit for a blank and will probably receive some credit if you write something in answer to an essay question. If you guess a letter – say "B" for a multiple-choice question – you may have guessed right. If you leave a blank as an answer to a multiple-choice question, the examiners may respect your feelings but it will not add a point to your score. Some exams may penalize you for wrong answers, so in such cases *only*, you may not want to guess unless you have some basis for your answer.

7) Suggestions
   a. Objective-type questions
      1. Examine the question booklet for proper sequence of pages and questions
      2. Read all instructions carefully
      3. Skip any question which seems too difficult; return to it after all other questions have been answered
      4. Apportion your time properly; do not spend too much time on any single question or group of questions

5. Note and underline key words – *all, most, fewest, least, best, worst, same, opposite*, etc.
6. Pay particular attention to negatives
7. Note unusual option, e.g., unduly long, short, complex, different or similar in content to the body of the question
8. Observe the use of "hedging" words – *probably, may, most likely*, etc.
9. Make sure that your answer is put next to the same number as the question
10. Do not second-guess unless you have good reason to believe the second answer is definitely more correct
11. Cross out original answer if you decide another answer is more accurate; do not erase until you are ready to hand your paper in
12. Answer all questions; guess unless instructed otherwise
13. Leave time for review

  b. Essay questions
    1. Read each question carefully
    2. Determine exactly what is wanted. Underline key words or phrases.
    3. Decide on outline or paragraph answer
    4. Include many different points and elements unless asked to develop any one or two points or elements
    5. Show impartiality by giving pros and cons unless directed to select one side only
    6. Make and write down any assumptions you find necessary to answer the questions
    7. Watch your English, grammar, punctuation and choice of words
    8. Time your answers; don't crowd material

8) Answering the essay question

Most essay questions can be answered by framing the specific response around several key words or ideas. Here are a few such key words or ideas:

M's: manpower, materials, methods, money, management
P's: purpose, program, policy, plan, procedure, practice, problems, pitfalls, personnel, public relations

  a. Six basic steps in handling problems:
    1. Preliminary plan and background development
    2. Collect information, data and facts
    3. Analyze and interpret information, data and facts
    4. Analyze and develop solutions as well as make recommendations
    5. Prepare report and sell recommendations
    6. Install recommendations and follow up effectiveness

  b. Pitfalls to avoid
    1. *Taking things for granted* – A statement of the situation does not necessarily imply that each of the elements is necessarily true; for example, a complaint may be invalid and biased so that all that can be taken for granted is that a complaint has been registered

2. *Considering only one side of a situation* – Wherever possible, indicate several alternatives and then point out the reasons you selected the best one
3. *Failing to indicate follow up* – Whenever your answer indicates action on your part, make certain that you will take proper follow-up action to see how successful your recommendations, procedures or actions turn out to be
4. *Taking too long in answering any single question* – Remember to time your answers properly

IX. AFTER THE TEST

Scoring procedures differ in detail among civil service jurisdictions although the general principles are the same. Whether the papers are hand-scored or graded by machine we have described, they are nearly always graded by number. That is, the person who marks the paper knows only the number – never the name – of the applicant. Not until all the papers have been graded will they be matched with names. If other tests, such as training and experience or oral interview ratings have been given, scores will be combined. Different parts of the examination usually have different weights. For example, the written test might count 60 percent of the final grade, and a rating of training and experience 40 percent. In many jurisdictions, veterans will have a certain number of points added to their grades.

After the final grade has been determined, the names are placed in grade order and an eligible list is established. There are various methods for resolving ties between those who get the same final grade – probably the most common is to place first the name of the person whose application was received first. Job offers are made from the eligible list in the order the names appear on it. You will be notified of your grade and your rank as soon as all these computations have been made. This will be done as rapidly as possible.

People who are found to meet the requirements in the announcement are called "eligibles." Their names are put on a list of eligible candidates. An eligible's chances of getting a job depend on how high he stands on this list and how fast agencies are filling jobs from the list.

When a job is to be filled from a list of eligibles, the agency asks for the names of people on the list of eligibles for that job. When the civil service commission receives this request, it sends to the agency the names of the three people highest on this list. Or, if the job to be filled has specialized requirements, the office sends the agency the names of the top three persons who meet these requirements from the general list.

The appointing officer makes a choice from among the three people whose names were sent to him. If the selected person accepts the appointment, the names of the others are put back on the list to be considered for future openings.

That is the rule in hiring from all kinds of eligible lists, whether they are for typist, carpenter, chemist, or something else. For every vacancy, the appointing officer has his choice of any one of the top three eligibles on the list. This explains why the person whose name is on top of the list sometimes does not get an appointment when some of the persons lower on the list do. If the appointing officer chooses the second or third eligible, the No. 1 eligible does not get a job at once, but stays on the list until he is appointed or the list is terminated.

X. HOW TO PASS THE INTERVIEW TEST

The examination for which you applied requires an oral interview test. You have already taken the written test and you are now being called for the interview test – the final part of the formal examination.

You may think that it is not possible to prepare for an interview test and that there are no procedures to follow during an interview. Our purpose is to point out some things you can do in advance that will help you and some good rules to follow and pitfalls to avoid while you are being interviewed.

What is an interview supposed to test?

The written examination is designed to test the technical knowledge and competence of the candidate; the oral is designed to evaluate intangible qualities, not readily measured otherwise, and to establish a list showing the relative fitness of each candidate – as measured against his competitors – for the position sought. Scoring is not on the basis of "right" and "wrong," but on a sliding scale of values ranging from "not passable" to "outstanding." As a matter of fact, it is possible to achieve a relatively low score without a single "incorrect" answer because of evident weakness in the qualities being measured.

Occasionally, an examination may consist entirely of an oral test – either an individual or a group oral. In such cases, information is sought concerning the technical knowledges and abilities of the candidate, since there has been no written examination for this purpose. More commonly, however, an oral test is used to supplement a written examination.

Who conducts interviews?

The composition of oral boards varies among different jurisdictions. In nearly all, a representative of the personnel department serves as chairman. One of the members of the board may be a representative of the department in which the candidate would work. In some cases, "outside experts" are used, and, frequently, a businessman or some other representative of the general public is asked to serve. Labor and management or other special groups may be represented. The aim is to secure the services of experts in the appropriate field.

However the board is composed, it is a good idea (and not at all improper or unethical) to ascertain in advance of the interview who the members are and what groups they represent. When you are introduced to them, you will have some idea of their backgrounds and interests, and at least you will not stutter and stammer over their names.

What should be done before the interview?

While knowledge about the board members is useful and takes some of the surprise element out of the interview, there is other preparation which is more substantive. It *is* possible to prepare for an oral interview – in several ways:

1) Keep a copy of your application and review it carefully before the interview

This may be the only document before the oral board, and the starting point of the interview. Know what education and experience you have listed there, and the sequence and dates of all of it. Sometimes the board will ask you to review the highlights of your experience for them; you should not have to hem and haw doing it.

2) Study the class specification and the examination announcement

Usually, the oral board has one or both of these to guide them. The qualities, characteristics or knowledges required by the position sought are stated in these documents. They offer valuable clues as to the nature of the oral interview. For example, if the job involves supervisory responsibilities, the announcement will usually indicate that knowledge of modern supervisory methods and the qualifications of the candidate as a supervisor will be tested. If so, you can expect such questions, frequently in the form of a hypothetical situation which you are expected to solve. NEVER go into an oral without knowledge of the duties and responsibilities of the job you seek.

3) Think through each qualification required

Try to visualize the kind of questions you would ask if you were a board member. How well could you answer them? Try especially to appraise your own knowledge and background in each area, *measured against the job sought*, and identify any areas in which you are weak. Be critical and realistic – do not flatter yourself.

4) Do some general reading in areas in which you feel you may be weak

For example, if the job involves supervision and your past experience has NOT, some general reading in supervisory methods and practices, particularly in the field of human relations, might be useful. Do NOT study agency procedures or detailed manuals. The oral board will be testing your understanding and capacity, not your memory.

5) Get a good night's sleep and watch your general health and mental attitude

You will want a clear head at the interview. Take care of a cold or any other minor ailment, and of course, no hangovers.

What should be done on the day of the interview?

Now comes the day of the interview itself. Give yourself plenty of time to get there. Plan to arrive somewhat ahead of the scheduled time, particularly if your appointment is in the fore part of the day. If a previous candidate fails to appear, the board might be ready for you a bit early. By early afternoon an oral board is almost invariably behind schedule if there are many candidates, and you may have to wait. Take along a book or magazine to read, or your application to review, but leave any extraneous material in the waiting room when you go in for your interview. In any event, relax and compose yourself.

The matter of dress is important. The board is forming impressions about you – from your experience, your manners, your attitude, and your appearance. Give your personal appearance careful attention. Dress your best, but not your flashiest. Choose conservative, appropriate clothing, and be sure it is immaculate. This is a business interview, and your appearance should indicate that you regard it as such. Besides, being well groomed and properly dressed will help boost your confidence.

Sooner or later, someone will call your name and escort you into the interview room. *This is it.* From here on you are on your own. It is too late for any more preparation. But remember, you asked for this opportunity to prove your fitness, and you are here because your request was granted.

What happens when you go in?

The usual sequence of events will be as follows: The clerk (who is often the board stenographer) will introduce you to the chairman of the oral board, who will introduce you to the other members of the board. Acknowledge the introductions before you sit down. Do not be surprised if you find a microphone facing you or a stenotypist sitting by. Oral interviews are usually recorded in the event of an appeal or other review.

Usually the chairman of the board will open the interview by reviewing the highlights of your education and work experience from your application – primarily for the benefit of the other members of the board, as well as to get the material into the record. Do not interrupt or comment unless there is an error or significant misinterpretation; if that is the case, do not hesitate. But do not quibble about insignificant matters. Also, he will usually ask you some question about your education, experience or your present job – partly to get you to start talking and to establish the interviewing "rapport." He may start the actual questioning, or turn it over to one of the other members. Frequently, each member undertakes the questioning on a particular area, one in which he is perhaps most competent, so you can expect each member to participate in the examination. Because time is limited, you may also expect some rather abrupt switches in the direction the questioning takes, so do not be upset by it. Normally, a board member will not pursue a single line of questioning unless he discovers a particular strength or weakness.

After each member has participated, the chairman will usually ask whether any member has any further questions, then will ask you if you have anything you wish to add. Unless you are expecting this question, it may floor you. Worse, it may start you off on an extended, extemporaneous speech. The board is not usually seeking more information. The question is principally to offer you a last opportunity to present further qualifications or to indicate that you have nothing to add. So, if you feel that a significant qualification or characteristic has been overlooked, it is proper to point it out in a sentence or so. Do not compliment the board on the thoroughness of their examination – they have been sketchy, and you know it. If you wish, merely say, "No thank you, I have nothing further to add." This is a point where you can "talk yourself out" of a good impression or fail to present an important bit of information. Remember, *you close the interview yourself.*

The chairman will then say, "That is all, Mr. _____, thank you." Do not be startled; the interview is over, and quicker than you think. Thank him, gather your belongings and take your leave. Save your sigh of relief for the other side of the door.

How to put your best foot forward

Throughout this entire process, you may feel that the board individually and collectively is trying to pierce your defenses, seek out your hidden weaknesses and embarrass and confuse you. Actually, this is not true. They are obliged to make an appraisal of your qualifications for the job you are seeking, and they want to see you in your best light. Remember, they must interview all candidates and a non-cooperative candidate may become a failure in spite of their best efforts to bring out his qualifications. Here are 15 suggestions that will help you:

1) Be natural – Keep your attitude confident, not cocky

If you are not confident that you can do the job, do not expect the board to be. Do not apologize for your weaknesses, try to bring out your strong points. The board is interested in a positive, not negative, presentation. Cockiness will antagonize any board member and make him wonder if you are covering up a weakness by a false show of strength.

2) Get comfortable, but don't lounge or sprawl

Sit erectly but not stiffly. A careless posture may lead the board to conclude that you are careless in other things, or at least that you are not impressed by the importance of the occasion. Either conclusion is natural, even if incorrect. Do not fuss with your clothing, a pencil or an ashtray. Your hands may occasionally be useful to emphasize a point; do not let them become a point of distraction.

3) Do not wisecrack or make small talk

This is a serious situation, and your attitude should show that you consider it as such. Further, the time of the board is limited – they do not want to waste it, and neither should you.

4) Do not exaggerate your experience or abilities

In the first place, from information in the application or other interviews and sources, the board may know more about you than you think. Secondly, you probably will not get away with it. An experienced board is rather adept at spotting such a situation, so do not take the chance.

5) If you know a board member, do not make a point of it, yet do not hide it

Certainly you are not fooling him, and probably not the other members of the board. Do not try to take advantage of your acquaintanceship – it will probably do you little good.

6) Do not dominate the interview

Let the board do that. They will give you the clues – do not assume that you have to do all the talking. Realize that the board has a number of questions to ask you, and do not try to take up all the interview time by showing off your extensive knowledge of the answer to the first one.

7) Be attentive

You only have 20 minutes or so, and you should keep your attention at its sharpest throughout. When a member is addressing a problem or question to you, give him your undivided attention. Address your reply principally to him, but do not exclude the other board members.

8) Do not interrupt

A board member may be stating a problem for you to analyze. He will ask you a question when the time comes. Let him state the problem, and wait for the question.

9) Make sure you understand the question

Do not try to answer until you are sure what the question is. If it is not clear, restate it in your own words or ask the board member to clarify it for you. However, do not haggle about minor elements.

10) Reply promptly but not hastily

A common entry on oral board rating sheets is "candidate responded readily," or "candidate hesitated in replies." Respond as promptly and quickly as you can, but do not jump to a hasty, ill-considered answer.

11) Do not be peremptory in your answers

A brief answer is proper – but do not fire your answer back. That is a losing game from your point of view. The board member can probably ask questions much faster than you can answer them.

12) Do not try to create the answer you think the board member wants

He is interested in what kind of mind you have and how it works – not in playing games. Furthermore, he can usually spot this practice and will actually grade you down on it.

13) Do not switch sides in your reply merely to agree with a board member

Frequently, a member will take a contrary position merely to draw you out and to see if you are willing and able to defend your point of view. Do not start a debate, yet do not surrender a good position. If a position is worth taking, it is worth defending.

14) Do not be afraid to admit an error in judgment if you are shown to be wrong

The board knows that you are forced to reply without any opportunity for careful consideration. Your answer may be demonstrably wrong. If so, admit it and get on with the interview.

15) Do not dwell at length on your present job

The opening question may relate to your present assignment. Answer the question but do not go into an extended discussion. You are being examined for a *new* job, not your present one. As a matter of fact, try to phrase ALL your answers in terms of the job for which you are being examined.

Basis of Rating

Probably you will forget most of these "do's" and "don'ts" when you walk into the oral interview room. Even remembering them all will not ensure you a passing grade. Perhaps you did not have the qualifications in the first place. But remembering them will help you to put your best foot forward, without treading on the toes of the board members.

Rumor and popular opinion to the contrary notwithstanding, an oral board wants you to make the best appearance possible. They know you are under pressure – but they also want to see how you respond to it as a guide to what your reaction would be under the pressures of the job you seek. They will be influenced by the degree of poise you display, the personal traits you show and the manner in which you respond.

ABOUT THIS BOOK

This book contains tests divided into Examination Sections. Go through each test, answering every question in the margin. We have also attached a sample answer sheet at the back of the book that can be removed and used. At the end of each test look at the answer key and check your answers. On the ones you got wrong, look at the right answer choice and learn. Do not fill in the answers first. Do not memorize the questions and answers, but understand the answer and principles involved. On your test, the questions will likely be different from the samples. Questions are changed and new ones added. If you understand these past questions you should have success with any changes that arise. Tests may consist of several types of questions. We have additional books on each subject should more study be advisable or necessary for you. Finally, the more you study, the better prepared you will be. This book is intended to be the last thing you study before you walk into the examination room. Prior study of relevant texts is also recommended. NLC publishes some of these in our Fundamental Series. Knowledge and good sense are important factors in passing your exam. Good luck also helps. So now study this Passbook, absorb the material contained within and take that knowledge into the examination. Then do your best to pass that exam.

EXAMINATION SECTION

EXAMINATION SECTION
TEST 1

DIRECTIONS: Each question or incomplete statement is followed by several suggested answers or completions. Select the one that best answers the question or completes the statement. *PRINT THE LETTER OF THE CORRECT ANSWER IN THE SPACE AT THE RIGHT.*

1. To enhance a student's acceptance of further instruction, the instructor should

    A. emphasize the student's inabilities
    B. keep the student informed of the progress made
    C. establish performance standards a little above the student's actual ability
    D. inform the student that others in the class are progressing faster

    1.____

2. The basis on which evaluation of student performance and accomplishment should be made is established during which step in the teaching process?

    A. Presentation B. Preparation
    C. Application   D. Review and evaluation

    2.____

3. Before the end of each instructional period, the instructor should

    A. conduct a subjective evaluation of the student's performance
    B. emphasize that mastery of the task is more important than complete understanding
    C. introduce the main features and objectives of the next lesson
    D. require the student to demonstrate the extent to which the lesson objectives have been met

    3.____

4. Evaluation of student performance and accomplishment during a lesson should be based on the

    A. student's actual performance as compared to a faultless performance
    B. student's background and past experiences
    C. direct comparison with the performance of other students in the class
    D. objectives and goals that were established in the lesson plan

    4.____

5. Which statement is TRUE regarding student evaluation?

    A. Evaluation of a student's learning should be an integral part of each classroom lesson.
    B. The preferred method of quizzing a student is by asking questions which can be answered by a *yes* or a *no*.
    C. Tests should be developed in such a manner that no one can get a perfect score.
    D. Ambiguous questions tend to force one to think therefore, they are acceptable when evaluating students.

    5.____

6. Suppose during a review and evaluation of things previously learned, a deficiency or fault exists in the knowledge or performances on which the present lesson is predicated. What should the instructor do?

    A. Correct the deficiency or fault before a new lesson is begun.
    B. Repeat the present lesson until the deficiency is corrected.

    6.____

C. Carefully note and point out the deficiency or fault and go on to the next new lesson.
D. Include remedial actions in the next new lesson.

7. At the beginning of the student's lesson, during early instruction, the instructor should

   A. avoid terms and phrases which are part of the new topic since they are new and strange to the student
   B. define the terms and phrases which will be used during the forthcoming lesson
   C. use colloquial expressions so the student can learn the language
   D. use picturesque expressions to brighten the instruction given

8. Which statement is TRUE regarding positive or negative approaches in instructional techniques?

   A. A negative teaching approach generally results in positive learning.
   B. Negative approaches are more effective than positive approaches.
   C. Positive approaches point out the pleasurable features before the critical possibilities are stressed.
   D. To be effective, instructors should ignore the existence of negative factors.

9. Which statement is TRUE regarding positive or negative approaches in instruction?

   A. Negative approaches are generally more effective than positive approaches.
   B. A positive approach is one which stresses all the critical possibilities before the potential and pleasurable features are presented.
   C. The positive approach of introducing new procedures after the student is acquainted with normal procedures is not likely to be discouraging or frightening for the student.
   D. A positive approach will stress that a procedure must be accomplished in a certain manner or serious consequences will result.

10. Which of these is an example of a positive approach in the first lesson of a student with no previous experience?

    A. Instruction must be vague for fear course may prove difficult.
    B. A series of inconsequential data is used.
    C. A series of review of previous term's work is introduced.
    D. Introducing the subject slowly and concisely.

11. The _____ method of presentation is desirable for a lesson on a skill such as the use of a computer.

    A. demonstration/performance   B. informal lecture
    C. formal lecture   D. guided discussion

12. In the teaching process, the _____ method of presentation is suitable for presenting new material, for summarizing ideas, and for showing relationships between theory and practice.

    A. demonstration/performance   B. guided discussion
    C. lecture   D. integrated instruction

13. The linear-programmed instruction method is based *primarily* on 13.____

    A. referral to previously learned subjects
    B. punishment for incorrect responses
    C. involvement in class discussions
    D. reinforcement (reward) for accurate performance

14. Students should perform an operation the right way the first few times because 14.____

    A. it establishes the basis for evaluation of the students' overall performance
    B. that is when habits are established
    C. it allows an earlier introduction of a new lesson
    D. it requires less supervision and coaching by the instructor

15. What is the PROPER sequence in which the instructor should employ the four basic steps in the teaching process? 15.____

    A. Explanation, trial and practice, evaluation, and review
    B. Explanation, demonstration, practice, and evaluation
    C. Presentation, trial and practice, evaluation, and review
    D. Preparation, presentation, application, and review and evaluation

16. An instructor who uses the student's previous experiences and knowledge as a starting point and leads into new ideas and concepts is teaching from the 16.____

    A. least frequently used to most frequently used
    B. simple to complex
    C. known to the unknown
    D. most frequently used to least frequently used

17. The method of arranging lesson material from the simple to complex, past to present, and known to unknown, is one that 17.____

    A. the instructor should avoid
    B. creates student thought pattern departures
    C. covers the areas only briefly in a normal discussion
    D. shows the relationships of the main points of the lesson

18. When teaching from the *known* to the *unknown,* an instructor is using the student's 18.____

    A. negative self-concepts
    B. anxieties and insecurities
    C. previous experiences and knowledge
    D. likes and dislikes

19. In organizing lesson material, which step should relate the coverage of material to the entire course? 19.____

    A. Conclusion
    B. Overview
    C. Development
    D. Introduction

20. In developing a lesson, the instructor must logically : organize explanations and demonstrations to help the student

    A. learn by trial-and-error practice of the procedures
    B. understand the relationships of the main points of the lesson
    C. experience a minimum amount of difficulty in memorizing the steps of a procedure
    D. learn by rote so that performance of the procedure will become automatic

21. Should an instructor be concerned about an apt student who makes very few mistakes?

    A. *Yes;* the student will lose confidence in the instructor unless the instructor invents deficiencies in the student's performance
    B. *No;* this is an indication that the student will perform flawlessly.
    C. *No;* the correction of such a student's mistakes is unimportant and unnecessary.
    D. *Yes;* faulty performance may soon appear due to student overconfidence.

22. What should an instructor do if a student is suspected of not fully understanding the principles involved in a task, even though the student can correctly perform the task?

    A. Require the student to apply the same elements to the performance of other tasks.
    B. Emphasize that mastery of the task is more important than complete understanding.
    C. Introduce a more complicated task and ask the student to explain the elements involved.
    D. Construct a specific and factual oral or written quiz which requires a simple *yes* or *no* answer.

23. When reviewing the lesson, the instructor should recapitulate what has been covered during the lesson to

    A. improve the student's grades, based upon the objectives and goals of the lesson plan and syllabus
    B. ensure that the student is aware of the progress made
    C. emphasize the competitive nature of the learning situation
    D. identify the blocks of learning which constitute the necessary parts of the total objective

24. Which of these should be omitted from an instructor's critique of a student's performance?

    A. Instruction in the form of direction and guidance
    B. Negative criticism that does not point toward improvement
    C. The student's strengths and successes
    D. The student's personal feelings

25. Which statement is TRUE about an instructor's critique of a student's performance?

    A. The student's personal feelings should not enter into the critique.
    B. It should be constructive and objective.
    C. It should treat every aspect of the performance in detail.
    D. By its nature, a critique is necessarily negative in content.

KEY (CORRECT ANSWERS)

1. B
2. D
3. D
4. D
5. A

6. A
7. B
8. C
9. C
10. D

11. D
12. D
13. D
14. B
15. D

16. C
17. D
18. C
19. B
20. B

21. D
22. A
23. D
24. B
25. B

TEST 2

DIRECTIONS: Each question or incomplete statement is followed by several suggested answers or completions. Select the one that BEST answers the question or completes the statement. *PRINT THE LETTER OF THE CORRECT ANSWER IN THE SPACE AT THE RIGHT.*

1. Which statement is TRUE about instructors' critiques? 1.___
    A. Instructors should rely on their position to make a critique more acceptable to their students.
    B. Before students willingly accept their instructors' critique, they must first accept the instructor.
    C. Critiques must be inflexible and not allow for variables.
    D. A comprehensive critique must treat every aspect of the student's performance in detail.

2. The purpose of a critique of the student's performance is to 2.___
    A. instill student confidence in the instructor's ability and authority
    B. provide direction and guidance to raise the level of the student's performance
    C. identify only the student's faults and weaknesses
    D. evaluate the student and assign a grade

3. Which statement is TRUE about an instructor's critique of a student's performance? 3.___
    A. The critique should be subjective rather than objective in nature.
    B. It is a step in the learning process, not in the grading process.
    C. By its nature, a critique is necessarily negative in content.
    D. The instructor's comments and recommendations should be general rather than specific.

4. An instructor's critique of a student's performance should 4.___
    A. treat every aspect of the performance in detail
    B. identify only the faults and weaknesses
    C. clearly express what was done well, what was done poorly, and how to improve the performance
    D. be conducted only in private

5. When an instructor critiques a student, it should ALWAYS be 5.___
    A. conducted immediately after the student's performance
    B. subjective rather than objective
    C. done in private
    D. designed and executed so that the instructor cannot allow for variables

6. When conducting a critique, the instructor should 6.___
    A. cover only a few well-made points rather than a large number of inadequately developed points
    B. cover all of the student's faults or weaknesses, large and small
    C. emphasize the points covered with dogmatic and absolute statements
    D. praise the student before criticizing, even if undeserved

7. When conducting a critique, the instructor should

   A. cover all of the student's faults or weaknesses, large and small
   B. avoid trying to cover too much material
   C. emphasize the points covered with dogmatic and absolute statements
   D. praise the student before criticizing, even if undeserved

   7.____

8. Of the following, which is a VALID reason for the use of proper oral quizzing during a lesson? It

   A. permits the instructor to devote more time to helping weak students rather than developing written tests
   B. helps the instructor determine the general intelligence level of the students
   C. promotes active student participation
   D. is unnecessary to grade the results

   8.____

9. To be effective in oral quizzing during the conduct of a lesson, a question should

   A. divert the student's thoughts to subjects covered in other lessons
   B. center on only one idea
   C. be easy for the student at that particular stage of training
   D. include a combination of where, how, and why

   9.____

10. During oral quizzing in a given lesson, effective questions should

    A. divert the student's thoughts to subjects covered in previous lessons
    B. relate to more than one thought or idea
    C. include a combination of who, what, when, or where
    D. be difficult for the student at that particular stage of training

    10.____

11. To answer a student's question, it is MOST important that the instructor

    A. clearly understand the qxiestion
    B. risk a guess rather than admit ignorance
    C. keep specifics to a minimum
    D. have complete knowledge of the subject

    11.____

12. If a student asks a question which the instructor CANNOT answer, the instructor should

    A. tell the student to reintroduce the question later, to allow time for the instructor to research the answer
    B. inform the student the question is irrelevant and not pertinent to the subject being covered
    C. admit not knowing the answer and promise to get the answer or help find the answer
    D. tell the student to find the answer in available references

    12.____

13. One desirable result of proper oral quizzing by the instructor is to

    A. establish a grade for the student
    B. reveal the effectiveness of the instructor's training procedures
    C. fulfill the requirements set forth in the overall objectives of the course
    D. reveal the essential information from which the student can determine progress

    13.____

14. Proper quizzing by the instructor during a lesson can have which of these results? 14.___

    A. It diverts the student's thoughts to unrelated subjects
    B. It permits the introduction of new material which was not covered previously.
    C. It identifies points which need more emphasis.
    D. It develops a feeling in the student of matching wits with the instructor.

15. In all quizzing as a portion of the instruction process, the questions should 15.___

    A. include catch questions to develop the student's perceptive power
    B. include unrelated subject matter to increase total comprehension
    C. include questions with more than one central idea to evaluate how completely a student understands the subject
    D. call for specific answers and be readily evaluated by the instructor

16. One of the MAIN advantages of selection-type (multiple choice) test items over supply-types (essay) test items is that the selection-type 16.___

    A. precludes comparison of students under one instructor with those under another instructor
    B. requires students to organize their knowledge
    C. would be graded objectively regardless of the student or the grader
    D. demands the ability of students to express ideas

17. Which statement is TRUE relative to effective multiple-choice type test items? 17.___

    A. Students should be able to select the correct response only if they know it is correct.
    B. It is not ethical to mislead the unknowledgeable student into selecting an incorrect alternative.
    C. Common errors or misconceptions should not be used as incorrect alternatives.
    D. Students should be able to select the correct response with even slight knowledge of the subject.

18. Which statement is TRUE about multiple-choice type test items that are intended to measure achievement at a higher level of learning? 18.___

    A. If there are less than four alternatives, the probability of guessing the correct response is decreased.
    B. It is unethical to mislead the unknowledgeable student into selecting an incorrect alternative.
    C. The use of common errors as distracting alternatives to divert the student from the correct response is ineffective and invalid.
    D. Some or all of the alternatives should be nearly correct but only one should be clearly correct.

19. In developing multiple-choice type test items and the alternative responses, it is 19.___

    A. proper to include as an alternative response a statement which itself is true but does not satisfy the requirements of the problem
    B. ineffective and invalid to use common errors as distracting alternatives
    C. more likely the test will contain ambiguities but will give more clues to the correct response
    D. ethical to mislead the unknowledgeable student into selecting an incorrect alternative

20. In a written test, the _____ type of test items makes it easier to compare the performance of students within the same class or in different classes. 20.____

    A. selection   B. true-false
    C. essay   D. supply

21. One of the MAJOR difficulties encountered in the construction of multiple-choice type test items is 21.____

    A. inventing distractors which will be attractive to students lacking knowledge or understanding
    B. phrasing the item in question form in lieu of statement form
    C. adapting the items to statistical item analysis
    D. keeping all responses approximately equal in length

22. The _____ type of test item creates the GREATEST probability of guessing. 22.____

    A. multiple-choice   B. true-false
    C. selection   D. supply

23. Which of the following principles should be followed in the development of true-false type tests? 23.____

    A. Include complex statements in the questions
    B. Include one or more ideas in each statement in the questions
    C. Avoid absolutes such as *all, every,* and *only*
    D. Establish patterns in the sequence of correct responses for easier scoring

24. A characteristic of supply-type (essay) test items is the 24.____

    A. ability of the student to express ideas is not required
    B. student's specific knowledge of subject matter is readily evaluated
    C. test results would be graded the same regardless of the student or the grader
    D. same test graded by different instructors would probably be given different scores

25. Which of the following is the MAIN disadvantage of supply-type (essay) test items? They 25.____

    A. increase the probability of student guessing
    B. make it possible to directly compare student accomplishment
    C. do not require students to organize their knowledge
    D. cannot be graded with uniformity

KEY (CORRECT ANSWERS)

1. B
2. B
3. B
4. C
5. A

6. A
7. B
8. C
9. B
10. D

11. A
12. C
13. B
14. C
15. D

16. C
17. A
18. D
19. A
20. A

21. A
22. B
23. C
24. D
25. D

TEST 3

DIRECTIONS: Each question or incomplete statement is followed by several suggested answers or completions. Select the one that BEST answers the question or completes the statement. *PRINT THE LETTER OF THE CORRECT ANSWER IN TE SPACE AT THE RIGHT.*

1. The characteristic of a written test which measures small differences in achievement between students is its 1.____

    A. validity
    B. comprehensiveness
    C. discrimination
    D. reliability

2. When a written test shows positive discrimination, it will 2.____

    A. distinguish between the students who are low and those who are high in achievement
    B. sample liberally what is being measured
    C. not measure what is intended
    D. include a representative and comprehensive sampling of the course objectives

3. A written test is said to be *comprehensive* when it 3.____

    A. includes all levels of difficulty
    B. measures knowledge of the same topic in many different ways
    C. samples liberally whatever is being measured
    D. shows a wide range of scores

4. A written test has *validity* when it 4.____

    A. measures small differences in the achievement of students
    B. samples liberally whatever is being measured
    C. yields consistent results
    D. actually measures what it is supposed to measure and nothing else

5. A written test which has *reliability* is one which 5.____

    A. yields consistent results
    B. samples liberally whatever is being measured
    C. measures small differences in the achievement of students
    D. actually measures what it is supposed to measure and nothing else

6. Development and assembly of *blocks of learning* in their proper relationship will provide a means for 6.____

    A. allowing the student to master the segments of the overall performance requirements individually and combining these with other related segments
    B. taking full advantage of both positive and negative transfer of learning
    C. eliminating the need to master initial instruction in the simple elements of a task before more advanced operations can be introduced
    D. both the instructor and student to easily correct faulty habit patterns

11

7. Which statement is TRUE regarding course syllabi? They should be

   A. followed rigidly if maximum benefit is to be derived from their use
   B. altered to suit the student's progress and the demands of special circumstances
   C. used primarily by inexperienced instructors
   D. used primarily when teaching students who have already received part of their training from another instructor

8. When it is impossible to conduct a scheduled lesson, it is preferable for the instructor to

   A. revise the lesson objective
   B. conduct a lesson that is not predicated completely on skills to be developed during the lesson which was postponed
   C. proceed to the next scheduled lesson, or if this is not practical, cancel the lesson
   D. postpone all lessons until the scheduled lesson can be completed

9. Which of the following statements is TRUE concerning extraneous blocks of instruction during a course of training?
   They

   A. assist in the attainment of the lesson's objective
   B. provide measurable objectives
   C. are usually necessary parts of the total objective
   D. detract from the completion of the final objective

10. In planning instructional activity, the SECOND step is to

    A. establish the overall objectives and standards
    B. identify the blocks of learning which constitute the necessary parts of the total objective
    C. develop lesson plans for each period or unit of instruction
    D. determine the personality and intelligence level of assigned students

11. In planning any instructional activity, the FIRST consideration should be to

    A. identify the blocks of learning which make up the overall objective
    B. determine the overall objectives and standards
    C. develop a sequence of training periods
    D. determine aptitudes of the students

12. In developing a lesson plan, which of these would CORRECTLY state the true objective of the lesson?

    A. To develop the student's skill in planning and following a pattern
    B. To explain and demonstrate the principles of planning and following a pattern
    C. To cover the principles of planning and following a pattern
    D. To learn the principles of planning and following a pattern

13. Which statement is TRUE regarding lesson plans?

    A. The use of standard prepared lesson plans for all students is most effective.
    B. Lesson plans should not contain elements of knowledge or skill previously learned.
    C. Lesson plans should clearly state the desired student learning outcomes.
    D. To be effective, lesson plans need not be in written form.

14. Which statement is TRUE about lesson plans? 14.____

    A. A good lesson plan will eliminate the need for a review of earlier lessons.
    B. The lesson should contain new facts, principles, procedures, or skills related to a previous lesson.
    C. The use of a rigidly prepared lesson plan should be used for an instruction.
    D. An effective lesson plan may be only a mental outline.

15. With regard to the characteristics of a well-planned lesson, each lesson should contain 15.____

    A. all the information needed to reach the objective of the training syllabus
    B. only one element of a simple principle, procedure, or skill
    C. new material that is related to the lesson previously presented
    D. information that is independent of earlier lessons

16. Which statement is TRUE regarding lesson plans? 16.____

    A. Rigidly followed lesson plans for all students is most effective for instruction.
    B. Lesson plans should not be directed toward the course objective, only to the lesson objective.
    C. Lesson plans should not contain material or skills previously learned.
    D. To be effective, lesson plans must be in written form.

17. If lesson plans are constructed in a proper manner, they will provide an outline for 17.____

    A. each lesson of the course without regard to the student/instructor relationship
    B. blocks of learning that become progressively larger, in scope
    C. the teaching procedure to be used in a single instructional period
    D. proceeding from the unknown to the known

18. With regard to the use of a lesson plan, which statement is TRUE? 18.____

    A. If the lesson plan is not leading to the desired results, the instructor should change the approach.
    B. A carefully thought-out lesson plan has little or no bearing on achieving teaching success.
    C. A lesson should provide as much information related to the subject as possible.
    D. An approach which has been successful with one group is always successful with another.

19. Which statement is TRUE regarding lesson plans? 19.____

    A. The rigid use of prepared lesson plans for all students is most effective.
    B. Lesson plans should not include review of earlier lessons.
    C. Lesson plans help instructors to keep a constant check on their own activity as well as that of their students.
    D. Lesson plans may be either *mental outlines* or in written form.

20. Which of these should be the FIRST step in preparing a lecture? 20.____

    A. Planning productive classroom activities
    B. Organizing the material
    C. Establishing the objective and desired outcomes
    D. Researching the subject

21. The preferred method for conducting a teaching lecture is to 21.___

    A. memorize the material to be presented
    B. speak extemporaneously from an outline
    C. speak impromptu with a minimum of specifics
    D. read from prepared material

22. Which teaching method provides no accurate means of checking student learning? 22.___
    _____ method.

    A. Lecture				B. Programmed instruction
    C. Guided discussion		D. Demonstration-performance

23. Which teaching method is particularly suitable for introducing a subject and is the most 23.___
    economical in terms of the time required to present a given amount of material? _____
    method.

    A. Programmed instruction		B. Demonstration-performance
    C. Guided discussion			D. Lecture

24. The teaching lecture is probably BEST delivered by 24.___

    A. reciting memorized material without the aid of a manuscript
    B. speaking extemporaneously from an outline
    C. speaking impromptu without preparation
    D. reading from a typed or written manuscript

25. In the teaching lecture, the use of which of these would detract from the instructor's dig- 25.___
    nity and reflect upon the student's intelligence?

    A. Simple words
    B. Free-and-easy colloquialisms
    C. Picturesque slang
    D. Errors in grammar and vulgarisms

KEY (CORRECT ANSWERS)

1. C
2. A
3. C
4. D
5. A

6. D
7. B
8. B
9. A
10. B

11. B
12. D
13. C
14. B
15. C

16. D
17. C
18. A
19. C
20. D

21. B
22. A
23. D
24. B
25. D

TEST 4

DIRECTIONS: Each question or incomplete statement is followed by several suggested answers or completions. Select the one that BEST answers the question or completes the statement. *PRINT THE LETTER OF THE CORRECT ANSWER IN THE SPACE AT THE RIGHT.*

1. The instructor can BEST inspire active student participation in informal lectures through the use of

    A. negative motivations   B. humor
    C. questions   D. visual aids

2. In regard to the teaching lecture, which of these statements is TRUE?

    A. The instructor must develop a keen perception for subtle responses and must be able to interpret the meaning of these reactions.
    B. Delivering the lecture in an extemporaneous or off-hand manner is not recommended.
    C. The teacher receives direct reaction from the student in the form of verbal or motor activity.
    D. New ideas should be introduced in the conclusion of the lesson.

3. The distinguishing characteristic of an informal lecture is the

    A. relative importance of the subject   B. use of visual aids
    C. student's participation   D. lack of a central idea

4. When a guided discussion is being conducted, the instructor should

    A. never use a reverse question in response to a student's question
    B. discourage students from asking questions
    C. make no comments during the discussion
    D. remember that the more intense the discussion and the greater the participation, the more effective the learning will be

5. When it appears students have adequately discussed the ideas presented during a guided discussion, one of the MOST valuable tools an instructor can use is

    A. a written test on the subject discussed
    B. an immediate recess or dismissal of the class
    C. a taped recording of the discussion
    D. an interim summary of what the students accomplished

6. Learning is produced in a guided discussion through the skillful use of

    A. demonstrations   B. lectures   C. negativism   D. questions

7. In preparing questions for a guided discussion, the instructor should remember that the purpose is to

    A. require that students research the topic
    B. evaluate and grade the student's knowledge
    C. bring about discussion to develop an understanding of the subject
    D. get answers to student questions

8. Which statement about the guided discussion method of teaching is TRUE?

   A. The instructor should answer all student questions never reverse or relay the questions to the class.
   B. The more intense the discussion and the greater the participation, the less effective the learning will be.
   C. Students without a background in the subject should be included in the discussion.
   D. Unless the students have some knowledge to exchange with each other, they cannot reach the desired learning outcomes.

9. In a guided discussion, learning is produced through

   A. explanations and demonstrations
   B. discussion of a topic in which students have little or no background
   C. the skillful use of questions
   D. tutorial instruction

10. During an introduction to a new subject, the instructor can more effectively stimulate group discussion by

    A. selecting a subject in which students lack knowledge
    B. creating a generally relaxed, informal atmosphere
    C. delivering a comprehensive lecture
    D. creating an atmosphere of sternness

11. The basic demonstration-performance method of instruction consists of several steps. In proper order, they are

    A. instructor tells -- student does; student tells -- student does; student does -- instructor evaluates
    B. instructor tells -- instructor does; student tells -- instructor does; student tells -- student does; student does -- instructor evaluates
    C. instructor does -- instructor tells; student does -- instructor tells; student does -- student tells; student does -- instructor evaluates
    D. instructor tells -- instructor does; student tells -- instructor does; student does -- instructor evaluates

12. What are the essential steps in the demonstration-performance method of teaching?

    A. Demonstration, practice, and evaluation
    B. Motivation, presentation, summary, and closure
    C. Explanation, demonstration, student performance, instructor supervision, and evaluation
    D. Demonstration, student performance, and evaluation

13. In the demonstration-performance method of instruction, which two separate actions are performed concurrently?

    A. Instructor demonstration and evaluation
    B. Student performance and instructor evaluation
    C. Instructor explanation and evaluation
    D. Instructor explanation and student demonstration

14. If, due to some unanticipated circumstances, the instructor's demonstration does not conform to the explanation, the instructor should

    A. lower the standards when the student performs the task
    B. *downplay* or ignore the discrepancy as being unimportant to the demonstration
    C. disguise the discrepancy with unrelated instruction
    D. immediately acknowledge and explain the discrepancy

15. Instructional aids used in the teaching-learning process should be

    A. self-supporting and should require no explanation
    B. selected prior to developing and organizing the lesson plan
    C. used to supplant the instructor's oral presentation of a lesson
    D. concentrated on the key points of the lesson

16. The use of instructional aids should be based on their ability to support a specific point in the lesson.
    What is the FIRST step to determine if and where instructional aids are necessary?

    A. Decide at what point in the lesson the student's interest must be rekindled.
    B. Clearly establish the lesson objective, being certain what must be communicated.
    C. Gather necessary data by researching for support material.
    D. Organize subject material into an outline or a lesson plan.

17. Instructional aids used in the teaching-learning process should NOT be used

    A. if detailed schematics are necessary to explain elaborate equipment
    B. as a crutch by the instructor
    C. for teaching more in less time
    D. in conjunction with verbal presentations

18. An instructor cannot retain the reputation of a professional if that person

    A. accepts students as they are with all their faults and problems
    B. does not demand higher pay
    C. instructs on a part-time basis
    D. gives the impression that interest in instruction is secondary to other activities

19. Which personal habit of an instructor is perhaps the MOST important one that affects the professional image?

    A. Common courtesy
    B. Manner of speech
    C. Attire
    D. Personal cleanliness

20. Which of these will make it impossible for the instructor to command the interested attention of the student?

    A. Limiting actions and decisions to standard patterns and practices
    B. Hiding some inadequacy behind a smokescreen of unrelated instruction
    C. Creating a relaxed, informal atmosphere in the classroom
    D. Insisting on correct techniques and procedures from the outset of training

KEY (CORRECT ANSWERS)

1. C
2. D
3. C
4. D
5. D

6. D
7. C
8. D
9. C
10. B

11. B
12. C
13. B
14. D
15. B

16. B
17. B
18. D
19. D
20. B

EXAMINATION SECTION
TEST 1

DIRECTIONS: Each question or incomplete statement is followed by several suggested answers or completions. Select the one that BEST answers the question or completes the statement. *PRINT THE LETTER OF THE CORRECT ANSWER IN THE SPACE AT THE RIGHT.*

1. The LARGEST percentage of a normal person's knowledge is acquired through which of these senses?

    A. Sight
    B. Smell and taste
    C. Touch
    D. Hearing

    1.____

2. Which of these learning experiences would be the MOST effective in the learning process?

    A. Those which present a minimum challenge to the student
    B. Experiences which involve the student's feelings, thoughts, and memories of past experiences
    C. Experiences which are totally new and unrelated to the learner's previous experiences
    D. Those in which the student need only commit something to memory

    2.____

3. A student's readiness to learn and understanding of the requirements involved in the learning situation are affected MOST by the

    A. student's intellectual level
    B. student's past experiences
    C. degree of difficulty involved in learning
    D. goals and incentives of other students in the class

    3.____

4. Learning is strengthened when accompanied by a pleasant or satisfying feeling. This principle is the law of

    A. intensity   B. recency   C. effect   D. primacy

    4.____

5. Which law of learning implies that a student will learn more from the real thing than from a substitute?
   The law of

    A. effect   B. recency   C. intensity   D. primacy

    5.____

6. Things most often repeated are BEST remembered because of which law of learning?
   Law of

    A. exercise   B. intensity   C. primacy   D. recency

    6.____

7. Which law of learning is recognized when an instructor carefully plans a summary school lesson or a critique? Law of

    A. intensity   B. recency   C. effect   D. exercise

    7.____

8. If a student has a strong purpose, a clear objective, and a well-fixed reason for learning something, it is the result of the law of

    A. readiness   B. effect   C. intensity   D. primacy

    8.____

21

9. The law of _____ learning states that learning is weakened when associated with an unpleasant feeling.

   A. readiness   B. primacy   C. intensity   D. effect

10. If students lack-motivation, their-progress will be LESS than if the law of _____ learning prevails.

    A. primacy   B. exercise   C. effect   D. readiness

11. Teaching the student to perform a task right the first time is an example of the law of

    A. readiness   B. recency   C. effect   D. primacy

12. The law of exercise is the basis of

    A. learning by rote
    B. the emotional reaction of the learner
    C. learning to do things right the first time
    D. practice and drill

13. A basic need that affects all of a person's perceptions is the need to

    A. avoid areas of any threat to success
    B. accomplish a higher level of learning
    C. maintain and enhance the person's own organized self
    D. acquire a formal education

14. What is the basis of all learning?

    A. Motivation   B. Perception
    C. Positive self-concept   D. Insight

15. Instruction, as opposed to the *trial and error* method of learning, is desirable because competent instruction speeds the learning process by

    A. teaching the relationship of perceptions as they occur
    B. relieving the student of the task of self-evaluation
    C. eliminating the practice of exploring and experimenting
    D. emphasizing only the important points of training

16. Which statement is TRUE about the perceptual process?

    A. Negative self-concepts have little or no effect on the perceptual process.
    B. An individual's beliefs and value structures have no effect on perceptions.
    C. All perceptions are affected by the need to preserve and perpetuate one's self.
    D. Fear favorably affects perceptions by widening a person's perceptual field.

17. *Insights,* as applied to learning, involve a person's

    A. awareness of those processes which are not immediately apparent
    B. grouping of associated perceptions into meaningful wholes
    C. ability to recognize the reason for learning a procedure
    D. self-concept or self-image

18. Perceptions result when a person 18.____

    A. responds to visual cues first, then aural cues, and relates these cues to ones previously learned
    B. groups together bits of information
    C. gives meaning to sensations being experienced
    D. responds correctly to self-evaluation

19. In the learning process, fear or the element of threat will 19.____

    A. accelerate the attainment of perceptions
    B. improve the student's ability to cope with the learning situation
    C. narrow the student's perceptual field
    D. intensify the student's desire to improve performance

20. Evoking student insights is one of the instructor's major responsibilities. 20.____
    This involves

    A. the grouping of perceptions into meaningful wholes
    B. a student's immediate grasp of theoretical principles as they are taught in school
    C. the analysis of a student by the instructor
    D. the ability of a student to master the rote performance of a task that has been learned

21. To predict how the student will interpret training experiences and instructions, the instructor must have knowledge of the student's 21.____

    A. intelligence and previous educational accomplishments
    B. readiness to learn
    C. basic need to maintain and enhance one's organized self
    D. precise kinds of commitments and philosophical outlooks

22. To enhance the instructor's relationship with students, an instructor should be aware that students have 22.____

    A. a tendency to shirk responsibility, because people are inherently lazy
    B. relinquished their role as individuals while enrolled in training programs
    C. drives and desires that they continually try to satisfy in one way or the other
    D. feelings of insecurity when receiving criticism, whether constructive or not

23. Select the TRUE statement concerning negative self-concepts. 23.____
    Negative self-concepts

    A. should be considered an asset to learning because they favorably affect the *ability to do*
    B. may be used to the advantage of an instructor who has a good understanding of psychology
    C. may inhibit the ability of the student to properly implement that which is perceived
    D. may be helpful because positive experiences often tend to contradict or destroy the self-concept

24. The student who has negative experiences which tend to contradict self-concepts is PROBABLY one who 24.___

    A. compensates for a personality conflict with the instructor
    B. attempts to suppress aggressive reactions
    C. will tend to reject instruction
    D. is psychologically motivated for further training

25. An instructor may foster the development of insights by 25.___

    A. introducing the student to at least two new tasks during each lesson
    B. always keeping the rate of learning consistent so that it is predictable
    C. pointing out the attractive features of the activity to be learned
    D. helping the student acquire and maintain a favorable self-concept

---

KEY (CORRECT ANSWERS)

1. A	11. B
2. B	12. A
3. B	13. C
4. C	14. B
5. C	15. D
6. A	16. C
7. A	17. B
8. D	18. C
9. D	19. D
10. D	20. A

21. C
22. C
23. B
24. C
25. D

TEST 2

DIRECTIONS: Each question or incomplete statement is followed by several suggested answers or completions. Select the one that BEST answers the question or completes the statement. *PRINT THE LETTER OF THE CORRECT ANSWER IN THE SPACE AT THE RIGHT.*

1. The factor which contributes MOST to a student's failure to remain receptive to new experiences or which creates a tendency to reject additional training is the student's 1._____

    A. physical organism
    B. goals and values
    C. basic needs
    D. negative self-concept

2. Select the CORRECT statement pertaining to motivation. 2._____

    A. The desire for personal gain is a form of negative motivation.
    B. Slumps in learning are often due to slumps in motivation.
    C. Motivation has little to do with learning.
    D. Negative motivations are as effective in promoting efficient learning as are positive motivations.

3. Which of these is a form of negative motivation? 3._____

    A. Reproof and threats
    B. The promise of achievement of rewards
    C. The belief that success is possible under certain circumstances
    D. Realizing that certain actions and operations may prevent injury or loss of life

4. Which of the following is *generally* the MORE effective way for the instructor to properly motivate students? 4._____

    A. Reinforce their self-confidence by requiring no tasks beyond their ability to perform
    B. Appeal to their pride and self-esteem
    C. Provide positive motivations by the promise or achievement of rewards
    D. Maintain pleasant personal relationships with students, even though it may be necessary to lower standards at times

5. Which of these may produce fears and be accepted by the student as threats? _____ motivations. 5._____

    A. Negative
    B. Positive
    C. Intangible
    D. Tangible

6. Motivations in the form of reproof and threats should be avoided with all but the student who is 6._____

    A. slow or discouraged
    B. bored or disinterested
    C. overconfident and impulsive
    D. timid and shy

7. Which statement is TRUE concerning motivations? 7._____

    A. Negative motivations characteristically are as effective as positive motivations.
    B. Motivations may be very subtle and difficult to identify.

25

C. There is little or no motivation in menial tasks such as digging a ditch.
D. Motivations must be tangible to be effective.

8. What effect does making each lesson a pleasurable experience have on the student? 8.___

   A. Fosters complacency
   B. Maintains a high level of motivation
   C. Tends to lower standards of performance
   D. Develops undesirable habit patterns

9. To promote efficient learning, the instructor should use 9.___

   A. positive and negative motivators as equally as possible
   B. positive motivators rather than negative motivators
   C. negative motivators more often than positive motivators
   D. only negative motivators

10. The dominant force which governs the student's progress and ability to learn is 10.___

    A. physical organism   B. insight
    C. perception   D. motivation

11. An instructor can MOST effectively maintain a high level of student motivation by 11.___

    A. setting performance standards to match the student's ability
    B. making things easy for the student
    C. making each lesson a pleasant experience for the student
    D. conducting lessons which offer no rewards

12. The HIGHEST level of learning has been achieved when a person is able to 12.___

    A. accomplish or perform each element of a procedure precisely
    B. accurately repeat verbally what has been learned
    C. understand each segment of a particular subject, procedure, or technique
    D. correlate an element which has been learned with other segments or blocks of learning or accomplishments

13. A person who has learned by rote is one who 13.___

    A. can repeat back something which has been taught, without being able to understand what has been learned
    B. understands what has been taught
    C. has achieved the skill to apply what has been taught
    D. is able to associate an element which has been learned with other segments of learning

14. The LOWEST level of learning has been attained when the student 14.___

    A. can repeat back something without understanding what has been learned
    B. understands what has been taught
    C. can apply what has been taught
    D. can associate an element which has been learned with other segments of learning

15. A leveling-off process or *learning plateau* in a student's progress is considered

    A. normal and should be expected after an initial period of rapid improvement
    B. abnormal since it means that learning has ceased
    C. abnormal and should not be brought to the student's attention
    D. normal if it does not stay level for significant periods of effort

16. On a graph showing the typical progress in learning, the initial leveling off of the learning curve is called a

    A. learning plateau   B. progress reversal
    C. learning gradient   D. progress advance

17. Which of these would be MOST profitable to a beginning student?

    A. Assignment of a grade on performance
    B. Evaluation of performance against a set standard
    C. Early evaluation to predict eventual proficiency
    D. Constructive critique to help eliminate errors

18. Which of the following would MOST likely be an indication that a student is reacting abnormally to stress?

    A. Automatic response to a given situation
    B. Extreme overcooperation
    C. Slow progress
    D. Hesitancy to act

19. The instructor can counteract anxiety in a student by

    A. ignoring the student's fears
    B. treating the student's fears as a normal reaction
    C. continuously citing the unhappy consequences of faulty performance
    D. discontinuing instruction in the tasks that cause anxiety

20. One of the SUREST ways to lose the student's confidence and attention is for the instructor to

    A. admit not knowing the answer to the student's question
    B. create the impression of *talking down* to the student
    C. acknowledge that both the student and instructor are important to each other
    D. refer to a checklist

21. Which of the following would MOST likely be an indication that a student is reacting abnormally to stress?

    A. Inappropriate laughter or singing
    B. Rapid thinking and reaction
    C. Automatic response to a given situation
    D. Slow changes in emotions

22. What technique can the instructor use to delay the onset of fatigue during class instruction?   22._____

    A. Introducing a number of different thoughts involving different theories and objectives
    B. Increasing the complexity of problems
    C. Lengthening the instruction periods
    D. Increasing the frequency of instruction periods

23. Which of the following is the MOST accurate statement concerning student concentration during classroom instruction?   23._____
    Concentration

    A. will be more pronounced when a number of tasks involving different elements and objectives are introduced
    B. is the primary consideration in determining the length and frequency of instruction periods
    C. is induced solely because of tenseness and can be minimized by a review of tasks already learned
    D. is a factor which depends more on mental alertness than on physical condition

24. When under stress, normal individuals USUALLY react   24._____

    A. by responding rapidly and exactly, often automatically, within the limits of their experience and training
    B. inappropriately such as extreme overcooperation, painstaking self-control, and inappropriate laughing or singing
    C. with very rapid changes in emotions, severe anger at the instructor, or others
    D. with marked changes in mood on different lessons such as excellent morale followed by deep depression

25. Which of the following would lead to lack of student confidence in the instructor?   25._____

    A. Too much help and encouragement given by the instructor to the slow student
    B. Unplanned periods of instruction or poor preparation
    C. A situation in which quick or brisk instruction is given
    D. An examination given on the first day of class

KEY (CORRECT ANSWERS)

1. D
2. B
3. A
4. D
5. A

6. C
7. B
8. B
9. B
10. D

11. C
12. D
13. A
14. A
15. A

16. A
17. D
18. D
19. B
20. B

21. A
22. A
23. B
24. A
25. B

TEST 3

DIRECTIONS: Each question or incomplete statement is followed by several suggested answers or completions. Select the one that BEST answers the question or completes the statement. *PRINT THE LETTER OF THE CORRECT ANSWER IN THE SPACE AT THE RIGHT.*

1. To deal with the problem of a sick student, the instructor should be aware that it is 1.____

    A. confined to the emotionally unstable student
    B. a temporary illness
    C. a reaction to apprehension that is only exhibited by the failing student
    D. due to a lack of confidence on the student's part

2. Students who grow impatient when learning the basic elements of a task are those who 2.____

    A. should have the preliminary training presented one step at a time with clearly stated goals for each step
    B. are less easily discouraged than the unaggressive students
    C. possess superior motivation
    D. should not be held back by insisting that the immediate goal be reached before they progress to the next step

3. Instruction that is keyed to the pace of a slow learner, but is applied to an apt student, will MOST likely result in 3.____

    A. anxiety
    B. confusion
    C. impatience
    D. a feeling of unfair evaluations

4. According to one theory, some forgetting is due to the practice of submerging an unpleasant experience into the subconscious.
   This is called 4.____

    A. repression   B. disuse
    C. interference   D. blanking

5. Concerning the factors involved in remembering, which statement is TRUE? 5.____

    A. Negativism promotes remembering.
    B. Repetition guarantees remembering.
    C. Practice guarantees remembering.
    D. Praise stimulates remembering.

6. One theory about forgetting is that an item is forgotten because a later experience has overshadowed it.
   This process is called 6.____

    A. repression   B. disuse
    C. interference   D. blanking

7. Which of these BEST ensures recall of material on tasks that have been taught?

   A. Practice of mere repetition
   B. Rote learning
   C. Meaningful teaching
   D. Negative motivations

8. Things learned previously by the student may either help or hinder the current learning task.
   This process GENERALLY is called

   A. insight
   B. interference
   C. transfer of learning
   D. correlation

9. Which statement is TRUE about transfer of learning?

   A. Positive transfer occurs if the learning of one skill interferes with retention or proficiency of another skill.
   B. Negative transfer occurs when students interpret new things in terms of what they already know.
   C. Positive transfer occurs when the learning of one skill helps the student learn another skill.
   D. Negative transfer occurs when the process refutes the interference theory of forgetting.

10. To ensure further learning and correct student performance after the completion of a course, it is the instructor's responsibility to

    A. allow incorrect performance at the beginning of the course to *get those errors out of the student's system*
    B. proceed to the next learning task even though the more simple tasks are performed incorrectly
    C. accept improper habits during the early phase of the course and correct these faults later
    D. insist on correct techniques and procedures from the outset of the course

11. To help the student achieve transfer of learning, the instructor should

    A. make certain the student understands that what is learned can be applied to other situations
    B. encourage rote learning
    C. discourage the use of imagination and ingenuity in applying knowledge and skills
    D. use instructional materials that precludes the formation of well-founded concepts and generalizations

12. Which generalization about motivated human nature has been made by noted psychologists?

    A. A human being will not exercise self-direction and self-control in the pursuit of committed goals.
    B. The average human being does not inherently dislike work.
    C. It is human nature to shirk responsibility.
    D. The capacity to exercise a relatively high degree of imagination, ingenuity, and creativity in solving common problems is rare in the human race.

3 (#3)

13. Before a student can concentrate on learning, which of the human needs must be satisfied?   13.____

    A. Self-fulfillment   B. Safety
    C. Social   D. Physical

14. Which of the student's human needs offers the GREATEST challenge to the instructor?   14.____

    A. Self-fulfillment   B. Physical
    C. Safety   D. Social

15. Among the various human needs, the individual is FIRST concerned with   15.____

    A. personal safety   B. social needs
    C. self-fulfillment   D. physical needs

16. After individuals are physically comfortable and have no fear for their safety, _____ needs become the PRIME influence on their behavior.   16.____

    A. social   B. egoistic
    C. materialistic   D. physical

17. When a student becomes bewildered and lost in the advanced phase of learning after completing the early phase without grasping the fundamentals, the defense mechanism is USUALLY in the form of   17.____

    A. rationalization   B. aggression
    C. flight   D. resignation

18. When students display the defense mechanism called aggression, they   18.____

    A. attempt to justify actions that otherwise would be unacceptable
    B. may refuse to participate in the activities of the class
    C. develop symptoms or ailments that give them satisfactory excuses for removing themselves from frustration
    D. become so frustrated they lose interest and give up

19. When students subconsciously use the defense mechanism called rationalization, they   19.____

    A. develop symptoms that give them excuses for removing themselves from frustration
    B. cannot accept the real reasons for their behavior
    C. become aggressive against something or somebody
    D. no longer believe it profitable or even possible to work further

20. When students become so frustrated they no longer believe it profitable or even possible to work further, they USUALLY display which defense mechanism?   20.____

    A. Resignation   B. Aggression
    C. Escape   D. Rationalization

21. Taking physical or mental flight is a defense mechanism that students use when they   21.____

    A. want to escape from frustrating situations
    B. cannot accept the real reasons for their behavior

C. become bewildered and lost in the advanced phase of training
D. attempt to justify actions that otherwise would be unacceptable

22. Although-defense mechanisms can serve a useful purpose, they also can be hindrances because they 22.____

   A. destroy feelings of failure
   B. alleviate the causes of problems
   C. provide feelings of adequacy
   D. involve self-deception and distortion of reality

23. When a student uses excuses to justify inadequate performance, it is an indication of the defense mechanism known as 23.____

   A. escape   B. rationalization
   C. aggression   D. resignation

24. When a student asks irrelevant questions or refuses to participate in class activities, it USUALLY is an indication of the defense mechanism known as 24.____

   A. escape   B. rationalization
   C. aggression   D. resignation

25. When a student engages in daydreaming, it is the defense mechanism of 25.____

   A. escape   B. rationalization
   C. aggression   D. resignation

KEY (CORRECT ANSWERS)

1.	B	11.	A
2.	A	12.	B
3.	C	13.	D
4.	A	14.	A
5.	C	15.	A
6.	B	16.	C
7.	C	17.	D
8.	C	18.	A
9.	C	19.	B
10.	D	20.	C

21. C
22. D
23. B
24. C
25. A

TEST 4

DIRECTIONS: Each question or incomplete statement is followed by several suggested answers or completions. Select the one that BEST answers the question or completes the statement. *PRINT THE LETTER OF THE CORRECT ANSWER IN THE SPACE AT THE RIGHT.*

1. Which statement is TRUE regarding true professionalism as an instructor? 1.____

    A. To achieve professionalism, actions and decisions must be limited to standard patterns and practices.
    B. Anything less than sincere performance destroys the effectiveness of the professional instructor.
    C. Professionalism is not necessarily based on intelligence or the ability to reason logically and accurately.
    D. A single definition of professionalism would encompass all of the qualifications and considerations which must be present.

2. Student confidence tends to be destroyed if instructors 2.____

    A. identify the student's errors and failures
    B. bluff whenever in doubt about some point
    C. acknowledge their own mistakes
    D. direct and control the student's actions and behavior

3. The professional relationship between the instructor and the student should be based upon the 3.____

    A. mutual acknowledgement that they are important to each other and both are working toward the same objective
    B. concept that making things easy for the student and accepting lower standards will improve the relationship
    C. need to disregard the student's personal faults, interests, or problems
    D. understanding that during the training course, the instructor's objectives are different from the student's

4. Which of these would MORE likely result in students becoming frustrated? 4.____

    A. Telling the students that their work is unsatisfactory with no explanation
    B. Neglecting to tell students what is expected of them and what they can expect
    C. Failing to point out to students how a particular lesson or course can help them reach an important goal
    D. Covering up instructor mistakes or bluffing when the instructor is in doubt

5. In the communication process, the communicator will be more successful in gaining and retaining the receiver's attention by 5.____

    A. varying the communicative approach
    B. providing an atmosphere which discourages questioning
    C. presenting the message in a manner that is totally foreign to the receiver's experiences
    D. relying on technical language to express ideas to the receiver

6. Which statement is TRUE regarding effective communication during student instruction? Effective communication

   A. has taken place when information is provided in such a way that it changes the behavior of the student
   B. has taken place when the student is able to repeat the information that has been received
   C. is when the student has accurately received the information even though the factors and principles are not yet understood
   D. at its best is when information is accurately transmitted and received

7. To communicate *effectively,* instructors must

   A. depend on a highly technical or professional background to ensure acceptance of the message
   B. reveal a positive and confident attitude while delivering their message
   C. rely on technical language to express ideas clearly to students
   D. limit the method of communication to one channel (hearing, seeing, or feeling) to avoid confusion

8. In the communication process, if a listener has difficulty in understanding the symbols the speaker is using, and indicates confusion, the speaker

   A. is encouraged and force is added to communication
   B. should avoid the use of concrete words
   C. should resort to the use of abstract words
   D. may become puzzled and uncertain

9. In the communication process, a speaker is encouraged and force is added to communication when the listener

   A. has difficulty in understanding and indicates confusion
   B. reacts favorably
   C. shows an attitude of passive neutrality
   D. has no experiences in common with the speaker

10. Effective communication has taken place when, and only when, the

    A. sender uses a vocabulary (written or oral) that is meaningful to the reader or listener
    B. communicator has convinced the listener there is a need to know the ideas presented
    C. receiver has the ability to question and comprehend the ideas that have been transmitted
    D. receivers react with understanding and change their behavior accordingly

11. The effectiveness of communication between the instructor and the student is measured by the

    A. facial expressions of the student during a lesson
    B. similarity between the idea transmitted and the idea received
    C. degree of attention the student gives to the instructor during a lesson
    D. level of motivation displayed by the student

12. Probably the GREATEST single barrier to effective communication in the teaching process is a lack of

    A. personality harmony between instructor and student
    B. quiet environment
    C. time available for communication
    D. a common experience level between the instructor and student

13. By the use of abstractions in the communication process, the communicator will

    A. narrow and gain better control of the image produced in the minds of listeners and readers
    B. not evoke in the listener's or reader's mind the specific items of experience the communicator intends
    C. be using words which refer to objects or ideas that human beings can experience directly
    D. bring forth specific items of experience in the minds of the receivers

14. Probably the GREATEST single barrier to effective communication is the

    A. confusion between the symbol and the thing symbolized
    B. making of statements which contain inaccuracies
    C. use of abstractions by the communicator
    D. lack of a common core of experience between communicator and receiver

15. A communicator's words cannot communicate the desired meaning to another person unless the

    A. listener or reader has had some experience with the objects or concepts to which these words refer
    B. words give the meaning that is in the mind of the receiver
    C. communicator makes extensive use of abstractions
    D. communicator avoids the use of words which relate to the receiver's past experience

16. The danger in using abstract words is that they

    A. will not evoke the specific items of experience in the listener's mind that the communicator intends
    B. control the image produced in the listener's mind
    C. refer only to things that people are familiar with or can relate to
    D. are overly concise in their meanings

17. Instructors who limit their thinking to the whole group without considering the individuals within that group are

    A. using a good lecture technique
    B. assuming all students have an average personality which really fits no one
    C. presenting information efficiently for maximum retention
    D. using an excellent time-saving measure

18. Which of the following is one of the ways in which anxiety or apprehension will affect a student? Anxiety

    A. tends to increase mental acuity and perceptiveness, but interferes with muscular coordination
    B. causes dispersal of the student's attention over such a wide range of matters as to interfere with normal reactions
    C. will speed up the learning process for the student if properly controlled and directed by the instructor
    D. may limit the student's ability to learn from perceptions

19. Faulty performance due to student overconfidence should be corrected by

    A. requiring the student to perform unpleasant tasks
    B. raising the standard of performance for each lesson
    C. withholding the evaluation of the student's progress
    D. praising the student only when it is deserved

20. Ridicule and reproof of a slow and apprehensive student is

    A. effective if the student understands the reason for being criticized in this manner
    B. ineffective in encouraging learning
    C. generally an effective psychological tool because students will work to avoid unpleasant experiences
    D. effective because students learn best when mistakes are pointed out in a forceful manner

21. When a student correctly understands the situation and knows the correct procedure for the task, but fails to act at the proper time, the student MOST probably

    A. will be unable to cope with the demands of the task
    B. is handicapped by indifference or lack of interest
    C. feels that the instructor is making unreasonable demands for performance and progress
    D. lacks self-confidence

22. What should an instructor do if a student's slow progress is due to discouragement and a lack of confidence?

    A. Assign subgoals which can be attained more easily than the normal learning goals
    B. Provide unlimited help and encouragement
    C. Raise the performance standards so that the student will gain satisfaction in meeting higher standards
    D. Emphasize the negative aspects of poor performance by pointing out the serious consequences

23. If a student's progress is slow due to discouragement and a lack of confidence, the instructor should

    A. provide unlimited help and encouragement
    B. accept the slow rate of progress and accept a substandard performance
    C. have the student practice elements of the task involved until confidence and ability are gained
    D. discontinue directing the student's attention to the unacceptable performance

24. The *usual* result when a student has made an earnest effort but is told that the work is not satisfactory, with no other explanation, is

 A. increased effort
 B. frustration
 C. regression
 D. increased motivation

25. When the instructor keeps the student informed of lesson objectives and completion standards, it minimizes the student's

 A. individuality
 B. insecurity
 C. motivation
 D. aggressiveness

KEY (CORRECT ANSWERS)

1.	B	11.	D
2.	B	12.	D
3.	A	13.	C
4.	B	14.	D
5.	A	15.	A
6.	D	16.	A
7.	B	17.	B
8.	D	18.	D
9.	B	19.	D
10.	B	20.	B

21. D
22. A
23. C
24. B
25. B

EXAMINATION SECTION
TEST 1

DIRECTIONS: Each question or incomplete statement is followed by several suggested answers or completions. Select the one that BEST answers the question or completes the statement. *PRINT THE LETTER OF THE CORRECT ANSWER IN THE SPACE AT THE RIGHT.*

1. The MOST desirable type of classroom discipline is BEST attained through which one of the following practices?

   A. Encouraging traits of self-discipline
   B. Including class behavior in the final rating
   C. Establishing the idea that rules and regulations will be strictly enforced
   D. Anticipating difficulty and sending the first few minor cases of breach of discipline to the chairman or dean
   E. Maintaining a permissive or a restrictive atmosphere in the classroom but never a mixture of both

1.____

2. If you find a student in one of your classes doing very poorly despite an obviously high potential, the MOST desirable procedure among the following to take is to

   A. refer the student to the guidance counselor
   B. ask the student to bring his parents to school to see you
   C. write a letter to his parents asking them to come to school to see you
   D. interview the student yourself before making any referrals or calling his parents
   E. fail him

2.____

3. The procedure of requiring students to stand and face the class when responding is

   A. *advisable* because it discourages calling out of answers
   B. *inadvisable* because it creates an ordeal for the shy student
   C. *advisable* because it increases audibility of answers
   D. *inadvisable* because a recalcitrant student would dispute the rule
   E. *advisable* because it trains the class in the American way of standing up and facing an adversary eye to eye

3.____

4. Of the following, the BEST procedure for obtaining the aim of a specific lesson is

   A. for the teacher to state the aim of the lesson and write it on the blackboard so that all will be sure to have it
   B. to elicit the aim from the class and have it written on the board
   C. for the teacher to dictate the aim of the lesson so that all students can get it in their notebooks
   D. to give the aim the previous day so that the students can prepare for the lesson
   E. to secure a class consensus on the aim by secret vote

4.____

5. Of the following, the BEST course of action for a new teacher who is having difficulty in presenting a particular type of lesson to take is to

   A. make an arrangement with an experienced teacher to observe his classes
   B. consult the chairman and request an opportunity for intervisitation
   C. try to adjust without outside help to avoid demonstrating weakness to colleagues

5.____

D. discuss the problem frankly with the class and ask for suggestions from the class
E. take in-service courses

6. Of the following, the BEST situation for using essay questions is where

   A. it is desired to test the ability of a pupil to organize his answers
   B. the class is made up chiefly of slow pupils
   C. *single shot* questions are needed to complete an examination
   D. it is desired to sample a large area of subject matter
   E. it is desired to sample a small area of subject matter

7. In a lesson in which a new topic is to be taught, which one of the following is the MOST desirable principle to follow?

   A. Make certain that all difficulties encountered by pupils in doing the previous homework assignment have been corrected before beginning the new topic.
   B. Allow sufficient time to include a suitable motivation of the new material, a development, and independent pupil practice.
   C. Introduce the new topic, but require pupils to study the textbook for a complete explanation.
   D. Insist that no questions be asked by pupils until the development is completed.
   E. Permit all students who have not completed the previous topic to continue on it and require only those who show the requisite ability and interest to take up the new topic.

8. A test may be said to be reliable when

   A. it consistently measures what it purports to measure
   B. it adequately deals with the types of educational outcomes to be measured at proper levels of difficulty for pupils
   C. there is a high correlation between test scores and criterion measures
   D. it can be obtained on time from publishers
   E. it measures accurately whatever it does measure

9. Of the following, the one which does NOT measure the concentration of scores in any set of scores or group of data is the

   A. mode   B. modulus   C. mean   D. median   E. middle

10. Of the following, the GREATEST advantage of short-answer tests is the

    A. ease with which the test items can be constructed
    B. ease with which such tests can be standardized
    C. wide sampling of the subject matter of the course
    D. ease with which the test results can be interpreted
    E. large number of questions that can be given as contrasted with the essay test

11. The MOST effective use of the talents and abilities of the able pupils in your subject area would be gained by which one of the following procedures?

    A. Give them extra homework assignments in order to earn better marks.
    B. Give them the responsibility of tutoring disadvantaged pupils.
    C. Give them monitorial duties, such as marking test papers.

D. Excuse them from class work which they grasp easily so they do enrichment work in other subject areas.
E. Have them serve as the teacher in as many class situations as possible.

12. The MAIN advantage of standardized tests is

    A. objectivity
    B. ease of marking for teachers
    C. marks may be compared with other groups
    D. it provides greater motivation for students
    E. they are held *secure*

13. A percentile score of 55 is

    A. a score equivalent to the arithmetic median of the scores
    B. equaled or exceeded by 45% of the scores in the distribution
    C. equivalent to a score of 55 out of 100
    D. the accepted norm
    E. equivalent to a raw score of 55

14. The process of reviewing homework daily is time-consuming. Of the following suggestions made by a group of teachers, which one is MOST sound pedagogically?

    A. Do not go over the homework at all.
    B. Go over, in class, only the problems with which pupils had trouble.
    C. Collect the homework of only one row at a time and return it corrected the next day.
    D. Collect the homework of the whole class once a week on a specific day.
    E. Before going on to the new lesson, be sure to go over all the homework.

15. Which one of the following is the BEST statement about a teacher's technique of questioning?

    A. No question should be so difficult that even the slowest pupil couldn't answer it.
    B. Each lesson should have at least one question which would require the pupils to do critical thinking.
    C. There should be a series of pivotal questions to highlight the chief learnings.
    D. Each question should be simple and short.
    E. At times, use the *whiplash* or *tugging* types with slow learners.

16. Of the following, the BEST statement concerning skill in questioning is that

    A. to make sure all students hear, the teacher should often repeat her question
    B. answers should be repeated because some children sit far away from the pupil who is answering
    C. each question should be addressed to a particular pupil by giving his name before asking the question
    D. to vary the kinds of questions, include the double question, particularly for bright students
    E. a question should be addressed to the entire class

17. Of the following, the LEAST effective method for obtaining pupil participation is to

A. give a warm-up drill to the entire class
B. group the class and give different assignments to each group
C. have pupils answer in concert
D. use experiences of pupils in the lesson development
E. ask thought-provoking pivotal questions

18. A test which is TOO difficult will usually yield scores that fall into a _____ distribution.   18.___

    A. bell-shaped   B. negatively skewed
    C. positively skewed   D. bimodal
    E. variety of patterns of

19. The MOST desirable routine procedure for going over homework is to   19.___

    A. compare answers orally with the class
    B. have students put their work on the board and explain it to the rest of the class
    C. have the teacher do each example together with the class
    D. collect it and mark it outside of class, returning it within a week
    E. ask students to raise their hands if they have the correct answer as it is announced by the teacher

20. Of the following characteristics of a good lesson plan, the one which applies LEAST is that it   20.___

    A. forms part of a larger unit
    B. helps give direction to the lesson
    C. be adhered to even if vital side issues appear
    D. focuses on a meaningful problem
    E. refers to previous lessons and learnings

21. The degree to which a test measures what it is supposed to measure is called its   21.___

    A. validity   B. coefficient of correlation
    C. objectivity   D. reliability
    E. consistency

22. Of the following audio-visual aids, the one that represents a MOST recent innovation in science teaching is   22.___

    A. single topic films   B. film strips
    C. 2x2 inch colored slides   D. 16 mm sound films
    E. 8 mm sound films

23. Of the following reasons for using charts as a teaching device in the classroom, the MOST desirable one is the   23.___

    A. ease with which large numbers of charts can be stored
    B. ability to use color for both functional and decorative effect
    C. ability to include many details about a topic on one chart
    D. ability to make comparisons between various things, places, distances, conditions, etc.
    E. ease with which they can be followed in a class discussion

24. Of the following techniques employed in questioning, the one that probably has the LEAST value for conceptual learning would be questions of a type that are

   A. varied in difficulty and directed to appropriate pupils
   B. rapid-fire and call for monosyllabic responses
   C. pivotal in nature and call for analysis
   D. questions of pupils that are directed back to other pupils by the teacher
   E. based on *why* rather than on *what*

24.____

25. Of the following reasons for including essay questions in an examination, the one that is probably MOST important is that this type of question

   A. provides greater coverage of material than other test items
   B. is easier to formulate than good objective-type questions
   C. provides opportunities for subjective evaluation of answers
   D. provides for pupil expression in an organized manner and in depth
   E. emphasizes thinking through rather than mere recall

25.____

26. Of the following practices for helping a beginning teacher in the classroom, the BEST would probably be to

   A. have informal discussions with colleagues at opportune times
   B. continue taking courses at the local colleges
   C. follow a planned program of intervisitation
   D. attend departmental conferences devoted to pedagogy
   E. ask the principal or chairman to sit in on his first month of teaching

26.____

27. Of the following reasons for using, at times, a single loop movie projector rather than a 16 mm movie projector, the one reason that is INCORRECT is that it(s)

   A. is faster to load and unload film
   B. can be used in a more flexible manner
   C. can be used without darkening the room
   D. sound track can produce sound of functional fidelity
   E. sound track can produce sound of higher fidelity

27.____

28. Of the following practices for training students to give reports in class, the one that is LEAST recommended is to

   A. insist that they read them
   B. limit their reports to a stated time
   C. encourage them to use simple illustrations
   D. permit reference to notes during a presentation
   E. prepare summary questions to test the agreement or understanding of the class

28.____

29. Of the following reasons for experimenting with team teaching methods, the one that is probably MOST valid from an educational point of view is that it

   A. would help meet the problem of teacher shortage
   B. would provide overburdened teachers with more free time
   C. makes provision for flexible scheduling and independent study by pupils
   D. can easily be incorporated into old as well as new school plants
   E. would provide more highly skilled teachers

29.____

30. In considering the roles of a homeroom teacher, the one of the following which would probably be considered LEAST important from an educational viewpoint is to

   A. give guidance since the school has licensed guidance counselors
   B. keep accurate and up-to-date records for students
   C. provide a program of tutorial assistance for students that need help
   D. maintain firm discipline while routine school matters are being handled
   E. establish liaison with the parents of the students

31. Of the following practices followed by teachers in doing project work, the one that probably has the LEAST merit is to

   A. require that every student submit an individual project
   B. display class projects in a science fair held in the school
   C. encourage students to work in committees on group projects
   D. provide opportunity for pupils to discuss their work on school time
   E. organize a project center where displays of the best work may be seen

32. If a teacher wanted to prepare seventy copies of a five-page test for two of his classes, he would probably find that the machine which was MOST practical for this purpose is a(n)

   A. polygraph   B. mimeograph   C. kymograph
   D. offset   E. xerox

33. Of the following, the one who was a Harvard psychologist and author of THE PROCESS OF EDUCATION and TOWARD A THEORY OF INSTRUCTION was

   A. James Conant   B. Jerome S. Bruner
   C. John H. Fischer   D. H. Bentley Glass
   E. James M. Hester

34. Of the following types of objective questions, the one that is considered MOST flexible and statistically reliable is the

   A. modified true-false   B. matching
   C. completion   D. multiple choice
   E. true-false

35. Of the following, probably the LEAST valuable way to begin a new topic or lesson is for the teacher to

   A. distribute a step-by-step outline of the topics or lesson
   B. explore some interest already possessed by the student
   C. elicit an explanation of the importance of the subject
   D. develop an overview of the subject
   E. refer to some current event

36. Motivation for a lesson is BEST when it

   A. makes a sharp transition from the previous lesson
   B. is dramatic
   C. raises a question that poses a problem for the class
   D. is succinct
   E. arouses emotions, preferably indignation or dissent .

37. In administering the Iowa Tests of Educational Development, the one factor among the following that is NOT a primary aim is to

    A. identify the intellectually gifted
    B. show parents the fixed limitations of their children
    C. serve as backgrounds for conferences between parents and counselors
    D. select students for remedial classes
    E. aid in ability grouping

38. The teacher might curtail continued and disturbing conversations during a recitation by doing all of the following EXCEPT

    A. walking around the room, making it a point to stand near potential talkers
    B. separating friends who encourage misbehavior in one another
    C. singling out the talkers and publicly admonishing and embarrassing them
    D. drawing the talkers into the group activity without a special reprimand
    E. motivating interest and participation through thought-provoking questions, cartoons, demonstrations, etc.

39. Of the following, the BEST reason for the assignment of suitable homework is that it provides

    A. each parent with an opportunity to learn what her child is learning
    B. all the necessary follow-up drill for teaching
    C. practice in reading skills
    D. further opportunities for application of skills or concepts taught
    E. an important objective basis for rating the child

40. Of the following, the one statement that is generally TRUE of the bright pupil is that he

    A. works up to his capacity
    B. is generally better in reading than in mathematics
    C. is more likely to succeed in his social relationships
    D. is likely to be physically superior as well
    E. is quick to form associations between words and ideas

41. Of the following, the MOST important reason why the adolescent period is frequently referred to as a time of conflict, turmoil, and rebellion is that

    A. adolescence is characterized by rapid physiological growth combined with radical changes in body chemistry
    B. adolescents normally meet with frustrations in their efforts to secure financial, personal, and social independence
    C. acne, obesity, skin blemishes, and the attainment of sexual maturity cause hypersensitivity
    D. adolescents experience difficulty in applying previous learnings because their mental and physical resources are drained by their extraordinary physiological changes
    E. the modern program of education has afforded the adolescent new insights into the failures and inadequacies of the *establishment*

42. The MOST important function of the warm-up drill at the beginning of a period is to

A. keep the class busy while the teacher is on hall patrol
B. give the teacher a chance to take attendance
C. provide meaningful drill for skills and concepts previously taught
D. help the teacher get a more accurate mark for each pupil
E. permit the slow learner to catch up with the previous work before the new lesson is begun

43. Of the following, the CHIEF value of the use of audiovisual materials with slow learners is that they

    A. are attractive and provide entertainment in the learning process
    B. lighten the teacher's load in planning for a lesson
    C. promote conceptual thinking by providing a basis of concrete reality
    D. can teach much more in a given lesson because they minimize the interruptions caused by extraneous pupil questions
    E. can be stopped or held at any point to permit intensive teaching or drill

44. Educational investigations have discovered a strongly positive correlation between a student's academic achievement and

    A. the small size of his class
    B. the excellence of his attendance
    C. his participation in extra-curricular activities
    D. his motivation
    E. his home environment

45. With regard to a homework assignment, of the following, it is LEAST defensible for it to

    A. be given in the last minute or two of the lesson
    B. be quite specific
    C. be varied for different class members
    D. involve material covered in previous lessons
    E. require independent research

46. Of the following, the MOST acceptable statement regarding the use of lesson plans in the junior high school is that

    A. they should not be consulted during the lesson since they distract pupils
    B. they are useful only to new teachers
    C. they require preparation anew each semester even in subject areas that are relatively static
    D. their content should be uniform throughout a school department so that they can be used by substitute teachers
    E. the department should draw up a uniform set of plans for all teachers so that instruction may be equalized for all classes

47. In designing a unit test question of the matching type, the LEAST desirable technique, of the following, would be to

    A. include two or three more responses than the number of premises
    B. provide at least twenty items in each list to minimize guessing
    C. keep both the premises and responses homogeneous

D. avoid extraneous clues
E. include items that are authentic and relate to the work in hand

48. If a teacher has completed about three-quarters of his lesson and suddenly discovers that there are only three minutes remaining of the period, of the following, the WISEST course of action for him would be to

    A. tell the pupils to refrain from asking questions and make every effort to complete the lesson
    B. select the most important items from the remaining one-quarter of the lesson and summarize them on the board
    C. have the pupils summarize the important ideas that had already been developed in the lesson and, thereafter, revise the next day's lesson plan
    D. complete as much of the lesson as possible and assign the incomplete portion for homework
    E. summarize succinctly for the class the last quarter of the lesson so that the lesson may be fully completed that day

49. In preparing pupils for a uniform examination which all teachers in the department have seen, the BEST procedure, of the following, is for a teacher to

    A. prime pupils on the key questions out of fairness, since other teachers will probably do the same
    B. make up similar questions but in different language and form and drill the class upon them
    C. reveal nothing about the scope or type of questions so that no pupils will have an unfair advantage
    D. give broad hints as to the test questions to slow learners only
    E. indicate to all pupils the scope of the examination and provide practice in questions on the topics covered in the examination

50. A book written by James B. Conant on American education is entitled

    A. THE EDUCATION OF AMERICAN TEACHERS
    B. THE TYRANNY OF TESTING
    C. THE SCHOOLS
    D. THE AMERICAN INTELLECT
    E. IS YOUR CHILD IN THE WRONG GRADE?

KEY (CORRECT ANSWERS)

1. A	11. B	21. A	31. A	41. B
2. D	12. C	22. A	32. E	42. C
3. C	13. B	23. E	33. B	43. C
4. B	14. B	24. B	34. D	44. D
5. B	15. C	25. D	35. A	45. A
6. A	16. E	26. C	36. C	46. C
7. B	17. C	27. E	37. B	47. B
8. E	18. C	28. A	38. C	48. B
9. B	19. B	29. C	39. D	49. E
10. C	20. C	30. D	40. E	50. A

TEST 2

DIRECTIONS: Each question or incomplete statement is followed by several suggested answers or completions. Select the one that BEST answers the question or completes the statement. *PRINT THE LETTER OF THE CORRECT ANSWER IN THE SPACE AT THE RIGHT.*

1. If the curricular demands of a course of study prevent the teacher from using adequate time to go over the questions on a uniform examination, the BEST procedure of the following would be for him to distribute review questions and

    A. answer papers and ask pupils to pick out questions for review at random
    B. make an analysis of frequency of errors on those done at home and review the questions most frequently missed first
    C. go over several questions each day over a period of weeks
    D. ask pupils to submit questions about their papers in writing and respond to a few of these each day
    E. model answers, together with scoring keys, which he drew up and used in marking their papers

1.____

2. Of the following, the MOST accurate statement regarding oral reports in junior high school classes is that they

    A. must be carefully supervised for form and content to be effective
    B. are worthwhile chiefly because they provide a change from the monotony of teacher domination
    C. are wasteful of time and provide learning neither for the speaker nor the audience
    D. should be prepared by pupils according to their own dictates to allow for maximum pupil expression
    E. should be extemporaneous and be used, wherever and whenever possible, in place of written reports

2.____

3. If a teacher is unsuccessful in eliciting the aim of a lesson through questioning in a few minutes, the MOST acceptable procedure, of the following, would be for the teacher to

    A. abandon the day's plan and reteach the previous day's work
    B. continue to rephrase pivotal questions to try to elicit the aim for as long as necessary
    C. state the aim and continue with the planned lesson
    D. give a homework assignment designed so as to help elicit the aim the next day
    E. lay this aside and take up the content of the lesson, knowing that the aim will be elicited from the students at an appropriate place in the lesson

3.____

4. Of the following, the MOST effective technique for determining whether a written homework assignment is clear is to

    A. examine in detail each of the assignments turned in the following day
    B. ask the class whether there are any questions about the assignment
    C. review intensively each of the directions in the assignment to make certain that these are understood
    D. have pupils copy the assignment at the beginning of the period to see whether questions arise
    E. discuss the assignment with the class and ask specific questions to test understanding

4.____

5. The developmental lesson is LEAST characterized by which one of the following? 5.___

   A. Medial and final summaries
   B. Lecture and demonstration
   C. The eliciting of factual information through questioning
   D. The eliciting and clarification of an aim with the help of a motivating technique
   E. The movement of the recitation arrow from pupil → pupil, pupil → teacher, teacher → pupil

6. In distributing questions in a class of pupils of average ability, of the following, it is usually BEST to 6.___

   A. start with non-volunteers to develop their interest
   B. ignore non-volunteers
   C. call on volunteers principally until the lesson gains momentum
   D. ask pupils not to volunteer so that each pupil in the class will feel responsible for staying attentive
   E. answer yourself the questions that the volunteers cannot answer

7. Assuming there are three marking periods per term, which one of the following is the BEST approach in arriving at a grade for a student for the second marking period? 7.___

   A. Average all test marks of the student for that marking period and assign the multiple of 5 which is closest to this average as his grade.
   B. Average all test marks for each student and assign a grade to a particular student which will indicate his relative standing in the class according to these averages.
   C. Using test marks, class work, and homework as a guide, assign as his grade your estimate of the percentage of the work that has been presented that the student has mastered to date.
   D. Average all test marks of the student since the beginning of the term and assign the multiple of 5 which is closest to this average as his grade.
   E. Averaging test marks, class work, and homework on a weighted basis of 3, 2, and 1, respectively, assign the multiple of 5 which is closest to this average as his grade.

8. The teacher is informed by the parent of one of his pupils that the child will be absent for the next three weeks because of illness. 8.___
   Which one of the following is the WISEST course of action for the teacher to follow?

   A. Offer to visit the child frequently during his illness to help him keep up with the class.
   B. Offer to tutor the child privately after he recovers at a nominal fee.
   C. Recommend the services of another teacher who will tutor the child for a fee.
   D. Have one of the children in his class volunteer to visit the sick child each day and transmit the content of the day's lesson and the assignment to him.
   E. Prepare an adequate number of written and study assignments for the child to do during his absence to minimize the effect of the loss of classroom instruction.

3 (#2)

9. Which one of the following methods for preventing cheating on tests is MOST effective? 9._____

   A. Mention several methods students use in cheating and warn the class that you will be watching carefully for them.
   B. Prepare two separate tests for alternate rows.
   C. Watch the class carefully and very severely punish the first offender to set an example for the rest.
   D. Call on the services of several Arista members to assist you in proctoring the test.
   E. Directly in front of the class, warn one of the students, whom you suspect to be a ringleader, that you will not tolerate cheating of any kind.

10. A test is considered RELIABLE if it 10._____

    A. measures what it is intended to measure
    B. predicts future behavior
    C. shows consistent growth from previous achievement test scores
    D. measures something consistently
    E. can be counted on to distinguish between the bright, the average, and the slow students

11. Of the following, the one statement that is generally TRUE of the slow learner is that he is 11._____

    A. slow in forming associations between words and ideas
    B. poor in reading but good in arithmetic
    C. more likely to develop into a delinquent
    D. in respect to the general population, at or about the 90th percentile in mechanical ability
    E. more capable of nonverbal reasoning than verbal reasoning

12. In day-to-day practice, the BEST procedure for handling medial summaries of a lesson is that they be 12._____

    A. stated briefly by the teacher
    B. developed into blackboard outlines
    C. elicited from students
    D. be given at the middle of the lesson
    E. developed into mimeographed sheets and be retained in a looseleaf binder

13. Of the following, probably the BEST way for the teacher to determine the true ability of a student is to 13._____

    A. consult frankly with his parents
    B. use a carefully standardized group intelligence test with age-grade equivalents
    C. review his records, observe him very carefully, and analyze his performance
    D. gain the confidence of a physician who has served the family for years
    E. send him to a college psychological testing center and have him take the full complement of tests

14. Of the following, the BEST basis for determining students' grades is usually 14._____

    A. tests *only*
    B. tests, homework, and class participation
    C. tests, homework, class participation, and conduct

D. tests and class participation
E. general estimate, based on their most recent and most successful performances

15. Of the following, the one MOST characteristic of the normally developing adolescent is   15.___

    A. continuous need for parental support
    B. development of emotional maturity
    C. desire for constant domination by siblings
    D. freedom from peer group identification
    E. emphasis on expression of individuality and independence

16. Assuming that a student asks a question which the teacher cannot immediately answer,   16.___
    the BEST way, among the following, for the teacher to handle the situation is to

    A. attempt to answer the question anyway
    B. admit he does not know and have the answer looked up and reported to the class at the same or next lesson
    C. state that the question will be answered at a future time
    D. accept the answer of a student who seems to know
    E. ignore the question as though he did not hear it, but then, later on, after finding the answer, refer incidentally to the question and give the answer

17. Of the following, the LEAST effective method for obtaining pupil participation is to   17.___

    A. permit pupils to volunteer to answer
    B. permit pupils to evaluate each others' answers
    C. permit pupils to help develop the wording of the aim of the lesson
    D. use the experiences of pupils in the lesson development
    E. permit pupils to answer in concert

18. Of the following, the record data MOST likely to indicate a slow learner would show that   18.___
    the pupil has

    A. repeated failure in mathematics
    B. a mental age considerably higher than the chronological age
    C. reading achievement at the 20th percentile
    D. been an only child of divorced parents
    E. a poor handwriting index

19. Group morale will be higher, as a rule, in classes that are run in which one of the follow-   19.___
    ing patterns?

    A. Democratic   B. Laissez-faire   C. Authoritarian
    D. Individual   E. Pupil-teacher

20. Of the following, the LEAST desirable procedure for the assignment of project work is   20.___
    that it should

    A. be requested by the student
    B. provide for teacher conferences with pupils
    C. be given only to superior or gifted students
    D. be a substitute for the daily requirements of the course
    E. take the place of homework

21. The LEAST acceptable of the following procedures for using test scores on teacher-made periodic tests is to

   A. prepare a chart or graph so that each pupil's marks are posted on the bulletin board
   B. train each pupil to keep an individual test score graph in his own notebook
   C. mount only perfect papers on the bulletin board
   D. train each pupil to keep a folder of his own corrected test papers
   E. group children in committees

21._____

22. Of the following, the BEST reason for parent-teacher interviews is that the teacher

   A. be enabled to communicate the importance of homework
   B. and the parent share the task of motivating the student
   C. be enabled to advise the parent about the child's needs
   D. be enabled to tell the parent about the child's strength
   E. may be enabled to explain the current philosophy of education, together with principles and practices, of the school

22._____

23. A good motivation for a class is always intended to accomplish all of the following EXCEPT

   A. develop a sustained drive
   B. create the feeling of an unsolved problem
   C. communicate the information basic to the lesson to be taught
   D. develop around needs of the adolescent
   E. refer to previous learnings or lessons

23._____

24. Which one of the following approaches to the teaching of democratic attitudes is the LEAST effective?

   A. Attitudes should be caught rather than taught.
   B. The learner should identify himself with outstanding democratic leaders.
   C. Direct teaching of moral values will be most productive.
   D. Experiences in democratic living will develop proper democratic attitudes.
   E. Participation in civic affairs shows democracy at work.

24._____

25. Which one of the following basic suggestions should one carry out FIRST to establish good class management?

   A. Train the class in distribution of material
   B. Discuss the aims of the year's work
   C. Make out a seating plan
   D. Survey the work of the semester
   E. Discuss the required rules for proper class behavior

25._____

26. Of the following, the MOST important element in a problem situation in terms of the pupil's learning is that

   A. the pupil must feel a need or desire to find a solution
   B. the problem situation must come from the experiences of the pupil
   C. there should not be a barrier between the pupil and the solution
   D. the problem should be clear-cut and solvable in only one way
   E. there should be a reward for finding the correct solution

26._____

27. Which one of the following is GENERALLY a sound principle of questioning for the teacher to follow?

    A. Speak very loudly to make sure all pupils hear you, especially those who are inattentive.
    B. Repeat pupils' answers to make sure all pupils have heard them.
    C. Distribute questions widely so that all or nearly all pupils have a chance to participate.
    D. Encourage chorus responses so that the teacher will know how many pupils know the answer
    E. Call only upon those who volunteer lest you hurt the feelings of non-volunteers by calling upon them and having them make a spectacle of themselves in front of the whole class

28. A good junior high school lesson will frequently employ which one of the following as its initial phase?

    A. Detailed correction of all parts of the previous night's homework
    B. Explanation of a new kind of problem by the teacher
    C. Warm-up drill for pupils
    D. *Sitting up tall* for extra credit
    E. Good joke with a double entendre

29. Which one of the following descriptions of routines is LEAST indicative of good classroom management?

    A. Initiating distribution of paper by pupil monitor's placing a pile on first desk of each row
    B. Adjusting of windows and shades by a pupil monitor
    C. Placing a sampling of homework examples on chalkboard for correction and discussion
    D. Having students choose seats and then preparing a seating plan for each class
    E. Having a pupil monitor check attendance in your Delaney Book

30. Which one of the following is a CORRECT statement concerning the administration of a pre-test?

    A. It unnecessarily consumes time to acquire information more readily discovered by the teacher by informal means.
    B. It should be confined to the beginning of the school year for the entire grade.
    C. It dispenses with the need for review.
    D. A pre-test is usually given only at the inception of a unit of several weeks' duration.
    E. It serves in part as a survey of individual and class background and readiness.

31. Which one of the following is an INCORRECT procedure in constructing a multiple-choice, short-answer test?

    A. Providing a separate answer sheet, particularly for a long test
    B. Placing a number of easy questions at the beginning of the test
    C. Insuring that correct choices are not obvious
    D. Arranging correct answers according to a pattern
    E. Providing for gradation of difficulty in the sequence of presentation of questions

32. Which one of the following is generally the LEAST effective method of informing pupils of homework assignments?   32._____

    A. Dictation of assignments by teacher
    B. Distribution of duplicated assignment sheets
    C. Recording on chalkboard by the teacher before the period begins
    D. Recording on chalkboard by pupil at the beginning of lesson
    E. Making a different student responsible each day for recording the assignment on the chalkboard

33. Of the following, the BEST technique in following up homework is: 33._____

    A. The homework should be marked as a test daily
    B. Several students should place their homework on the chalkboard daily
    C. Very little, if any, class time should be consumed in going over homework
    D. Only those exercises and problems with which pupils have difficulty should normally be explained
    E. A monitor in each row should check the homework daily

34. Which one of the following is the LEAST valid method of evaluating a pupil's understanding and readiness for advanced work?   34._____

    A. Asking the parent how long the pupil takes to do homework assignments
    B. Observing the pupil as he works on practice material in class
    C. Listening to the pupil's explanation of how he arrived at an answer
    D. Analyzing the pupil's test papers
    E. Examining the pupil's responses as an individual and as a group member

35. When a parent keeps an appointment to visit a teacher to complain about the progress of her child, the teacher may PROPERLY do which one of the following?   35._____

    A. Tell the parent that many children in the class are failing.
    B. Ask the parent whether she has carefully supervised her child's homework.
    C. Be fully prepared for the interview by carefully studying the pupil's complete school record.
    D. Point out that the pupil was probably not held to a high standard in previous grades.
    E. Inform the parent that she's lucky that her child has not been kicked out or suspended up to this time.

36. Which one of the following is usually a pedagogically UNSOUND procedure in utilizing a filmstrip with a junior high school class?   36._____

    A. Including a follow-up related to the filmstrip in the home study assignment
    B. Employing the filmstrip as a review device
    C. Having pupils read and explain the captions
    D. Showing a complete filmstrip of 47 frames in one period
    E. Asking three or more pithy questions relating the filmstrip to the ongoing unit

37. Of the following possible techniques for use in connection with audio-visual aids, the BEST is for the   37._____

    A. students to take notes during the showing of a film
    B. teacher to explain the film during its showing

C. teacher to make auxiliary use of the chalkboard during the showing of the film
D. teacher to stop the film at certain crucial points to emphasize important knowledges or skills
E. class to observe the film without interruption and be questioned about it thereafter

38. Of the following, which one represents the LEAST effective disciplinary technique? 38.___

   A. Compelling pupils under threat of punishment to observe class rules
   B. Helping pupils to enjoy classwork through the use of meaningful activities
   C. Providing wide participation for all pupils in the work and administration of the class
   D. Discouraging lateness to class by starting each period with an interesting activity
   E. Having the homework assignment and/or two or three motivating questions on the board as the class enters the room

39. Which one of the following is a GOOD practical procedure for a teacher to utilize in maintaining discipline? 39.___

   A. Learn the names of all pupils as quickly as possible at the beginning of the year.
   B. Disregard most minor infractions to avoid magnifying their importance.
   C. Prepare a list designating punishments for various infractions and follow it rigidly.
   D. Avoid displaying a sense of humor during the first few weeks of the term.
   E. Maintain a posture of strictness and rigidity for the first third of the term.

40. Of the following, the LEAST desirable technique in performing a demonstration is for the 40.___

   A. teacher to accompany the demonstration with a detailed commentary
   B. apparatus used to be on a large scale
   C. apparatus to be pre-tested
   D. teacher to rehearse the demonstration so that he can perform it easily and smoothly
   E. teacher to have at hand all the apparatus needed for the experiment before he begins his demonstration

41. Of the following, the LEAST desirable technique in performing a demonstration is for the 41.___

   A. teacher to accompany the demonstration with a detailed commentary
   B. apparatus used to be on a large scale
   C. apparatus to be pre-tested
   D. teacher to rehearse the demonstration so that he can perform it easily and smoothly
   E. teacher to have at hand all the apparatus needed for the experiment before he begins his demonstration

42. Learning is MOST apt to happen when the 42.___

   A. pupil understands the importance of what he is doing
   B. pupil is told all the necessary facts by a knowledgeable teacher
   C. pupil handles things
   D. academic standards of the school are kept high
   E. standards of discipline are high and firmly enforced

43. Of the following, the one MOST serious objection to laboratory lessons, as they are usually conducted, is that 43.____

    A. many of the activities are unsafe for unskilled pupils
    B. there is little opportunity for creativity and solving of problems
    C. there is usually insufficient apparatus for individual work by pupils
    D. most of the experiments cannot be performed in a 40-minute laboratory period
    E. they are stereotyped and often on an elementary level, needing little or no demonstration or discovery

44. Whenever possible, a filmstrip should be used rather than a sound motion picture on the same subject because 44.____

    A. it takes less time to show it
    B. it is usually more sequential
    C. it can be used to focus attention more readily where the teacher desires it
    D. the absence of a soundtrack removes a distraction
    E. it is usually better prepared since it deals directly with the topic

45. In order to complete the course of study with a class of slow learners, the teacher should 45.____

    A. skip certain sections which are too difficult
    B. have pupils take copious notes from the blackboard to be studied at home
    C. have pupils read the textbook in class under his direction
    D. plan for varied methods of study of the essential concepts of each unit
    E. make a precis of the remaining work and distribute it in mimeographed form to the students

46. Of the following possible questions for various science lessons, the one which BEST meets the criteria for a good teaching question is: 46.____

    A. Isn't it a fact that the stamen contains the anther?
    B. What about the piston?
    C. What is diastrophism and what theory is used to explain it?
    D. What is the word that denotes a central part or thing about which other parts of things are grouped? It is a six-letter word that begins with *n* and ends with *s*.
    E. Why do glaciers reach beyond the snow line?

47. The MOST important value of a lesson plan book is to 47.____

    A. insure continuity of instruction in the event of the teacher's absence
    B. permit the supervisor to evaluate the quality of work done
    C. enable the teacher to give thought to the work that will be carried on in the class
    D. enable the teacher to dictate important statements
    E. assure that there will be no repetition of work previously covered

48. Reinforcing learning can BEST be achieved when drill is 48.____

    A. given to all pupils regardless of achievement
    B. given in intensive doses
    C. individualized
    D. given without motivation
    E. consistent, continuous, and culminating

49. Thought-provoking answers are MOST easily achieved when   49.____

    A. a pupil's name is called before a question is asked
    B. a question is repeated several times in varied forms
    C. a question is asked and then a pupil is called upon to recite
    D. pupils anticipate the question
    E. pupils are advised to think before they speak

50. The teaching effectiveness of class discussions can be improved by all of the following   50.____
    EXCEPT having

    A. pupils face one another in speaking
    B. a competent recorder write main contributions on the blackboard
    C. the brighter pupils offer most of the contributions
    D. the group evaluate its own performance in terms of previously accepted objectives
    E. pupils ask questions of each other and of the teacher

KEY (CORRECT ANSWERS)

1. B	11. A	21. A	31. D	41. A
2. A	12. C	22. B	32. A	42. A
3. C	13. C	23. C	33. D	43. B
4. E	14. B	24. C	34. A	44. C
5. B	15. B	25. E	35. C	45. D
6. C	16. B	26. A	36. D	46. E
7. C	17. A	27. C	37. E	47. C
8. E	18. C	28. C	38. A	48. C
9. B	19. A	29. B	39. A	49. C
10. D	20. C	30. E	40. B	50. C

EXAMINATION SECTION
TEST 1

DIRECTIONS: Each question or incomplete statement is followed by several suggested answers or completions. Select the one that *BEST* answers the question or completes the statement. *PRINT THE LETTER OF THE CORRECT ANSWER IN THE SPACE AT THE RIGHT.*

1. A chemical agent which will prevent the growth of germs is called a(n) 1.____

    A. toxin B. antiseptic C. septic D. astringent

2. Creams should be removed from jars with 2.____

    A. the corner of a towel B. a spatula
    C. the fingers D. a pledget

3. An agent which causes the contraction of living organic tissue and thus checks bleeding is called a(n) 3.____

    A. antiseptic B. disinfectant C. styptic D. glycerine

4. When not in use, sanitized instruments should be kept in 4.____

    A. the pocket B. a dry sanitizer
    C. an insecticide D. a deodorizer

5. Bacteria will be destroyed by 5.____

    A. glycerine B. intense heat
    C. pumice D. freezing

6. Bacteria can enter the body through 6.____

    A. hair B. nails
    C. broken skin D. unbroken skin

7. Instruments which must be sanitized regularly should be made of 7.____

    A. brass B. stainless steel
    C. tin plated copper D. aluminum

8. Pathogenic bacteria create 8.____

    A. immunity B. disease C. anti-toxins D. hormones

9. Milium is the technical name for a 9.____

    A. whitehead B. blackhead C. pimple D. dry skin

10. Pediculosis capitis is the technical term for 10.____

    A. head lice B. itch mites
    C. flies D. mosquitoes

11. Frequent washings with strong soaps may cause the scalp to become   11.____

   A. healthy   B. oily   C. dry   D. flexible

12. The hair and scalp may often be reconditioned with heating cap treatments and   12.____

   A. lemon rinses   B. porosity treatments
   C. scalp massage   D. stripping treatments

13. A tint to which peroxide has been added   13.____

   A. penetrates the hair shaft
   B. gives an orange tone to the hair
   C. coats the hair shaft
   D. lightens the hair

14. A temporary coating of color applied to the hair is called a   14.____

   A. compound dyestuff   B. metallic tint
   C. progressive tint   D. color rinse

15. A penetrating tint is one which penetrates and deposits color permanently into the   15.____

   A. cuticle   B. medulla   C. cortex   D. follicle

16. Hair containing no red or gold tones is known as _____ hair.   16.____

   A. drab   B. lightened
   C. brunette   D. tinted

17. Hair should NEVER be thinned close to the   17.____

   A. sides   B. crown   C. ends   D. scalp

18. The hair should be wet if hairshaping is done with   18.____

   A. shears   B. clippers
   C. razor   D. thinning scissors

19. Thinning the hair involves   19.____

   A. shortening   B. blunt cutting
   C. decreasing its bulk   D. trimming the ends

20. Removal of split hair ends may be accomplished by   20.____

   A. ruffing   B. slithering
   C. blunt cutting   D. feathering

21. Featheredging the neckline is BEST accomplished with   21.____

   A. a coarse toothed comb   B. a lighted wax taper
   C. a razor   D. points of the shears

22. Shortening and thinning the hair at the same time is known as   22.____

   A. clipping   B. ruffing   C. tapering   D. back-combing

23. In basic hair shaping, the length of the strands of hair should NOT vary by more than 23._____

    A. 2 inches   B. 1/4 inch   C. 1 inch   D. 1 1/2 inches

24. Before hair is set, it is important that it be 24._____

    A. shaped   B. clipped   C. ruffed   D. shingled

25. The BEST time to apply scalp manipulations in shampooing is 25._____

    A. before the head has been lathered
    B. after the head has been lathered
    C. after the head has been rinsed
    D. after the head has been dried

KEY (CORRECT ANSWERS)

1.	B	11.	C
2.	B	12.	C
3.	C	13.	A
4.	B	14.	D
5.	B	15.	C
6.	C	16.	A
7.	B	17.	D
8.	B	18.	C
9.	A	19.	C
10.	A	20.	C

21.	D
22.	C
23.	B
24.	A
25.	B

TEST 2

DIRECTIONS: Each question or incomplete statement is followed by several suggested answers or completions. Select the one that BEST answers the question or completes the statement. PRINT THE LETTER OF THE CORRECT ANSWER IN THE SPACE AT THE RIGHT.

1. When shampooing lightened hair, use 1.___

   A. a mild shampoo and tepid water
   B. hot water
   C. liquid dry shampoo
   D. strong shampoo

2. When pressing hair over a loose scalp, use 2.___

   A. large sections   B. more oil
   C. small sections   D. more pressure

3. The EASIEST type of hair to press is _____ hair. 3.___

   A. coarse   B. wiry
   C. fine   D. gray

4. The PROPER position to hold a strand of hair while it is being wound is to hold it 4.___

   A. in a downward position
   B. to one side
   C. up and out from the scalp
   D. in a slanting position

5. Cold wave curls are wrapped without tension to 5.___

   A. give a loose wave
   B. give a tight wave
   C. allow the hair to contract
   D. prevent overprocessing

6. The neutralizing time in cold permanent waving is comparable to one of the following in heat permanent waving: 6.___

   A. steaming time   B. cooling time
   C. wrapping time   D. test curl time

7. In giving a cold wave to tinted hair, you must expect 7.___

   A. the true hair shade to appear   B. some discoloration
   C. the hair to become darker   D. some hair breakage

8. Cold wave solution applied to the scalp may cause scalp 8.___

   A. discoloration   B. irritation   C. tension   D. wens

9. End papers used in winding hair ends for a cold permanent wave must be 9.___

   A. non-porous   B. moisture proof
   C. porous   D. dampened with a fixative

10. If tension is used in winding the hair, the action of the cold wave solution may be

    A. retarded
    B. accelerated
    C. stopped entirely
    D. neutralized

11. The deciding factor in determining the processing time in cold permanent waving is the hair

    A. texture   B. pigment   C. porosity   D. density

12. Sectioning and winding the hair for a cold permanent wave usually begins at the _____ area.

    A. crown
    B. frontal
    C. nape
    D. temple

13. Before starting a cold permanent wave, the hair should be shampooed and thoroughly

    A. lubricated
    B. saturated
    C. rinsed
    D. neutralized

14. A cosmetology license issued by the division of licenses is *not* needed for an operator who gives only

    A. shampoos
    B. scalp treatments
    C. manicures
    D. facials

15. The texture of hair that requires the LONGEST processing time in cold permanent waving is _____ hair.

    A. fine   B. wiry   C. bleached   D. dyed

16. A preparation used in beauty culture that is *highly* inflammable is

    A. brilliantine
    B. astringent
    C. hair lacquer
    D. cold-wave lotion

17. A bluing rinse may be given

    A. to tone down over-hennaed hair
    B. to give a platinum shade to bleached hair
    C. to take the yellow out of gray or white hair
    D. for all the above purposes

18. Upon entering a beauty shop, you find that the operator, in preparation for a patron, has assembled, gauze, orris powder, shaker, hair tonic, cotton, hair brush. You would surmise that the preparation is for a

    A. scalp treatment for oily hair
    B. scalp treatment for dry hair
    C. pre-shampoo treatment
    D. dry shampoo

19. Comb pressing is known as a _____ press.

    A. regular   B. marcel   C. hard   D. soft

20. A substance that is NOT present in hair is

    A. carbon   B. hydrogen   C. nitrogen   D. kaoline

21. Of the following, the MOST recent development in correcting broken and bitten nails is the application of

    A. "Nail Fix"
    B. "Patti Nails"
    C. artificial nails
    D. Revlon's "Lactol"

22. Electrolysis permanently removes hair by destroying the hair

    A. shaft   B. root   C. bulb   D. papilla

23. The purpose of the neutralizer in the cold-wave process is to

    A. fix the curl
    B. expand the hair
    C. soften the hair
    D. remove the oil from the hair

24. Which of the following statements is INCORRECT?

    A. A knowledge of hair porosity is important to a beauty operator who does hair tinting.
    B. The ends of the hair take tint slower than the rest of the hair
    C. 28% ammonia water is used in some bleaching mixtures.
    D. Powdered magnesium carbonate is sometimes used when bleaching hair with hydrogen peroxide and ammonia water.

25. Which of the following statements is INCORRECT?

    A. Metallic hair tints are recommended by professional beauticians.
    B. It is sometimes necessary to pre-soften hair in giving a hair tint.
    C. A beautician should know when it is advisable to use a hair filler
    D. Under proper conditions bleached hair can usually be given a successful permanent wave.

KEY (CORRECT ANSWERS)

1.	A	11.	A
2.	C	12.	C
3.	A	13.	B
4.	D	14.	C
5.	C	15.	B
6.	B	16.	C
7.	B	17.	D
8.	B	18.	D
9.	C	19.	D
10.	A	20.	D

21. B
22. D
23. A
24. B
25. A

EXAMINATION SECTION
TEST 1

DIRECTIONS: Each question or incomplete statement is followed by several suggested answers or completions. Select the one that BEST answers the question or completes the statement. PRINT THE LETTER OF THE CORRECT ANSWER IN THE SPACE AT THE RIGHT.

1. Which of the following statements are CORRECT? 1.____
    I. The skin is the same thickness over the entire body.
    II. Hair is an appendage of the nails.
    III. Keratin is the horny substance of which hair is made.
    IV. The amount of pigment contained in the cortex determines the color of hair.
   The CORRECT answer is:

   A. I, II   B. I, III   C. III, IV   D. II, IV

2. Which of the following statements is (are) CORRECT? 2.____
    I. Keratosis is a form of skin disease characterized by thinning epidermis.
    II. An acute disease is one of long duration.
    III. Canities is caused by fever, shock, nervousness, or senility.
    IV. Eczema is a contagious, parasitic disease of the skin, with crust formations, emitting a mousy odor.
   The CORRECT answer is:

   A. III only   B. I only   C. II, III   D. III, IV

3. Which of the following statements is (are) INCORRECT? 3.____
    I. Lanolin is a beneficial ingredient in tissue creams.
    II. The eyes should be covered with pads when exposing the face to therapeutic lights.
    III. Muscle toning treatments are recommended for oily skin.
    IV. Massage helps to eliminate the waste products of metabolism.
   The CORRECT answer is:

   A. III only   B. IV only   C. I, II   D. III, IV

4. Which of the following statements is (are) INCORRECT? 4.____
    I. A dry shampoo cleanses the hair by absorbing the dirt and oil.
    II. Cocoanut oil is a desirable ingredient in shampoos because it helps to form a thick lather.
    III. A gasoline shampoo is dangerous because it is inflammable.
    IV. Vinegar and lemon rinses help to neutralize the alkaline soap residue on the hair and scalp.
   The CORRECT answer is:

   A. I only   B. I, II, III
   C. I, II, III, IV   D. None of the above

2 (#1)

5. Which of the following statements is (are) CORRECT?
   I. The most hygienic way to stimulate the circulation of the scalp is by scratching it.
   II. In the treatment for alopecia, the high-frequency current is applied with a glass rake electrode but without sparks.
   III. The cosmetologist is most concerned with the treatment of scalp diseases.
   IV. A shampoo rarely accompanies a scalp treatment.
   The CORRECT answer is:

   A. I only   B. II only   C. I, III, IV   D. II, III

6. Which of the following statements is (are) INCORRECT?
   I. Ordinary household ammonia can be used to mix with peroxide for bleaching purposes.
   II. The newer growth near the scalp is most resistant to a hair dye.
   III. It is better to be lavish than sparing in the use of hair tint.
   IV. A synthetic hair dye is progressive in action; whereas a hair color restorer acts instantaneously.
   The CORRECT answer is:

   A. II only   B. I, II, III   C. II, III, IV   D. I, III, IV

7. Which of the following statements is (are) INCORRECT?
   I. Pointed neck lines are suggested for long, slender necks.
   II. The principal difference between a shingle bob and a feather-edge is the height at which the hair is cut.
   III. The thumb is uppermost on the scissors when shingling or feather-edging.
   IV. In singeing the hair, the lighted taper is passed over loose hair.
   The CORRECT answer is:

   A. II only   B. I, II, III   C. II, III, IV   D. I, III, IV

8. Which of the following statements are CORRECT?
   I. It is better to oversteam than to understeam the hair.
   II. It is always advisable to make a test curl.
   III. Hair of a porous nature is the most difficult to wave.
   IV. A vinegar rinse will help to remove snarls occasioned by oversteamed or kinky hair.
   The CORRECT answer is:

   A. I, II   B. I, III   C. III, IV   D. II, IV

9. Which of the following statements are INCORRECT?
   I. Recommend beauty treatments which offer the greatest profits, without considering the benefits to the patron.
   II. A spiral permanent wave can be substituted for a croquignole permanent wave.
   III. Trade practices and secrets can be revealed to the public.
   IV. An operator is justified in condemning her competitors.
   The CORRECT answer is:

   A. I, II, III, IV   B. I, II, III
   C. II, III, IV   D. I, III, IV

10. Which of the following statements are CORRECT?
    I. The skin is the organ of protection, absorption, elimination, heat regulation, respiration, and sensation.
    II. Age has no effect on the elasticity of the skin.
    III. The skin is the seat of the organ of touch.
    IV. The sebaceous glands secrete an oily substance called sebum.

    The CORRECT answer is:

    A. I, II, III
    B. II, III, IV
    C. I, III, IV
    D. I, II, IV

KEY (CORRECT ANSWERS)

1. C
2. A
3. A
4. D
5. B
6. D
7. D
8. D
9. A
10. C

TEST 2

DIRECTIONS: Each question or incomplete statement is followed by several suggested answers or completions. Select the one that BEST answers the question or completes the statement. PRINT THE LETTER OF THE CORRECT ANSWER IN THE SPACE AT THE RIGHT.

1. Which of the following statements is (are) CORRECT?   1.____
    I. Keloid is a wartlike growth commonly located in the eyelids.
    II. A communicable disease is one that can be transmitted from person to person.
    III. Alopecia areata is baldness at time of birth.
    IV. Pityriasis is the term applied to an excessively oily condition of the scalp.
   The CORRECT answer is:

   A. I, II, III   B. II, III, IV   C. III, IV   D. II only

2. Which of the following statements is (are) CORRECT?   2.____
    I. Fine skin requires less cleansing treatments than coarse skin.
    II. Astringent lotion lubricates the underlying tissues.
    III. Makeup of all kinds should correspond to the natural coloring of the individual.
    IV. Cleansing creams are absorbed by the skin.
   The CORRECT answer is:

   A. III only   B. II, III   C. I, III   D. IV only

3. Which of the following statements is (are) INCORRECT?   3.____
    I. Corns should be removed when giving a pedicure.
    II. Alcohol is a good remedy for perspiring hands.
    III. Hydrogen peroxide solution is used as a germicide in manicuring.
    IV. The nail blade has a vascular supply while the matrix has none.
   The CORRECT answer is:

   A. II only   B. I, II, III   C. II, III, IV   D. I, III, IV

4. Which of the following statements is (are) INCORRECT?   4.____
    I. A peroxide rinse is used to give the hair a reddish tint.
    II. Henna rinse and henna compound have the same base.
    III. Tar shampoos are advised for light hair only.
    IV. Egg shampoos are advised for bleached, dry and brittle hair.
   The CORRECT answer is:

   A. I, II   B. I only   C. III, IV   D. I, III

5. Which of the following statements is (are) CORRECT?   5.____
    I. Synthetic organic dyes are penetrating dyes.
    II. Metallic dyes only coat the hair shaft.
    III. Any person can receive a hair dye with perfect safety.
    IV. A predisposition test is only applied if a lesion or an inflammation of the scalp is present.
   The CORRECT answer is:

   A. I, II, III   B. II, III, IV   C. I only   D. I, II

6. Which of the following statements is (are) INCORRECT?
    I. A correct haircut will emphasize the attractive features and minimize the defects.
    II. Alcohol may be used for sterilizing clippers and shears.
    III. Bangs are best suited to a face with a high forehead.
    IV. The hair should be thinned before a marcel wave.
   The CORRECT answer is:

   A. I, II   B. II, III   C. I, II, IV   D. III only

7. Which of the following statements are CORRECT?
    I. Medium warm irons are employed for croquignole marcel waving.
    II. Start a croquignole marcel wave at the back of the head.
    III. In marcelling, the hair should be picked up with a comb, not with an iron.
    IV. Brushing and combing injure marcel waves.
   The CORRECT answer is:

   A. I, II   B. II, III   C. III, IV   D. I, IV

8. Which of the following statements is (are) INCORRECT?
    I. All systems of heat permanents are dependent upon moisture, alkali, contraction and expansion of the hair.
    II. Average healthy hair can be stretched about twenty percent of its own length.
    III. The hydroscopic quality of hair means its ability to absorb liquids.
    IV. When hair becomes too kinky from a permanent wave, hot oil treatments will help.
   The CORRECT answer is:

   A. I, II, III, IV   B. I, II, III
   C. II, III   D. None of the above

9. Which of the following statements is (are) CORRECT?
    I. An operator can discuss controversial issues in a beauty shop.
    II. The borrowing and lending of supplies and instruments are to be encouraged.
    III. Do not represent a marcel wave to be the same as a finger wave.
    IV. Inferior supplies can be substituted for standard goods.
   The CORRECT answer is:

   A. I, II, IV   B. I, II   C. III only   D. II, III, IV

10. Which of the following statements are INCORRECT?
    I. The appendages of the skin are the nails, hair, sebaceous and sudoriferous glands.
    II. Skin absorbs water readily.
    III. Health, age, and occupation have no influence on the texture of the skin.
    IV. Elimination is an important function of the skin.
   The CORRECT answer is:

   A. I, II   B. II, III   C. III, IV   D. I, IV

KEY (CORRECT ANSWERS)

1. D
2. A
3. D
4. D
5. D

6. D
7. B
8. D
9. C
10. B

COSMETOLOGY
EXAMINATION SECTION
TEST 1

DIRECTIONS: Each question or incomplete statement is followed by several suggested answers or completions. Select the one that *BEST* answers the question or completes the statement. *PRINT THE LETTER OF THE CORRECT ANSWER IN THE SPACE AT THE RIGHT.*

1. Which of the following statements are INCORRECT?
    I. Hot packs are recommended for acne rosacea treatments.
    II. Dandruff is considered a disease if the shedding of scales is excessive.
    III. An albino is a person with an abnormal deficiency of pigment in the skin, hair, and eyes.
    IV. Oily foods tend to aggravate a dry condition of the skin.
   The answer is:

   A. I, II, III   B. I, III, IV   C. I, IV   D. II, IV

2. Which of the following statements are CORRECT?
    I. Skin bleaching lubricates the skin.
    II. Heat causes the skin to contract.
    III. Facials may be given once a week if necessary.
    IV. Vanishing creams are non-absorbent and serve as a powder base.
   The answer is:

   A. I, II   B. II, III   C. III, IV   D. II, IV

3. Which of the following statements are INCORRECT?
    I. The shape of the nail is determined by the shape of the finger.
    II. The nail should be filed from the center to the corners.
    III. Hangnails are a splitting of the epidermis at the side of the finger.
    IV. Liquid polish is injurious to the nail.
   The answer is:

   A. II, IV   B. II, III   C. I, III   D. I, IV

4. Which of the following statements is (are) CORRECT?
    I. Yellow streaks in white hair may be caused by acid in the system.
    II. Water that is too hot dries the scalp.
    III. Water is composed of hydrogen and oxygen.
    IV. Heated oil is not good for general use on the hair.
   The answer is:

   A. IV only   B. I, II, III   C. I, II, IV   D. II, III, IV

5. Which of the following statements is (are) INCORRECT?
    I. Ammonia added to a bleach always gives a reddish tint.
    II. Tinting of hair has been practiced in recent years only.
    III. When changing the color of the hair which has a uniform color, it is necessary to dye first that portion which was last treated with the softener.
    IV. White henna is a bleach.
   The answer is:

   A. III only   B. I, II, III   C. I, II, IV   D. II, III, IV

6. Which of the following statements are CORRECT?
    I. The treatment for trichoptilosis is clipping or singeing.
    II. A number one hair clipper makes the shortest cut.
    III. A good hair comb is made of hard rubber.
    IV. Use a fresh neck strip and towel for each customer.
   The answer is:

   A. I, II, III, IV
   B. I, II, III
   C. I, III, IV
   D. II, III, IV

7. Which of the following statements are INCORRECT?
    I. Marcelling cannot be accomplished with kinky hair.
    II. It is not necessary to stretch the hair in order to produce a lasting wave.
    III. It is necessary to use a hot iron on bleached hair.
    IV. The temperature of the irons should not be the same for every texture of hair.
   The answer is:

   A. I, II, III
   B. I, II, IV
   C. I, III, IV
   D. II, III, IV

8. Which of the following statements are CORRECT?
    I. Always start a finger wave at the back of the head.
    II. Finger waving is easier to accomplish if the proper waving lotion is used.
    III. The hair should be thoroughly combed before finger waving.
    IV. After the finger wave is formed, it is not necessary to reset waves into a soft coiffure.
   The answer is:

   A. I, II
   B. I, III
   C. II, III
   D. III, IV

9. Which of the following statements are INCORRECT?
    I. A successful permanent wave can be given over a hair restorer.
    II. In a croquignole permanent wave, the protectors are attached to the head before the hair is wound.
    III. There is no difference between a wet and dry winding since both are treated with pads.
    IV. A spiral permanent wave is usually wound from the hair ends to the scalp.
   The answer is:

   A. I, II, III
   B. II, III, IV
   C. I, III, IV
   D. I, II, IV

10. Which of the following statements are CORRECT?
    I. Operators should accept tips.
    II. The operator should not try to sell the patron additional services while giving her a facial.
    III. The operator can discuss personal matters while giving a beauty treatment.
    IV. Promptness in keeping appointments helps to retain patrons.
   The answer is:

   A. I, III
   B. II, III
   C. I, IV
   D. II, IV

KEY (CORRECT ANSWERS)

1. C
2. C
3. A
4. B
5. C

6. C
7. A
8. C
9. C
10. D

TEST 2

DIRECTIONS: Each question or incomplete statement is followed by several suggested answers or completions. Select the one that BEST answers the question or completes the statement. *PRINT THE LETTER OF THE CORRECT ANSWER IN THE SPACE AT THE RIGHT.*

1. Which of the following statements are INCORRECT?
   I. Corium, derma, and true skin are the same.
   II. The skin is an external non-flexible covering of the body.
   III. Dermatology is the study of the hair.
   IV. The skin is an organ of elimination.
   The answer is:

   A. I, III B. II, III C. I, IV D. II, IV

2. Which of the following statements is (are) CORRECT?
   I. Pityriasis is the presence of white scales in the hair and scalp.
   II. Pityriasis is the technical name for dandruff.
   III. The symptoms of pityriasis capitis are itching scalp, dry dandruff and a partial loss of hair.
   IV. Certain ingredients in cosmetics may cause a dermatitis.
   The answer is:

   A. I only B. I, II C. I, II, III D. I, II, III, IV

3. Which of the following statements are INCORRECT?
   I. Tissue cream is used to nourish the skin.
   II. A double chin is due to a lack of adipose tissue.
   III. All eyebrows should be arched the same way.
   IV. Petrissage is a kneading movement.
   The answer is:

   A. I, II B. II, III C. II, IV D. III, IV

4. Which of the following statements are CORRECT?
   I. Onychophagy should be treated as a disease.
   II. Nails filed long and given oil manicures will aid in keeping them from splitting.
   III. Onychia is inflammation of the nail matrix.
   IV. If a nail is torn, cut or injured, a new one will always grow.
   The answer is:

   A. I, II B. II, III C. II, IV D. III, IV

5. Which of the following statements are INCORRECT?
   I. Always stimulate the scalp before each shampoo.
   II. Sage tea is a bleach.
   III. A vinegar rinse will cause hair to snarl.
   IV. An egg shampoo is recommended for overbleached hair.
   The answer is:

   A. I, II B. II, III C. II, IV D. III, IV

6. Which of the following statements is (are) CORRECT?
   I. Hair can be dyed from a darker to a lighter shade.
   II. Ten-volume peroxide may be used just as effectively in bleaching hair as seventeen-volume.
   III. Hair may be tinted a lighter shade than the natural shade by just applying a lighter shade of tint.
   IV. Progressive dyes are slow working dyes.
   The answer is:

   A. I only   B. IV only   C. I, II, III   D. I, II, IV

7. Which of the following statements is (are) INCORRECT?
   I. A razor is never used for tapering and thinning.
   II. Neck dusters are never sterilized.
   III. It is advisable to singe the hair before shampooing.
   IV. Hair is always shampooed before cutting.
   The answer is:

   A. III only   B. IV only   C. I, II, III   D. I, II, IV

8. Which of the following statements are CORRECT?
   I. Round curls give a fluffy effect to fine, thin hair.
   II. Marcel waves should never be brushed.
   III. A hot iron should never be used when marcelling gray hair.
   IV. A Francois marcel and croquignole marcel are given in the same way.
   The answer is:

   A. I, II   B. II, III   C. I, III   D. II, IV

9. Which of the following statements are INCORRECT?
   I. Fine hair has more elasticity than coarse hair.
   II. Dyed hair should be steamed longer than normal hair.
   III. A full twist will give a marcel effect while a flat wrap will give a round curl effect on a spiral wrap permanent.
   IV. The steaming time on fine and coarse hair is the same, provided the wrap is different.
   The answer is:

   A. I, II   B. II, III   C. I, II, III   D. I, II, III, IV

10. Which of the following statements are CORRECT?
    I. Elasticity of hair is weakened by bleaching.
    II. Oversteamed hair can be restored to its original texture.
    III. All bleached hair can be given a successful permanent wave.
    IV. The width of the wave depends upon the amount of hair used in each strand.
    The answer is:

    A. I, II   B. I, III   C. I, IV   D. I, II, IV

KEYS (CORRECT ANSWERS)

1. B
2. D
3. B
4. B
5. B

6. B
7. D
8. C
9. D
10. C

EXAMINATION SECTION
TEST 1

DIRECTIONS: Each question or incomplete statement is followed by several suggested answers or completions. Select the one that *BEST* answers the question or completes the statement. *PRINT THE LETTER OF THE CORRECT ANSWER IN THE SPACE AT THE RIGHT.*

1. The coarseness or fineness of hair is determined by its
   A. porosity   B. diameter   C. melanin   D. elasticity

2. If the papilla is destroyed, then the hair will
   A. grow again   B. grow longer
   C. grow thinner   D. never grow again

3. Hair pigment is derived from the color-forming substances in the
   A. skin   B. liver   C. blood   D. lymph

4. Normal hair when wet, can be stretched *approximately*
   A. 50%   B. 20%   C. 75%   D. 40%

5. The cause of dry skin can be traced to a lack of
   A. pores   B. sebum   C. hormones   D. enzymes

6. The small openings of the sweat glands on the skin are called
   A. follicles   B. capillaries   C. pores   D. roots

7. The sebaceous glands of the skin secrete
   A. melanin   B. lymph   C. oil   D. perspiration

8. The skin is thickest on the
   A. palms and soles   B. ears
   C. eyebrows   D. face

9. A shaping which resembles the outline of a wave but which does not have a definite ridge and formation is called a _____ wave.
   A. skip   B. halo
   C. interlocking   D. shadow

10. To produce a good wave line, it is necessary that you have
    A. wavy hair   B. a planned pattern
    C. straight hair   D. a test curl

11. A pin curl placed immediately behind or below a ridge to form a wave is called a(n) _____ curl.

    A. cascade B. ridge
    C. upward D. reverse

11.____

12. A combination of a ridge against which is placed a series of overlapping pin curls followed by another ridge and series of pin curls is called a(n) _____ wave.

    A. halo B. skip
    C. interlocking D. vertical

12.____

13. The elevation or crest of a wave is known as the wave

    A. ridge   B. stem   C. spiral   D. crown

13.____

14. The diameter of the pin curl will determine the

    A. width of the wave B. depth of the wave
    C. direction of the ridge D. direction of the wave

14.____

15. The proper results in comb pressing will be retarded by the application of too much

    A. wrist movement B. pressing oil
    C. heat D. tension

15.____

16. The type of hair which usually requires the MOST heat in thermal waving is _____ hair.

    A. fine B. tinted
    C. false D. coarse

16.____

17. Fish hooks in thermal curling may be the direct result of forming _____ curls.

    A. incomplete B. tight
    C. overlapping D. loose

17.____

18. When forming a thermal curl, the iron is inserted at *approximately* a _____- degree angle.

    A. 45 B. 60
    C. 75 D. 30

18.____

19. For the protection of the patron's scalp in thermal waving, the operator should

    A. dampen the hair roots
    B. hold a finger under the curl
    C. hold the hair up and away from the scalp
    D. click the iron frequently

19.____

20. A lightener retouch is applied to

    A. the entire hair shaft B. the hair ends
    C. the new growth of the hair D. a virgin head of hair

20.____

21. The process of adding artificial color to the hair is known as hair

    A. toning   B. tinting   C. oxidizing   D. lightening

21.____

22. White henna is a(n)

    A. powdered magnesium carbonate
    B. organic dye
    C. lightening agent
    D. oil bleach

23. Lightened hair requires special care because it may be

    A. less porous
    B. excessively oily
    C. excessively elastic
    D. dry and fragile

24. Hair breakage may result if a lighteneer is applied over hair previously treated with

    A. cholesterol
    B. sulphur ointment
    C. cream rinse
    D. a metallic hair dye

25. An aniline derivative hair dye is an example of

    A. compound henna
    B. penetrating hair tint
    C. vegetable hair tint
    D. metallic hair tint

KEY (CORRECT ANSWERS)

1.	B	11.	B
2.	D	12.	B
3.	C	13.	A
4.	D	14.	B
5.	B	15.	B
6.	C	16.	D
7.	C	17.	A
8.	A	18.	A
9.	D	19.	B
10.	B	20.	C

21.	B
22.	B
23.	D
24.	D
25.	B

TEST 2

DIRECTIONS: Each question or incomplete statement is followed by several suggested answers or completions. Select the one that BEST answers the question or completes the statement. PRINT THE LETTER OF THE CORRECT ANSWER IN THE SPACE AT THE RIGHT.

1. The part of the hair which MOST readily absorbs the hair tint is the   1.____
   - A. side of the head
   - B. back of the head
   - C. hair ends
   - D. hair near the scalp

2. Facial massage is beneficial because it simultates the   2.____
   - A. salivary glands
   - B. pituitary glands
   - C. blood circulation
   - D. thyroid glands

3. Improper cleansing of the skin may cause the development of   3.____
   - A. blackheads   B. lentigo   C. furuncles   D. lesions

4. A clay pack is recommended for a skin that has   4.____
   - A. moles   B. warts   C. lesions   D. blackheads

5. Friction in massage requires the use of _____ movements.   5.____
   - A. pinching
   - B. slapping
   - C. deep stroking
   - D. light stroking

6. Effleurage is used in massage for _____ effects.   6.____
   - A. cooling
   - B. soothing and relaxing
   - C. heating
   - D. magnetic

7. A scalp that can be moved easily with finger manipulation is called _____ scalp.   7.____
   - A. loose
   - B. dry
   - C. free
   - D. galvanic

8. Hair pieces are BEST cleaned with a(n) _____ shampoo.   8.____
   - A. liquid dry
   - B. powder dry
   - C. soap
   - D. egg

9. Color rinses produce a _____ hair.   9.____
   - A. lighter shade to dark
   - B. temporary coloring to the
   - C. yellowish tinge in gray
   - D. permanent coloring to the

10. Soapless oil shampoo is composed of _____ oil.   10.____
    - A. sulfonated
    - B. crude
    - C. lanolin
    - D. mineral

82

11. A liquid dry shampoo may contain 11.____

    A. orris root B. henna mixture
    C. liquid soap D. a cleansing fluid

12. Waves are formed by 12.____

    A. half circles going in opposite directions
    B. half circles going in same direction
    C. two ridges directed to the right
    D. two ridges directed to the left

13. A wave shaped toward the face is called a 13.____

    A. French twist B. forward wave
    C. pompadour D. skip wave

14. The strand of hair from the scalp up to but not including the first curvature of the curl is 14.____
    called the

    A. hair cuticle B. curl ridge
    C. curl stem D. curl base

15. In setting hair, if the comb does NOT penetrate to the scalp, the wave will 15.____

    A. be more lasting B. not last
    C. be frizzy D. be deeper

16. The opening and blending of the hair setting, curls, waves, etc., into the finished coiffure 16.____
    is called a

    A. planned pattern B. natural growth pattern
    C. style setting D. comb-out

17. For a side part, the finger waving usually is started on the 17.____

    A. thin side of the hair B. back of the head
    C. heavy side of the hair D. crown of the head

18. Combing the short hairs toward the scalp is known as 18.____

    A. featheredging B. back combing
    C. effileing D. tipping

19. The BEST results in finger waving are obtained when the hair is 19.____

    A. straight B. naturally wavy
    C. frizzy D. kinky

20. To form pin curls that will be lasting and springy, it is necessary that the hair be wet, flat 20.____
    and

    A. very oily B. excessively curly
    C. away from the base D. stretched

21. In order that we form good pin curls, the hair must 21.____

    A. be slightly twisted B. have a natural wave
    C. be flat and smooth D. lie away from the base

22. The choice of setting lotion should be governed by 22.____
    A. its lightening qualities
    B. the color of the lotion
    C. the texture of the patron's hair
    D. its lacquer content

23. A good comb-out of a hair style is simplified by 23.____
    A. the use of a good setting lotion
    B. a planned hair-set
    C. combing hair slightly damp
    D. using curls with small center openings

24. In mixing the tint with the developer, use a _____ dish. 24.____
    A. brass   B. copper
    C. glass   D. bronze

25. A developer is an oxidizing agent such as 25.____
    A. ammonia   B. hydrogen peroxide
    C. dye softener   D. dye solvent

KEY (CORRECT ANSWERS)

1. C	11. D
2. C	12. A
3. A	13. B
4. D	14. C
5. C	15. B
6. B	16. D
7. A	17. C
8. A	18. B
9. B	19. B
10. A	20. D

21. C
22. C
23. B
24. C
25. B

EXAMINATION SECTION
TEST 1

DIRECTIONS: Each question or incomplete statement is followed by several suggested answers or completions. Select the one that *BEST* answers the question or completes the statement. *PRINT THE LETTER OF THE CORRECT ANSWER IN THE SPACE AT THE RIGHT.*

1. A substance having the ability to check the growth and multiplication of bacteria without destroying them, is called a(n) 1.____

    A. germicide   B. deodorant   C. antiseptic   D. disinfectant

2. A disinfectant can be applied with safety to 2.____

    A. the body
    C. clothing
    B. instruments
    D. an opening in the skin

3. Pathogenic bacteria are 3.____

    A. beneficial
    C. harmless
    B. harmful
    D. not disease producing

4. Asteatosis is an 4.____

    A. abundance of the sebaceous secretions
    B. absence of the sebaceous secretions
    C. abundance of the sudoriferous secretions
    D. absence of the sudoriferous secretions

5. A vinegar rinse is a(n) _____ rinse. 5.____

    A. alkaline
    C. acid
    B. neutral
    D. coloring

6. A dry shampoo is given with 6.____

    A. liquid soap
    C. powdered soap
    B. powdered orris root
    D. an antiseptic

7. The study of the nervous system and its disorders is called 7.____

    A. myology   B. dermatology   C. histology   D. neurology

8. The dead cells of the stratum corneum 8.____

    A. never shed
    C. shed according to season
    B. constantly flake off
    D. are difficult to remove

9. The skin is an absorbing organ to 9.____

    A. a limited extent
    C. no extent
    B. a great extent
    D. liquids only

10. Inflammation of the skin is known as

    A. dermatology B. dermatosis
    C. dermatologist D. dermatitis

11. Astringent tonics or ointments are most effective on

    A. normal skin B. dry skin
    C. oily skin D. sunburned skin

12. The use of strong soaps should be avoided on _____ skin.

    A. oily B. normal
    C. freckled D. dry

13. Face powders are intended to improve the _____ of the skin.

    A. texture B. appearance
    C. color D. function

14. Dry, brittle nails are aggravated by

    A. hot oil treatments B. tissue cream
    C. alkaline soaps D. cuticle cream

15. A group of similar cells performing the same function is called a(n)

    A. organ B. tissue C. gland D. system

16. In cleaning the free edge of the nail, abrasions are less likely to occur if the operator uses a(n)

    A. metal cleaner B. small brush
    C. orangewood stick D. bone instrument

17. The harmless types of hair colorings are the

    A. metallic dyes B. vegetable dyes
    C. aniline dyes D. compound hennas

18. The medical term for gray hair is

    A. albinism B. canities C. leucoderma D. lentigo

19. The addition of a few drops of a 28% solution of ammonia to peroxide will

    A. hasten its bleaching action
    B. stop its bleaching action
    C. lessen its bleaching action
    D. make the bleach more lasting

20. The treatment for trichoptilosis is

    A. thinning B. shingling C. clipping D. bobbing

21. Located at the back and lower part of the cranium is the

    A. frontal bone B. occipital bone
    C. parietal bone D. temporal bone

22. In machine permanent waving, coarse hair requires 22.____

    A. the same steaming time as fine hair
    B. less steaming time than fine hair
    C. more steaming time than fine hair
    D. double the steaming time for fine hair

23. The technical name for baldness is 23.____

    A. alopecia   B. pityriasis   C. dermatitis   D. albinism

24. Scalp treatments are NOT intended to 24.____

    A. preserve the health of the hair
    B. correct dandruff or loss of hair
    C. stimulate glandular activity
    D. cure infectious diseases of the scalp and hair

25. Processing in cold waving should be determined by 25.____

    A. the amount of hair   B. test curl
    C. texture of hair   D. previous waving time

KEY (CORRECT ANSWERS)

1.	C	11.	C
2.	B	12.	D
3.	B	13.	B
4.	B	14.	C
5.	C	15.	B
6.	B	16.	C
7.	D	17.	B
8.	B	18.	B
9.	A	19.	A
10.	D	20.	C

21. B
22. B
23. A
24. D
25. C

TEST 2

DIRECTIONS: Each question or incomplete statement is followed by several suggested answers or completions. Select the one that BEST answers the question or completes the statement. PRINT THE LETTER OF THE CORRECT ANSWER IN THE SPACE AT THE RIGHT.

1. It is advisable to brush hair before giving a shampoo because it

    A. saves combing after shampoo
    B. stimulates the scalp
    C. helps the operator to give the shampoo more rapidly
    D. saves one soaping

2. When bacteria get into the body, they are usually destroyed by

    A. white blood cells B. red blood cells
    C. lymph   D. plasma

3. Nails are composed of keratin, which is also found in the

    A. muscles   B. hair shaft   C. glands   D. bones

4. Eyelashes should NOT be tinted with hair dye because

    A. it may cause injury to the eyes
    B. it may not match the hair
    C. it may be too strong and make them too dark
    D. the operator may not be experienced in using it

5. Overbleached hair is difficult to permanent-wave because it has lost its

    A. melanin   B. elasticity   C. medulla   D. cortex

6. A spiral flat wave is

    A. twisted   B. half-twisted
    C. wound from ends to roots   D. wound from roots to ends

7. Excessive perspiration may be caused by

    A. cold   B. mental excitement
    C. lack of exercise   D. relaxation

8. A condition in which the cuticle splits around the nail is known as

    A. felon   B. onychia   C. hangnail   D. infection

9. A comedone extractor is a small instrument for removing

    A. scars   B. pimples   C. milia   D. blackheads

10. Nails are composed of a horny protein substance called

    A. cortex   B. keratin   C. allergens   D. cicatrix

11. The amount of melanin in the hair determines the

    A. texture   B. strength   C. elasticity   D. color

12. A disinfectant can also be used as an antiseptic if it is   12.____

    A. diluted
    B. concentrated
    C. applied full strength in smaller quantity
    D. mixed with a germicide

13. Hair is more resistant to dye   13.____

    A. behind the ears   B. at the back of the head
    C. at the crown   D. at the forehead and temples

14. A license which entitles an operator to work in a city beauty shop is issued by the   14.____

    A. department of health   B. department of state
    C. department of labor   D. city bureau of licenses

15. If, during the manicure, the skin is cut, the operator should apply   15.____

    A. powdered alum   B. formalin
    C. styptic pencil   D. herpicide

16. Pediculosis is treated by the application of   16.____

    A. tincture of larkspur   B. oil of wintergreen
    C. lanolin   D. vinegar

17. To disentangle oversteamed hair, one should use a(n)   17.____

    A. alkaline rinse   B. peroxide rinse
    C. neutral rinse   D. acid rinse

18. Of the following, the harmless types of hair colorings are the   18.____

    A. aniline dyes   B. compound henna
    C. metallic dyes   D. vegetable dyes

19. Which of these statements about bone is untrue?   19.____

    A. The technical term for bone is os.
    B. Bone is composed of animal and mineral matter.
    C. Bone is pink externally and white internally.
    D. The two types of bone tissue are dense and cancellous.

20. Which of these statements is untrue?   20.____

    A. Boiling water destroys all bacteria except spores.
    B. Spore-forming bacteria can be destroyed by exposure to steam at 15 pounds pressure.
    C. Dry heat is often used in the beauty shop.
    D. A disinfectant solution can be changed to an antiseptic by dilution.

21. Chemicals should be stored in   21.____

    A. open containers in a dark, dry and cool place
    B. closed containers in a dark, dry and cool place
    C. closed containers in a light, damp and cool place
    D. closed containers in a dark, damp and warm place

22. How should coarse hair and fine hair be wound for cold-waving? 22.___

    A. Coarse hair should be wound in smaller curls than fine hair.
    B. Coarse hair should be wound in larger curls than fine hair.
    C. Coarse hair cannot be cold-waved as easily as fine hair.
    D. Coarse hair takes a shorter time than fine hair for cold-waving.

23. Which of these statements is untrue? The 23.___

    A. ends of the bones are covered with cartilage
    B. occipital bone is located at the crown
    C. cranium consists of 10 bones
    D. mandible bone is bone of the lower jaw

24. Ringworm on the skin is caused by a 24.___

    A. bacterium   B. fungus   C. protozoan   D. worm

25. Cold applications tend to 25.___

    A. decrease the supply of blood in the area to which they are applied
    B. dilate the blood vessels
    C. bring a greater supply of blood to the area to which they are applied
    D. increase the pressure on the nerve endings

KEY (CORRECT ANSWERS)

1. B		11. D	
2. A		12. A	
3. B		13. C	
4. A		14. B	
5. B		15. A	
6. D		16. A	
7. B		17. D	
8. C		18. D	
9. D		19. C	
10. B		20. C	

21. B
22. A
23. B
24. B
25. A

EXAMINATION SECTION
TEST 1

DIRECTIONS: Each question or incomplete statement is followed by several suggested answers or completions. Select the one that BEST answers the question or completes the statement. *PRINT THE LETTER OF THE CORRECT ANSWER IN THE SPACE AT THE RIGHT.*

1. Which of the following is defined as the study of hair? 1.____
   A. Trichology B. Onychology
   C. Dermatology D. Epidemiology

2. Which of the following represent the chief purposes of hair? 2.____
   A. Oil reduction and protection B. Adornment and sweat diversion
   C. Adornment and protection D. Sweat diversion and protection

3. _____ is the technical term for eyelash hair. 3.____
   A. Cilia B. Barba C. Capilli D. Flagella

4. Hair is composed primarily of what substance? 4.____
   A. Collagen B. Keratin C. Melanin D. Glycogen

5. The chemical composition of hair varies with which of the following? 5.____
   A. Hair color B. Hair thickness
   C. Hair length D. Hair growth pattern

6. Which of the following is the MOST prominent type of hair on the human body? 6.____
   A. Cilia B. Lanugo
   C. Vellus hair D. Terminal hair

7. At a right angle to the direction of hair growth, an imaginary line known as the Line of _____ separates the follicle bulb at the widest part of the papilla into an upper and lower region. 7.____
   A. Auber B. Symmetry C. Proportion D. Demarcation

8. What type of hair is thick, may have a medulla, can vary in length, and is primarily found on the head or face? 8.____
   A. Cilia B. Lanugo
   C. Vellus hair D. Terminal hair

9. Which of the following represents the two main divisions of the hair? 9.____
   A. Bulb and follicle B. Hair root and papilla
   C. Hair root and hair shaft D. Hair shaft and follicle

10. In what region is the hair root located?
    A. Within the cortex   B. Under the cuticle
    C. Above the skin surface   D. Below the skin surface

11. Which of the following represents the three main structures associated with the hair root?
    A. Follicle, bulb, and papilla   B. Follicle, bulb, and medulla
    C. Follicle, bulb, and matrix   D. Follicle, papilla, and medulla

12. What structure is a tube-like depression in the skin that encases the hair root?
    A. Bulb   B. Papilla   C. Follicle   D. Medulla

13. Which of the following is the club-shaped structure that forms the lower part of the hair root?
    A. Bulb   B. Papilla   C. Follicle   D. Medulla

14. In what region is the papilla located?
    A. Above the hair root   B. Below the medulla
    C. At the skin surface   D. At the bottom of the follicle

15. Which of the following is defined as the small involuntary muscle that is attached to the underside of the follicle?
    A. Epicranius   B. Arrector pili
    C. Tendinous aponeurosis   D. Galea aponeurotica

16. Which of the following glands are commonly referred to as oil glands?
    A. Apocrine   B. Endocrine   C. Sebaceous   D. Sudoriferous

17. The sebaceous glands secrete an oily substance referred to as
    A. serum   B. sebum   C. plasma   D. sweat

18. To what are sebaceous glands connected?
    A. Dermis   B. Epidermis   C. Hair roots   D. Hair follicles

19. Which of the following represents the three layers of hair?
    A. Cuticle, cortex, and bulb   B. Cuticle, root, and medulla
    C. Cuticle, cortex, and medulla   D. Cuticle, bulb, and medulla

20. The scale-like cells of the cuticle protect what region?
    A. Root   B. Scalp
    C. Outside horny layer   D. Inner structure of the hair

21. The hair pigment is found in what layer?
    A. Cortex   B. Cuticle   C. Medulla   D. Papilla

22. The innermost layer of the hair is referred to as the _____, or medulla.
    A. cortex   B. cuticle
    C. pitch marrow   D. protective layer

23. Which of the following statements is TRUE regarding the papilla?   23.____
    If the papilla is destroyed, the hair will
    A. regrow
    B. grow back gray
    C. grow in thicker
    D. never grow again

24. How often are eyebrows and eyelashes replaced?   24.____
    A. Daily
    B. Weekly
    C. Monthly
    D. Every 4-5 months

25. The strength, texture, and natural color of hair is primarily dependent upon   25.____
    which of the following?
    A. Heredity
    B. Diet
    C. Exposure to sunlight
    D. pH of hair care products

KEY (CORRECT ANSWERS)

1. A
2. C
3. A
4. B
5. A

6. C
7. A
8. C
9. C
10. D

11. A
12. C
13. A
14. D
15. B

16. C
17. B
18. D
19. C
20. D

21. A
22. C
23. D
24. D
25. A

TEST 2

DIRECTIONS: Each question or incomplete statement is followed by several suggested answers or completions. Select the one that BEST answers the question or completes the statement. *PRINT THE LETTER OF THE CORRECT ANSWER IN THE SPACE AT THE RIGHT.*

1. As illustrated in the image shown at the right, which of the following is a condition in which a person is born with an absence of coloring matter in the hair shaft and no marked pigment coloring in the skin or irises of the eye?
   A. Vitiligo
   B. Lanugo
   C. Albinism
   D. Melanism

   1.____

2. Which of the following statements is TRUE regarding gray hair?
   Gray hair
   A. sheds easily
   B. forms in response to age
   C. forms in response to stress
   D. grows that way from the bulb

   2.____

3. What is the PRIMARY cause of gray hair?
   A. Vitamin deficiency
   B. Stress
   C. Normal aging process
   D. Chronic medical condition

   3.____

4. Which of the following statements is TRUE regarding vellus hair?
   Vellus hair is
   A. curly   B. coarse   C. pigmented   D. non-pigmented

   4.____

5. Which of the following represents the three phases of hair growth?
   A. Anagen, catagen, biogen
   B. Anagen, biogen, telogen
   C. Catagen, biogen, telogen
   D. Anagen, catagen, telogen

   5.____

6. Which of the following is known as the growing phase of hair growth?
   A. Biogen   B. Anagen   C. Catogen   D. Telogen

   6.____

7. Which of the following is known as the transitional phase of hair growth?
   A. Biogen   B. Anagen   C. Catogen   D. Telogen

   7.____

8. Hair continues to grow for what period of time?
   A. 3-6 months   B. 6-12 months   C. 1-2 years   D. 2-6 years

   8.____

9. The transitional phase of hair growth lasts for what period of time?
   A. 1-2 days   B. 3-5 days   C. 5-7 days   D. 1-2 weeks

   9.____

2 (#2)

10. Which of the following statements is TRUE regarding the follicle during catagen?
    During catagen, the follicle
    A. thickens
    B. lengthens
    C. decreases in volume
    D. increases in volume

    10.____

11. The lower part of what structure is destroyed during the transitional phase of the hair life cycle?
    A. Papilla   B. Hair root   C. Hair bulb   D. Hair follicle

    11.____

12. Which of the following is known as the resting phase of hair growth?
    A. Biogen   B. Anagen   C. Catogen   D. Telogen

    12.____

13. As illustrated in the image shown at the right, a whorl is formed when hair grows in what pattern?
    A. Tuft
    B. Circular
    C. Clockwise
    D. Conflicting

    13.____

14. As illustrated in the image shown at the right, what is formed when a tuft of hair is standing up?
    A. Whirl
    B. Cowlick
    C. Curl
    D. Point

    14.____

15. Which of the following represents the three hair shapes?
    A. Round, oval, and spherical
    B. Round, spherical, and concentric
    C. Round, oval, and almost flat
    D. Round, spherical, and almost flat

    15.____

16. If a person has straight hair, the hair itself is in what shape?
    A. Round   B. Oval   C. Almost flat   D. Spherical

    16.____

17. Which of the following determines the shape of hair a person will have?
    A. A person's diet
    B. A person's nationality
    C. The size of the hair root
    D. The direction of hair as it projects out of the follicle

18. The degree of coarseness or fineness of hair refers to the hair
    A. texture   B. porosity   C. elasticity   D. density

19. What type of hair has the GREATEST diameter?
    A. Fine   B. Coarse   C. Thick   D. Gray

20. _____ refers to the hair's ability to absorb moisture.
    A. Texture   B. Porosity   C. Elasticity   D. Density

21. _____ refers to the ability of the hair to stretch and return to its normal form without breaking.
    A. Texture   B. Porosity   C. Elasticity   D. Density

22. For hair with _____, it may take a longer amount of time for chemicals to penetrate hair.
    A. fine texture
    B. medium texture
    C. good porosity
    D. poor porosity

23. A miniaturization of certain scalp follicles contributes to what condition?
    A. Alopecia areata
    B. Telogen effluvium
    C. Postpartum alopecia
    D. Androgenetic alopecia

24. The hair loss process is a gradual conversion of terminal hair follicles to which of the following?
    A. Lanugo-like follicles
    B. Vellum-like follicles
    C. Dome-shaped follicles
    D. Horseshoe-shaped follicles

25. Which of the following statements is TRUE regarding androgenetic alopecia? Androgenetic alopecia
    A. alters follicle structure
    B. increases follicle numbers
    C. does not change follicle size
    D. does not alter the number of follicles

KEY (CORRECT ANSWERS)

1.	C	11.	D
2.	D	12.	D
3.	C	13.	B
4.	D	14.	B
5.	D	15.	C
6.	B	16.	A
7.	C	17.	D
8.	D	18.	A
9.	D	19.	B
10.	C	20.	B

21. C
22. D
23. D
24. B
25. D

TEST 3

DIRECTIONS: Each question or incomplete statement is followed by several suggested answers or completions. Select the one that BEST answers the question or completes the statement. *PRINT THE LETTER OF THE CORRECT ANSWER IN THE SPACE AT THE RIGHT.*

1. As illustrated in the image shown at the right, alopecia areata is defined as
    A. male pattern baldness
    B. baldness due to chronic medical condition
    C. sudden hair loss in round or irregular patches
    D. hair loss due to repetitive pulling or twisting of hair

   1.____

   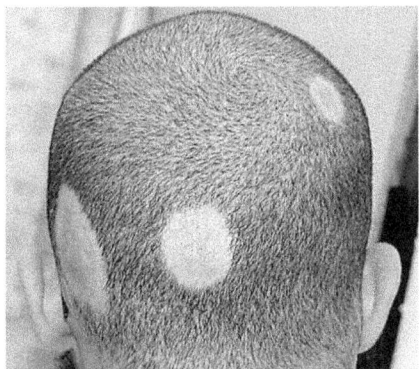

2. Which of the following statements is TRUE regarding telogen effluvium? Telogen effluvium
    A. is incurable
    B. is hereditary
    C. can be reversed
    D. only affects men

   2.____

3. As illustrated in the image shown at the right, excessive application of chemicals or excessive use of hot combs can lead to what condition?
    A. Androgenetic alopecia
    B. Alopecia areata
    C. Traumatic alopecia
    D. Traction alopecia

   3.____

   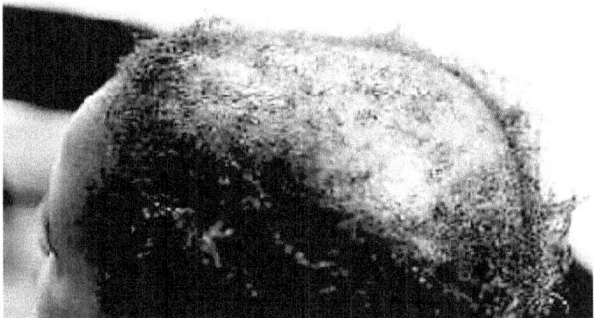

4. In what manner can a cosmetologist recognize miniaturized hairs on a client's scalp?
   Hair has _____ ends.
    A. flat   B. split   C. pointed   D. rounded

   4.____

5. What is an easy way to recognize androgenetic alopecia among females?
    A. A widening hair part
    B. Horseshoe-shaped balding pattern
    C. Fuller diameter ponytail
    D. Smaller diameter ponytail

   5.____

6. The degree of hair loss in men can be evaluated by rating which of the following?
   A. Pattern and density
   B. Pattern and texture
   C. Texture and density
   D. Texture and elasticity

7. Regarding male pattern baldness, the scalp is divided into what three regions?
   A. Front, mid-area, and apex
   B. Front, apex, and vertex
   C. Front, mid-area, and vertex
   D. Front, vertex, and parietal

8. As illustrated in the image shown at the right, which of the following is a condition characterized by an abnormal development of hair on areas of the body that normally only contain vellus hair?
   A. Hyperhidrosis
   B. Hypertrichosis
   C. Monilethrix
   D. Fragilitas cranium

9. Which of the following is the technical term for "split ends"?
   A. Monilethrix
   B. Hyperhidrosis
   C. Hypertrichosis
   D. Trichoptilosis

10. As illustrated in the image shown at the right, what condition is identified by nodular swellings along the hair shaft?
    A. Trichorrhexis
    B. Trichoptilosis
    C. Monolethrix
    D. Hypertrichosis

11. As illustrated in the picture shown at the right, which of the following is an autosomal disorder characterized by a beaded appearance of the hair due to periodic thinning of the shaft?
    A. Trichorrhexis
    B. Trichoptilosis
    C. Monilethrix
    D. Hypertrichosis

12. Which of the following is characterized by brittle hair?
    A. Hyperhidrosis   B. Hypertrichosis
    C. Monilethrix   D. Fragilitas cranium

13. The medical term for dandruff is
    A. trichorrhexis   B. trichoptilosis
    C. monolethrix   D. pityriasis

14. Tinea is commonly carried by scales or hairs containing which of the following?
    A. Bacteria   B. Viruses   C. Fungi   D. Protozoa

15. Tinea is the medical term for
    A. ringworm   B. scabies   C. dandruff   D. psoriasis

16. As illustrated in the image shown at the right, which of the following conditions is caused by head lice?
    A. Pityriasis
    B. Pediculosis
    C. Monolethrix
    D. Trichorrhexis

17. Which of the following are required for a healthy scalp?
    A. Cleanliness and stimulation   B. Cleanliness and conditioning
    C. Conditioning and stimulation   D. Stimulation and treatment

18. For a normal scalp, how often should a scalp massage be performed?
    A. Hourly   B. Daily   C. Weekly   D. Monthly

19. The mouths of hair follicles are _____ shaped.
    A. tube   B. funnel   C. cylindrical   D. spherical

20. Which of the following is responsible for the shine and silkiness of the hair?
    A. Cortex   B. Cuticle   C. Medulla   D. Papilla

21. What type of chemical bonds allow the hair to be curled using rollers?
    A. Hydrogen   B. Salt   C. Disulfide   D. Ionic

22. Hair that flows in the same direction is referred to as a hair
    A. wave   B. stream   C. current   D. flow

23. In order for chemicals to penetrate the healthy cuticle layer, they must have which of the following?
    A. Strongly acidic pH
    B. Mildly acidic pH
    C. Neutral pH
    D. Alkaline pH

24. Which of the following is a process in which living cells mature and begin their journey up the hair shaft?
    A. Osmosis
    B. Mitosis
    C. Meiosis
    D. Trichosis

25. The measurements of individual hair strands on 1 square inch of the scalp is referred to as
    A. texture
    B. porosity
    C. elasticity
    D. density

KEY (CORRECT ANSWERS)

1.	C	11.	C
2.	C	12.	D
3.	C	13.	D
4.	C	14.	C
5.	D	15.	A
6.	A	16.	B
7.	C	17.	A
8.	B	18.	C
9.	D	19.	B
10.	A	20.	B

21.	A
22.	B
23.	D
24.	A
25.	D

TEST 4

DIRECTIONS: Each question or incomplete statement is followed by several suggested answers or completions. Select the one that BEST answers the question or completes the statement. *PRINT THE LETTER OF THE CORRECT ANSWER IN THE SPACE AT THE RIGHT.*

1. Hydrogen chemical relaxers break disulfide bonds and convert them into what type of bonds?
    A. Hydrogen   B. Lanthionine   C. Ionic   D. Covalent

    1.____

2. Scalp massage is contraindicated with clients who have what medical condition?
    A. Diabetes
    B. Fibromyalgia
    C. Severe hypertension
    D. Migraine headaches

    2.____

3. Hair products are classified as either alkaline solution or an acidic solution based on the amount of which of the following?
    A. Hydrogen   B. Oxygen   C. Nitrogen   D. Sulfur

    3.____

4. Red-colored hair contains an iron containing pigment called
    A. anthocyanin
    B. betaxanthin
    C. tricosiderin
    D. astaxanthin

    4.____

5. A scalp treatment should never be performed if which of the following are present on the scalp?
    A. Moles   B. Freckles   C. Vitiligo   D. Abrasions

    5.____

6. What enzyme is a transmembrane protein which is essential to both the synthesis of eumelanin and pheomelanin and is directly linked to hair color?
    A. Tyrosinase
    B. Hydrolase
    C. Isomerase
    D. Oxid-reductase

    6.____

7. During the catagen phase, the hair follicle shrinks to _____ of the normal length.
    A. ½   B. ¼   C. $1/6$ D. $1/8$

    7.____

8. Which hair structure is only present in large thick hairs?
    A. Medulla   B. Papilla   C. Cortex   D. Cuticle

    8.____

9. Hair grows approximately _____ cm per year and any individual hair is unlikely to grow more than one meter long.
    A. 5   B. 10   C. 15   D. 20

    9.____

10. During the telogen phase, the hair does not grow but stays attached to the follicle while what structure stays in a resting phase below?
    A. Cortex
    B. Medulla
    C. Dermal papilla
    D. Arrector pili muscle

    10.____

11. If a person has wavy hair, the cross-section of the hair would appear
    A. round   B. oval   C. almost flat   D. spherical

12. If a person has curly hair, the cross-section of the hair would appear
    A. round   B. oval   C. almost flat   D. spherical

13. The average hair density is roughly _____ hairs per square inch.
    A. 500   B. 1,700   C. 2,200   D. 3,400

14. Porous hair can easily absorb water because what layer is raised?
    A. Cuticle   B. Cortex   C. Medulla   D. Papilla

15. High-grade proteins such as fish, eggs, cheese, milk, and meat are particularly beneficial because they are rich in what two substances that are essential for healthy hair growth?
    A. Iron and calcium
    B. Nitrogen and sulfur
    C. Magnesium and calcium
    D. Iron and nitrogen

16. What type of blood vessels supply and nourish the papilla?
    A. Arteries   B. Veins   C. Capillaries   D. Arterioles

17. Redheads often look as though they have thick hair because it tends to be of what texture?
    A. Fine   B. Medium   C. Coarse   D. Porous

18. What term has been introduced to identify the hair fiber shedding event as a separate process during hair follicle cycling?
    A. Anagen   B. Catagen   C. Exogen   D. Kenogen

19. Empty hair follicle after shedding of the hair fiber, but before the onset of renewed anagen are in a stage termed
    A. anagen   B. catagen   C. exogen   D. kenogen

20. Hair disorders are fundamentally caused by changes in hair follicle _____ and/or changes to the hair growth cycle.
    A. elasticity   B. porosity   C. texture   D. density

21. As illustrated in the image shown at the right, which of the following is a fungal infection of the hair shaft in which hard nodule made of fungus cling to hair fibers and can cause hair loss?
    A. Folliculitis
    B. Piedra
    C. Pityriasis
    D. Pediculosis

22. As illustrated in the image shown at the right, which of the following is a condition in which hair abruptly falls out in large patches a month or two after a personal shock such as surgery or severe stress?
    A. Alopecia areata
    B. Telogen effluvium
    C. Postpartum alopecia
    D. Androgenetic alopecia

23. Hirsutism, a condition in which women develop male-pattern hair (facial hair) is usually due to an increase in what hormone?
    A. Estrogen
    B. Progesterone
    C. Testosterone
    D. Aldosterone

24. Postpartum alopecia, hair loss after delivering a baby, is a form of what condition and usually resolves without treatment?
    A. Alopecia areata
    B. Telogen effluvium
    C. Postpartum alopecia
    D. Androgenetic alopecia

25. What part of the hair follicle, the short middle section, extends from the insertion of the arrector pili muscle to the entrance of the sebaceous gland duct?
    A. Isthmus
    B. Infundibulum
    C. Bulb
    D. Suprabulb

KEY (CORRECT ANSWERS)

1. B
2. C
3. A
4. C
5. D

6. A
7. C
8. A
9. B
10. C

11. B
12. C
13. C
14. A
15. B

16. C
17. C
18. C
19. D
20. D

21. B
22. B
23. C
24. B
25. A

EXAMINATION SECTION
TEST 1

DIRECTIONS: Each question or incomplete statement is followed by several suggested answers or completions. Select the one that BEST answers the question or completes the statement. *PRINT THE LETTER OF THE CORRECT ANSWER IN THE SPACE AT THE RIGHT.*

1. Which of the following is the outermost layer of skin, sometimes referred to as cuticle or scarf skin, and does not contain any blood vessels?
    A. Dermis
    B. Epidermis
    C. Subcutaneous tissue
    D. Sclerodermis

2. What underlying layer of skin is also referred to as derma curium cutis or true skin?
    A. Dermis
    B. Epidermis
    C. Subcutaneous tissue
    D. Sclerodermis

3. In what layer of the epidermis does skin cell growth occur through mitosis or cell division? Stratum
    A. basale
    B. lucidum
    C. corneum
    D. spinosum

4. What layer of the epidermis is sometimes considered to be part of the stratum germinativum and includes cells that have absorbed melanin to distribute pigmentation to other cells? Stratum
    A. basale
    B. lucidum
    C. corneum
    D. spinosum

5. What layer of the epidermis is evident only on the palms of the hands and the soles of the feet where there are no hair follicles? Stratum
    A. basale
    B. lucidum
    C. corneum
    D. spinosum

6. What layer of the epidermis, sometimes called the horny layer, is the toughest part of the epidermis and composed of keratin protein cells that are continually shed and continually replaced by new cells below? Stratum
    A. basale
    B. lucidum
    C. corneum
    D. spinosum

7. What layer of skin is a fatty layer that acts as a shock absorber to protect the bones and to help support the delicate structures such as blood vessels and nerve endings?
    A. Dermis
    B. Epidermis
    C. Subcutaneous tissue
    D. Sclerodermis

8. The _____ keeps the skin smooth, prevents dirt and grime from entering the outer layer of the epidermis, and also prevents the skin from drying or chapping.
    A. Acid mantle
    B. Dermis
    C. Subcutaneous tissue
    D. Sebaceous glands

9. Which of the following is distributed through all epidermal cells and forms an effective barrier from the penetration of ultraviolet rays to the deeper layers of the skin and tans the skin to protect it from burning rays of the sun?
   A. Albumin B. Keratin C. Melanin D. Collagen

10. Which enzyme found in melanosomes is important for the production of melanin?
    A. Lipase B. Kinase C. Tyrosinase D. Peroxidase

11. Which of the following, illustrated in the image shown at the right, is characterized by a pigmented or erythematous, flat lesion on the epidermis?
    A. Macule
    B. Papule
    C. Nodule
    D. Vesicle

12. Which of the following, illustrated in the image shown at the right, is characterized by a peaked or dome-shaped surface lesion measuring less than 5mm in diameter?
    A. Macule
    B. Papule
    C. Nodule
    D. Vesicle

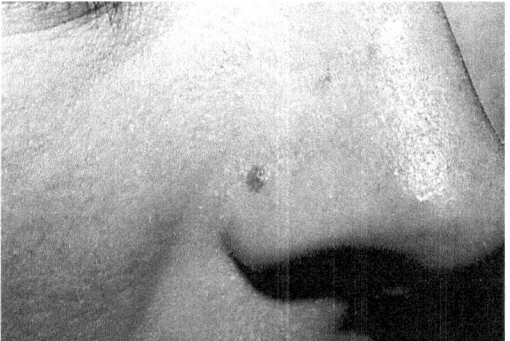

13. What skin disorder, illustrated in the image shown at the right, is characterized by an elevated, dome-shaped lesion greater than 5 mm in diameter?
    A. Nodule
    B. Plaque
    C. Vesicle
    D. Bulla

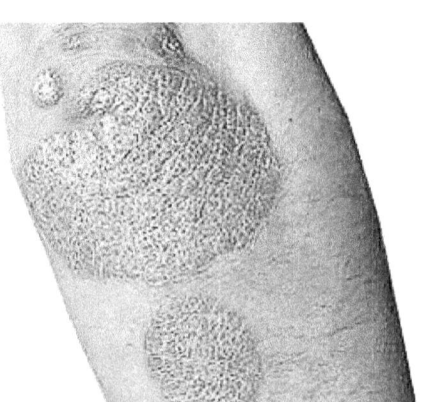

14. What skin disorder, illustrated in the image shown at the right, is characterized by fluid-filled blisters less than 5 mm in diameter?
    A. Nodule
    B. Plaque
    C. Vesicle
    D. Bulla

14.____

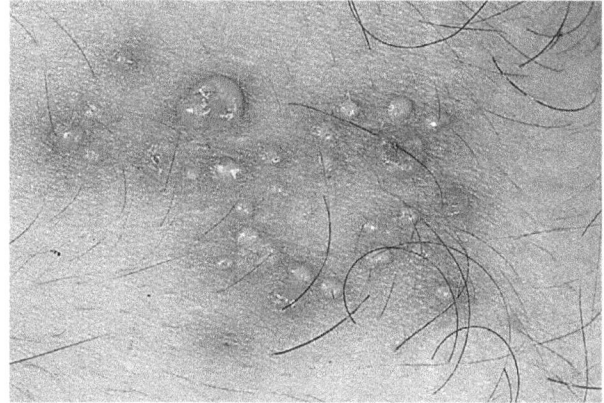

15. What skin disorder, illustrated in the image shown at the right, is characterized by fluid-filled blisters greater than 5 mm in diameter?
    A. Nodule
    B. Plaque
    C. Vesicle
    D. Bulla

15.____

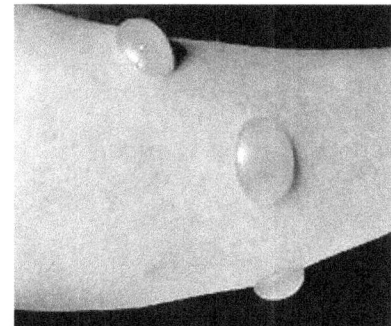

16. As illustrated in the image shown at the right, a wheal is an edematous, transient papule or plaque caused by fluid infiltration in what layer of the skin?
    A. Dermis
    B. Epidermis
    C. Sclerodermis
    D. Subcutaneous tissue

16.____

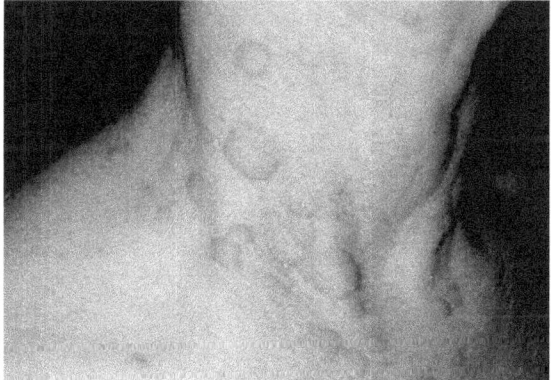

17. What skin disorder, illustrated in the image shown at the right, is characterized by fluid-filled blisters with inflammatory cells?
    A. Scales
    B. Pustules
    C. Vesicles
    D. Bulla

17.____

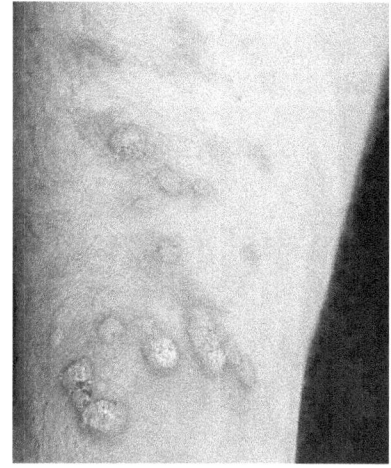

18. Hyperkeratosis, as illustrated in the image shown at the right, is characterized by increased thickness of what layer of the epidermis producing a scaled appearance on the skin?
    A. Stratum basale
    B. Stratum lucidum
    C. Stratum corneum
    D. Stratum spinosum

18.____

19. Which of the following is defined as intercellular connections made of proteins and are structures that assist in holding cells together?
    A. Desmosomes B. Melanosomes
    C. Corneocytes D. Keratinocytes

19.____

20. What type of melanin is red and yellow in color and normally produced by people with light-colored skin?
    A. Eumelanin B. Pheomelanin
    C. Neuromelanin D. Tyromelanin

20.____

21. What type of melanin is dark brown to black in color and is normally produced by people with dark-colored skin?
    A. Eumelanin B. Pheomelanin
    C. Neuromelanin D. Tyromelanin

21.____

22. Which of the following is defined as a fibrous, connective tissue made from protein that is found in the reticular layer of the dermis?
    A. Elastin B. Collagen C. Melanin D. Keratin

22.____

23. Which of the following is defined as epidermal cells that are composed of keratin, lipids, and other proteins that comprise 95% of the epidermis?
    A. Desmosomes B. Melanosomes
    C. Corneocytes D. Keratinocytes

23.____

24. Which of the following is defined as hardened, waterproof, protective keratinocytes that are dried out "dead" protein cells that lack nuclei?
    A. Desmosomes B. Leukocytes
    C. Corneocytes D. Melanocytes

24.____

25. Elastin is a protein fiber found in what layer of the skin that gives skin its elasticity and firmness?
    A. Dermis B. Epidermis
    C. Hypodermis D. Subcutaneous tissue

25.____

KEY (CORRECT ANSWERS)

1.	B	11.	A
2.	A	12.	B
3.	A	13.	B
4.	D	14.	C
5.	B	15.	D
6.	C	16.	A
7.	C	17.	B
8.	A	18.	C
9.	C	19.	A
10.	C	20.	B

21. A
22. B
23. D
24. C
25. A

TEST 2

DIRECTIONS: Each question or incomplete statement is followed by several suggested answers or completions. Select the one that BEST answers the question or completes the statement. *PRINT THE LETTER OF THE CORRECT ANSWER IN THE SPACE AT THE RIGHT.*

1. Which of the following types of cells are located in the dermis and respond to allergies by releasing histamines?
   A. Mast   B. Merkel   C. Leukocytes   D. Langerhans

   1.____

2. Which skin condition, illustrated in the image shown at the right, is an acquired skin disease characterized by white patches caused by a loss of pigment?
   A. Vitiligo
   B. Lentigo
   C. Albinism
   D. Leukoderma

   2.____

   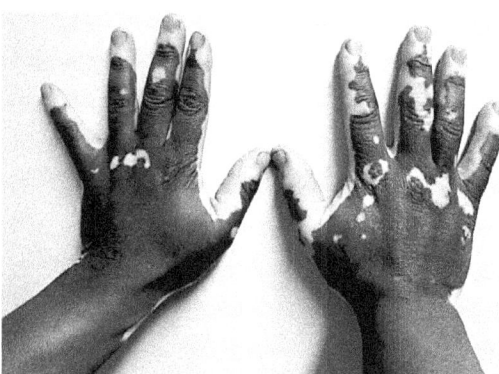

3. A "blister" is another name for which of the following?
   A. Cyst   B. Pustule   C. Papule   D. Vesicle

   3.____

4. _____ is defined as the mechanical or chemical process of removing dead skin to stimulate new cell growth.
   A. Desquamation   B. Exfoliation
   C. Permeation   D. Hydrolysis

   4.____

5. What skin condition, as illustrated in the image shown at the right, is a pigmentation disorder commonly referred to as a freckle?
   A. Nevus
   B. Vitiligo
   C. Lentigo
   D. Scleroderma

   5.____

   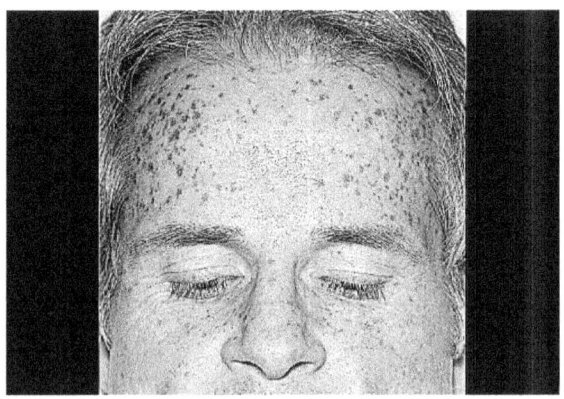

6. What region of the body can be characterized by the absence of apocrine glands?
   A. The nipples   B. The genitals
   C. The armpits   D. The soles of the feet

   6.____

7. Which of the following is a medical condition that results in the failure of the skin to produce melanin?   7._____
   A. Vitiligo   B. Albinism   C. Leukoderma   D. Scleroderma

8. _____ are the receptors responsible for reporting deep pressure and pain.   8._____
   A. Thermoreceptors   B. Ruffini's corpuscles
   C. Pacinian corpuscles   D. Meissner's corpuscles

9. _____ are the receptors responsible for reporting long-term pressure and heat.   9._____
   A. Chemoreceptors   B. Ruffini's corpuscles
   C. Pacinian corpuscles   D. Meissner's corpuscles

10. If a patient has a verruca on their skin, what is present on their skin?   10._____
    A. Wart   B. Pimple   C. Rash   D. Abrasion

11. _____ are the receptors responsible for reporting light pressure and cold.   11._____
    A. Krause's end bulbs   B. Ruffini's corpuscles
    C. Pacinian corpuscles   D. Meissner's corpuscles

12. Langerhans cells, which help protect the body from infection, are found in the stratum _____ layer of the skin.   12._____
    A. basale   B. lucidum   C. corneum   D. spinosum

13. Which of the following is defined as a male hormone that is found in both men and women that influences the amount of sebum that is produced?   13._____
    A. Melanin   B. Keratin   C. Collagen   D. Androgen

14. Which of the following is produced by the sudoriferous glands?   14._____
    A. Pus   B. Water   C. Sweat   D. Sebum

15. _____ is defined as the chemical conversion of living cells into dead protein.   15._____
    A. Desquamation   B. Exfoliation
    C. Permeation   D. Keratinization

16. Which pigment disorder, as illustrated in the image shown at the right, is commonly referred to as a birthmark?   16._____
    A. Nevus
    B. Vitiligo
    C. Lentigo
    D. Scleroderma

17. Which of the following is a medical condition caused by excess secretion of the sebaceous glands commonly associated with oily skin types?
    A. Hyperhidrosis   B. Seborrhea   C. Steatoma   D. Anhidrosis

17.____

18. _____ is defined as a mechanical abrasion of the epidermis that occurs when insect bites, scabs, or acne breakouts are scratched?
    A. Desquamation   B. Exfoliation
    C. Excoriation   D. Keratinization

18.____

19. Which of the following refers to an allergic reaction that produces an eruption of wheals?
    A. Hives   B. Carbuncle   C. Acne   D. Rosacea

19.____

20. A _____ is defined as a plugged sebaceous gland with an opening that is not widely dilated.
    A. whitehead   B. blackhead   C. furuncle   D. carbuncle

20.____

21. Foul-smelling perspiration caused by the yeast and bacteria that break down the sweat on the surface of the skin is referred to as
    A. anhidrosis   B. hyperhidrosis
    C. bromhidrosis   D. fungihidrosis

21.____

22. Eccrine glands are primarily responsible for which of the following processes?
    A. Sebum secretion   B. Collagen production
    C. Thermoregulation   D. Hormone regulation

22.____

23. Which acid promotes skin drying and cell turnover?
    A. Azaleic   B. Glycolic   C. Salicylic   D. Hyaluronic

23.____

24. According to the Fitzpatrick prototype scale, what skin type almost always burns and tans minimally?
    A. Type 1   B. Type 2   C. Type 3   D. Type 4

24.____

25. Which medical condition, as illustrated in the image shown at the right, is commonly referred to as baby acne?
    A. Milia
    B. Rosacea
    C. Lentigo
    D. Nevus

25.____

KEY (CORRECT ANSWERS)

1.	A	11.	D
2.	A	12.	D
3.	D	13.	D
4.	B	14.	C
5.	C	15.	D
6.	D	16.	A
7.	B	17.	B
8.	C	18.	C
9.	B	19.	A
10.	A	20.	A

21.	C
22.	C
23.	A
24.	B
25.	A

TEST 3

DIRECTIONS: Each question or incomplete statement is followed by several suggested answers or completions. Select the one that BEST answers the question or completes the statement. *PRINT THE LETTER OF THE CORRECT ANSWER IN THE SPACE AT THE RIGHT.*

1. Hair is primarily composed of what substance? 1._____
   A. Keratin   B. Collagen   C. Albumin   D. Magnesium

2. Which of the following is defined as a tube-like depression in the skin that encases the hair root? 2._____
   A. Bulb   B. Papilla   C. Follicle   D. Arrector pili

3. Which of the following refers to the club-shaped structure that forms the lower part of the hair root? 3._____
   A. Bulb   B. Papilla   C. Follicle   D. Arrector pili

4. The innermost layer of the hair is referred to as the pith marrow or 4._____
   A. cortex   B. cuticle   C. medulla   D. follicle

5. The growing phase of hair growth is referred to as which of the following? 5._____
   A. Biogen   B. Anagen   C. Telogen   D. Catagen

6. The transitional phase of hair growth is referred to as which of the following? 6._____
   A. Biogen   B. Anagen   C. Telogen   D. Catagen

7. The resting phase of the hair growth cycles is referred to as which of the following? 7._____
   A. Biogen   B. Anagen   C. Telogen   D. Catagen

8. Which of the following is defined as the hair's ability to absorb moisture? 8._____
   A. Density   B. Elasticity   C. Porosity   D. Viscosity

9. Scientists believe that approximately 95% of hair loss is caused by what progressive condition? 9._____
   A. Alopecia totalis   B. Alopecia areata
   C. Alopecia universalis   D. Androgenetic alopecia

10. Alopecia areata is defined as 10._____
    A. slow baldness
    B. male pattern baldness
    C. sudden hair loss in round or irregular patches
    D. hair loss due to repetitive pulling or twisted

11. When testing for telogen effluvium, the client is said to have active shedding if more than how many hairs come out? 11._____
    A. 1-3   B. 3-5   C. 5-10   D. 10-20

12. What topical solution can be applied to the scalp that has been medically proven to regrow hair?   12.____
    A. Follicidil   B. Minoxidil   C. Finasteride   D. Methacrylate

13. Hair is made up of what five elements?   13.____
    Carbon, nitrogen, hydrogen,
    A. oxygen, and sulfur   B. copper, and oxygen
    C. oxygen, and sodium   D. sulfur, and chlorine

14. The color of hair is generally related to which of the following?   14.____
    A. Texture of hair   B. Porosity of hair
    C. Health of the hair   D. Number of hairs on the head

15. Among the various natural hair colors, what color is generally the thickest and has the highest density?   15.____
    A. Red   B. Black   C. Brown   D. Blonde

16. At any one time, approximately what percentage of hair is in the anagen phase?   16.____
    A. 60%   B. 70%   C. 80%   D. 90%

17. Canities is the technical term for which of the following?   17.____
    A. Gray hair   B. Dandruff
    C. Beaded hair   D. Brittle hair

18. Which of the following refers to a prescription medication that is taken orally for the treatment of androgenetic alopecia?   18.____
    A. Follicidil   B. Minoxidil   C. Finasteride   D. Methacrylate

19. What medical condition, as illustrated in the image shown at the right, is characterized by dry, sulfur-yellow, cuplike crusts on the scalp?   19.____
    A. Tinea capitis
    B. Tinea favosa
    C. Pityriasis steatoides
    C. Pityriasis capitis simplex

20. What medical conditions, as illustrated in the image shown at the right, is characterized by greasy or waxy dandruff?   20.____
    A. Tinea capitis
    B. Tinea favosa
    C. Pityriasis steatoides
    D. Pityriasis capitis simplex

21. What medical condition, as illustrated in the image shown at the right, is characterized by dry dandruff?
    A. Tinea capitis
    B. Tinea favosa
    C. Pityriasis steatoides
    D. Pityriasis capitis simplex

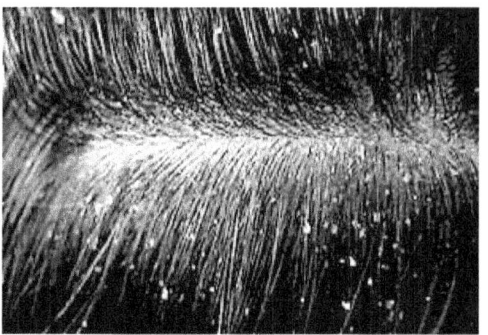

21._____

22. Which of the following refers to hairs that may split at any part of their length?
    A. Pityriasis
    B. Monilethrix
    C. Trichoptilosis
    D. Fragilitas crinium

22._____

23. A furuncle is an acute, localized bacterial infection of which of the following?
    A. Sweat pore
    B. Sebaceous gland
    C. Hair follicle
    D. Sudoriferous gland

23._____

24. Inflammation of the subcutaneous tissue, known as a carbuncle, is generally caused by what form of bacteria?
    A. Legionnaires
    B. Salmonella
    C. Staphylococcus
    D. Cryptosporidium

24._____

25. What medical condition, as illustrated in the image shown at the right, is a contagious skin disease caused by the itch mite?
    A. Carbuncle
    B. Scabies
    C. Ringworm
    D. Tinea capitis

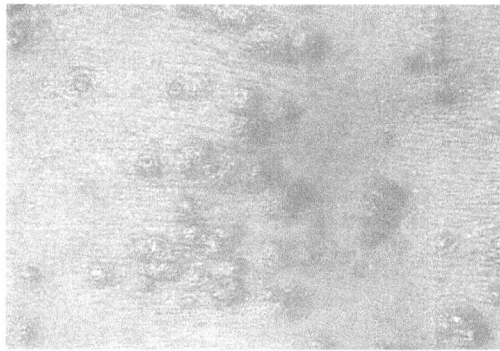

25._____

KEY (CORRECT ANSWERS)

1. A
2. C
3. A
4. C
5. B

6. D
7. C
8. C
9. D
10. C

11. B
12. B
13. A
14. D
15. D

16. D
17. A
18. C
19. B
20. C

21. D
22. D
23. C
24. C
25. B

TEST 4

DIRECTIONS: Each question or incomplete statement is followed by several suggested answers or completions. Select the one that BEST answers the question or completes the statement. *PRINT THE LETTER OF THE CORRECT ANSWER IN THE SPACE AT THE RIGHT.*

1. Small follicles are indicative of what type of skin?   1.____
   A. Dry   B. Oily   C. Normal   D. Combination

2. What skin type has an unhealthy acid mantle and skin barrier function?   2.____
   A. Dry   B. Oily   C. Normal   D. Combination

3. Follicles going from smaller to medium just on the edge of the T-zone by the nose is characteristic of what skin type?   3.____
   A. Dry   B. Oily   C. Normal   D. Combination

4. Skin that lacks oxygen is referred to as what type of skin?   4.____
   A. Dry   B. Oily   C. Combination   D. Asphyxiated

5. Touching the skin with your fingers during a skin analysis helps to determine whether or not the skin is   5.____
   A. dry   B. oily   C. rough   D. dehydrated

6. Which of the following describes skin damage or a skin condition caused by sun exposure?   6.____
   A. Actinic   B. Alipidic   C. Lipophilic   D. Lipophobic

7. Which of the following describes skin that does not produce enough sebum, indicated by the absence of visible pores?   7.____
   A. Actinic   B. Alipidic   C. Lipophilic   D. Lipophobic

8. Which of the following is a condition in which the skin appears red due to the presence of small, dilated, red blood vessels visible on the face?   8.____
   A. Combination skin   B. Couperose skin
   C. Rosacea   D. Erythema

9. Wrinkling as a result of photodamage and the aging process is measured according to which of the following?   9.____
   A. Fitzpatrick scale   B. Glogau scale
   C. Rubin classification   D. Monheit and Fulton system

10. What is used to measure the skin's ability to tolerate sun exposure?   10.____
    A. Fitzpatrick scale   B. Glogau scale
    C. Rubin classification   D. Monheit and Fulton system

2 (#4)

11. Which of the following is used to classify photodamage by the depth of skin changes or damage?   11._____
    A. Fitzpatrick scale
    B. Glogau scale
    C. Rubin classification
    D. Monheit and Fulton system

12. For what reason are occlusive products used?   12._____
    A. Reduce pore clogging
    B. Reduce oil loss
    C. Reduce water loss
    D. Increase sebum production

13. What skin condition, as illustrated in the image shown at the right, is characterized by skin redness as a result of inflammation?   13._____
    A. Combination skin
    B. Couperose skin
    C. Rosacea
    D. Erythema

14. Approximately what percentage of water is found in healthy skin?   14._____
    A. 30-40%   B. 40-50%   C. 50-70%   D. 70-80%

15. What medical condition, as illustrated in the image shown at the right, is characterized by a bacterial infection of the hairy parts of the face and neck?   15._____
    A. Sycosis
    B. Impetigo
    C. Furunculosis
    D. Herpes Zoster

16. Which of the following is defined as baldness due to scarring of the skin by chemical or physical means in which the hair follicle is permanently damaged and there is no treatment?   16._____
    A. Alopecia totalis
    B. Alopecia universalis
    C. Cicatrical alopecia
    D. Traction alopecia

17. _____ is a naturally occurring fungus that lives on the human skin and causes dandruff.   17._____
    A. Aspergillus
    B. Fusarium
    C. Cryptococcus
    D. Malassezia

18. Which of the following would be considered to be an internal factor causing dandruff?
    A. Hormonal imbalance
    B. Lack of proper cleansing
    C. Infrequent shampooing
    D. Increased activity of bacteria or fungi

18.____

19. Which of the following would be considered to be an external factor causing dandruff?
    A. Stress and tension   B. Poor nutrition
    C. Poor scalp stimulation D. Glandular problems

19.____

20. A crack in the skin that penetrates to the dermis is referred to as a(n)
    A. abrasion   B. laceration   C. fissure   D. puncture

20.____

21. In order for chemicals to penetrate a healthy cuticle layer, they must have which of the following?
    A. Low pH   B. Acidic pH   C. Neutral pH   D. Alkalkine pH

21.____

22. Of the 20 twenty amino acids required for hair production, how many can the human body actually produce?
    A. 6   B. 11   C. 15   D. 19

22.____

23. What type of chemical bond accounts for about one-third of the hair's overall strength?
    A. Hydrogen   B. Peptide   C. Salt   D. Disulfide

23.____

24. What type of chemical bond holds the chains of amino acids together and the position of these bonds determines the curl that is present in the hair?
    A. Hydrogen   B. Peptide   C. Salt   D. Sulfur

24.____

25. What type of chemical bond can be easily broken by weak alkaline or acidic solutions and changes in pH, however, can be reformed by normalizing the pH level of the hair?
    A. Hydrogen   B. Peptide   C. Salt   D. Sulfur

25.____

KEY (CORRECT ANSWERS)

1.	A		11.	C
2.	A		12.	C
3.	C		13.	D
4.	D		14.	C
5.	C		15.	A
6.	A		16.	C
7.	B		17.	D
8.	B		18.	A
9.	B		19.	C
10.	A		20.	C

21. D
22. B
23. A
24. D
25. C

GLOSSARY OF COSMETOLOGY

Compiled of words used in connection with beauty culture, defined in the sense of anatomical, medical, electrical, and beauty culture relationship only. Key to pronunciation will be found at bottom of each page.

A

abdomen (ăb-dō'měn): the belly; the cavity in the body between the thorax and the pelvis.
abducens (ab-dū'sênz): drawing away from.
abducent nerve (ăb-dū'sênt nûrv): the sixth cranial nerve; a small motor nerve supplying the external rectus muscle of the eye.
abductor (ăb-dŭk't ēr): a muscle that draws a part away from the median line (opp., adductor).
ability (â-bĭl'ĭ-tē): quality or state of being able to perform.
abnormal (âb-nôr'mâl): irregular; contrary to the natural law or customary order.
abnormality (âb-nôr-măl'ĭ-tē): the state of being abnormal; a deformity or malformation.
abortion (ă-bôr'shûn): act of giving premature birth; miscarriage.
abortion, artificial (är-tĭ-fi'sh'l): induced abortion.
abortionist (ă-bôr'shŭn-ĭst): one who practices abortion.
abrade (ăb-rād'): to rub off; to remove by friction or chafing; to roughen by friction.
abrasion (ă-brā'zhûn): scraping of the skin; excoriation.
abreast (ă-brĕst'): in line with; side by side with; up to the mark.
abscess (ăb'sĕs): a circumscribed cavity containing pus.
absorb (ăb-sôrb'): to suck in; to swallow up; engulf.
absorbent (ăb-sôr'bênt): anything that absorbs.
absorption (ăb-sôrp'shûn): assimilation of one body by another; act of absorbing.
absurd (ăb-sûrd'): inconsistent with reason.
acceleration (ăk-sĕl-ēr-ā'shûn): an increase in rapidity.
accelerator (ăk-sĕl'ēr-ā-tēr): any agent which hastens or quickens action.
accessory (ăk-sĕs'ô-r ē): any person or thing which aids subordinately, or assists.
accentuate (ăk-sĕn'tū-āt): to bring out distinctly; emphasize.
accessory nerve (nûrv): spinal accessory nerve; eleventh cranial nerve; affects the sterno-cleido-mastoid and trapezius muscles of the neck.
accidental (ăk-sĭ-dĕn'tâl): happening by chance.
accretion (â-krē'shôn): an accumulation of foreign matter in any cavity.
acetic (ă-sĕt'ĭk): pertaining to vinegar; sour.
acid (ăs'ĭd): a sour substance; any chemical compound having a sour taste.
acid rinse (ăs'ĭd rĭns): a solution of water and lemon juice or vinegar.
acidosis (ăs-ĭ-dō'sĭs): a condition in which there is an excess of acid products in the blood or excreted in the urine.
acidum boricum (ăs'ĭ-dûm bôr'ĭ-kûm): boric acid.
acne (ăk'nē): inflammation of the sebaceous glands from retained secretion.
acne albida (ăl'bĭ-dă): milium; white-head.
acne artificialis (är-tĭ-fĭsh-al'ĭs): pimples due to external irritants or drugs taken internally.
acne atrophica (ă-trŏf'ĭ-kă): acne in which the lesions leave a slight amount of scarring.
acne cachecticorum (kă-kĕk-tĭ-kôr-ŭm): pimples occurring in the subjects having anemia or some debilitating constitutional disease.

fāte, câre, ăm, finâl, ärm, àsk, sofă; ēve, évent, ĕnd, recênt, evēr; īce, ĭll; ōld, ŏbey, ôrb, ŏdd, cônnect, sŏft, fōod, fŏot; ūse, ûrn, ŭp, circûs

acne hypertrophica (hī-pēr-trŏf'ĭ-kă): pimples in which the lesions on healing leave conspicuous pits and scars.
acne indurata (ĭn-dū-rā'tă): deeply seated pimples with hard tubercles occurring chiefly on the back.
acne keratosa (kĕr-ă-tō'să): an eruption of papules consisting of horny plugs projecting from the hair follicles, accompanied by inflammation.
acne punctata (pŭnk-tá'tă): appear as red papules in which are usually found blackheads.
acne pustulosa (pŭs-tū-lō'să): acne in which the pustular lesions predominate.
acne rosacea (rō-zā'shē-ă): a form of acne usually occurring around the nose and cheeks, due to congestion, in which the capillaries become dilated and sometimes broken.
acne simplex (sĭm'plĕks): acne vulgaris; simple uncomplicated pimples.
acne vulgaris (vŭl-găr'ĭs): acne simplex; simple uncomplicated pimples.
acoustic (ă-ko͞os'tĭk): auditory; eighth cranial nerve; controlling the sense of hearing.
acquire (â-kwīr'): to receive; to attain; to master.
acrolein (ă-krō'iê-ĭn): a light volatile oily liquid giving off irritant vapor.
actinic (ăk-tĭn'ĭk): relating to the chemically active rays of the spectrum.
action (ăk'shŭn): the performance of a function.
activity (ăk-tĭv'ĭ-tē): natural or normal function or operation; physical motion or exercise of force.
acute (ă-kūt'): attended with severe symptoms; having a short and relatively short course; not chronic, said of a disease.
ad (ăd): a prefix denoting to, toward, addition, intensification.
adapt (ă-dăpt): to make suitable; to alter so as to fit for a new use.
adaptable (ă-dăpt'ă-b'l): capable of or given to adapting one's self to new conditions and uses.
adductor (â-dŭk'tēr): a muscle that draws a part toward the median line.
adenoma sebaccum (â-dĕn-ō'măsē-bā'sē-ûm): small tumor of translucent appearance, originating in the sebaceous glands.
adhere (ăd-hēr'): to remain in contact; to unite.
adipose (ăd'ĭ-pōs): relating to fat.
adipose tissue (tĭsh'û): fatty tissue; areolar connective tissue containing fat cells; subcutaneous tissue.
adjust (â-jŭst'): to make exact; to fit; to bring into proper relations.
adnata, alopecia (ă-nă'tă): baldness at birth.
adolescence (ăd-ō-lĕs'êns): state or process of growing from childhood to manhood or womanhood.
adrenal (ăd-rē'năl): an endocrine gland situated on the top of the kidneys.
adult (ă-dŭlt'): grown up to full age, size or strength.
adulterate (ă-dŭl'tēr-āte): to falsify; to alter, make impure by combining other substances.
aeration (ā-ēr-ā'shŭn): airing; saturating a fluid with air, carbon dioxide or other gas; the change of venous into arterial blood in the lungs.
aerobic (ā-ēr-ō'bĭk): unable to live without oxygen.
aesthetic, esthetic (ĕs-thĕt'ĭk): relating to sensation, either mental or physical; appreciation of beauty and art.
afferent (ăf'êr-ênt): bearing or carrying toward the center, or inward.
afferent nerves (nûrvz): convey stimulus from the external organs to the brain.
affinity (â-fĭn-ĭ-tē): attraction; in chemistry, the force which impels certain atoms to unite with certain others to form compounds.
agent (ā'jĕnt): an active power which can produce a physical, chemical, or medicinal effect

fāte, câre, ăm, finâl, ärm, ȧsk, sofă; ēve, évent, ĕnd, recênt, evẽr; īce, ĭll; ōld, óbey, ôrb, ŏdd, cônnect, sŏft, fo͞od, fo͝ot; ūse, ûrn, ŭp, circûs

agnail (ăg′nāl): hangnail.
air circulator (ăr sûr′kû-lā-tēr): a fan circulating cold air, attached to the permanent waving machine.
al (âl): a word termination denoting belonging to, of, or pertaining to.
ala (ā′lă); pl. **alae** (-lē): a wing-like structure, as the wing of the nose.
alae nasi (ā′lē nā′zī): the wing cartilage of the nose.
albida, acne (ăl′bĭ-dă): whitehead; milium.
albinism (ăl-bĭ-nĭz′m): congenital leukoderma or absence of pigment in the skin and its appendages; it may be partial or complete.
albino (ăl-bī′nō): a subject of albinism; a person with very little or no pigment in the skin, hair, or iris.
albumen, albumin (ăl-bū′měn): white of an egg; found also in milk and vegetables.
albuminous (ăl-bū′mĭ-nûs): relating in any way to albumen.
alcohol (ăl′kŏ-hŏl): a readily evaporating colorless liquid with a pungent odor and burning taste; powerful stimulant and antiseptic.
aliment (ăl′ĭ-mênt): nourishment; food or anything which feeds or adds to a substance in natural growth.
alimentary (âl-ĭ-měn′tă-rē): nourishing; relating to food or nutrition; the alimentary canal extends from the mouth to the anus.
alkali (ăl′kă-lī): an electropositive substance; capable of making soaps from fats; used to neutralize acids.
alkaline (ăl′kă-līn): having the properties of an alkali.
allergic (â-lûr′jĭk): sensitive to; susceptible.
allure (ăl-lūr′): to attract.
almond (ä′mûnd, ăl′mûnd): the kernel or seed of the fruit.
alopecia (ăl-ō-pē′shē-ă): deficiency of hair; baldness.
alopiecia, adnate (ăd-nă ′tă): baldness at birth].
alopecia areata (ā-rḗ-ă′tă): baldness in spots or patches.
alopecia cicatrisata (sĭ-kă-trĭ-sä′tă): baldness in irregular spots or patches, due to atrophy of the skin in the areas.
alopecia dynamica (dī năm′ĭ-kă): loss of hair due to destruction of the hair follicle by ulceration or some other disease process.
alopecia follicularis (fŏl-ĭk-u-lăr′ĭs): loss of hair due to inflamed hair follicles.
alopecia localis (lō-kā′lĭs): loss of hair occurring in patches on the course of a nerve at the site of an injury.
alopecia maligna (mă-lĭg′nă): a term applied to any form of alopecia that is severe and persistent.
alopecia premature (prē-mă-tū′ră): baldness beginning before middle age.
alopecia seborrheica (sěb-ôr-ē′ŭ-kă): baldness caused by diseased sebaceous glands.
alopecia senilis (sē-nĭl′ĭs): baldness occurring in old age.
alopecia syphilitica (sĭf-ĭl-it′ĭ-kă): loss of hair resulting from syphilis; usually a symptom of the second stage of the disease.
alopecia universalis (ū-nĭ-vēr-să′lĭs): a condition manifested by general falling out of the hair of the body.
alternating (ă ′tēr-nāt-īng): reversing periodically and rapidly in direction of flow, as in electricity.
alternating current, A.C. (kŭr′ânt): a current which rises and falls in strength of flow, alternating in opposite directions at regular intervals.

fāte, câre, ăm, finâl, ärm, ȧsk, sofă; ēve, évent, ěnd, recênt, evẽr; īce, ĭll; ōld, ŏbey, ôrb, ŏdd, cônnect, sŏft, fo͞od, fo͝ot; ūse, ûrn, ŭp, circûs

alum, alumen (ăl′ŭm, ă-lū′mên): sulphate of potassium and aluminum; an astringent; used as a styptic.

aluminum (ă-lū′mĭ-nûm): a whitish metal with a low specific gravity; noted for its lightness and its resistance to oxidation.

alveola (ăl-vē′ō-lă); pl., **alveolae** (-lē): a small hollow; alveolae border, the portion of the jaws bearing the teeth; branch of the internal maxillary artery.

amber (ăm′bēr): the fossil resin of pine trees found in northern Europe; it becomes negatively electrified in friction; the oil is sometimes used as a stimulant.

ameliorate (ă-mēl′yô-rāt): to make better; improve.

amino acid (ăm′ĭ-nō ăs ′ĭd): an important constituent of proteins.

amitosis (ăm-ĭ-tō′sĭs): cell multiplication by direct division of the nucleus in the cell.

ammeter (ăm′mē-tēr): an instrument for measuring the amperage of a current.

ammonia (ă-mō′nē-ă): a colorless gas with a pungent odor; very soluble in water.

amperage (ăm-pâr′âj, ăm′pēr-âj): the strength of an electric current.

ampere (ăm-pâr′): the unit of measurement of strength of an electric current.

amyl acetate (âm′ĭl ăs′ê-tât): banana oil; a colorless, aromatic and inflammable liquid employed as a solvent in making nail polishes.

anabolism (ăn-ăb′ô-lĭz′m): constructive metabolism; the process of assimilation of nutritive mater and its conversion into living substance.

analysis (ă-năl′ĭ-sĭs): a process by which the nature of a substance is recognized and is chemical composition determined.

analyze (ăn′ă-līz): to make an analysis.

anaphoresis (ăn-ă-fôr-ē′sĭs): the process of forcing liquids into the tissues from the negative toward the positive pole.

anaplasty (ăn′ă-plăs-tē): an operation for the restoration of lost parts; grafting.

anaplerosis (ăn-ă-plē-rō′sĭs): plastic surgery; replacement of defective parts caused by injury or disease.

anatomy (ă-năt′ō-mē): the science of the organic structure of the body.

anemia, anaemia (ă-nē′mē-ă): a condition in which the blood is deficient in red corpuscles, or in hemoglobin, or both.

anesthesia, anaesthesia (ăn-ĕs-thē′sē-ă, -zhē-ă): a state of being painless.

anesthetic, anaesthetic (ăn-ēs-thĕt′ĭk): a substance administered to make the body incapable of feeling pain.

angiology (ăn-jē-ŏl′ŏ-jē): the science of the blood vessels and lymphatics.

angioma (ăn-jē-ō′mă): a tumor formed of blood vessels and lymphatics.

Angstrom (ăng′strôm): a unit of measurement for the wavelength of light.

angular artery (ăng′û-lăr är′tēr-ē): supplies the lacrimal sac and the eye muscle.

angulus (ăng′û-lûs); pl., **anguli** (-lī): an angle or corner.

anidrosis, anhidrosis (ăn-ĭ-drō′sĭs): a deficiency in perspiration.

aniline (ăn′ĭ-lĭn, -lēn): a product of coal tar used in the manufacture of artificial dyes.

anion (ăn′ī-ôn): the ion which carries a charge of negative electricity; the element which, during electrolysis of a chemical compound, appears at the positive pole or anode.

annular finger (fĭn′gēr): ring finger.

anode (ăn′ōd): the positive terminal of an electric source.

anomalous (ă-nŏm′ă-lûs): abnormal; unusual; irregular.

anterior (ăn-tē′rē-ēr): situated before or in front of.

anthrax (ăn′thrâks): malignant pustule; gangrenous carbuncle-like lesion.

antibody (ăn′tĭ-bŏd-ĭ): a substance in the blood which builds resistance to disease.

antidote (ăn′tĭ-dōt): an agent preventing or counteracting the action of a poison.

fāte, câre, ăm, finâl, ärm, ȧsk, sofă; ēve, évent, ĕnd, recênt, evēr; īce, ĭll; ōld, ŏ́bey, ôrb, ŏdd, cônnect, sŏft, fo͞od, fo͝ot; ūse, ûrn, ŭp, circûs

anti-perspirant (ăn-tĭ-pēr-spī'rănt): a strong astringent liquid or cream used to stop the flow of perspiration in the region of the armpits, hands, or feet.
antiseptic (ăn-tĭ-sĕp'tĭk): a chemical agent that prevents the growth of bacteria.
antitoxin (ăn-tĭ-tôk'sĭn): a substance in serum which binds and neutralizes toxin (poison).
antrum (ăn'trŭm): a cavity or hollow space, especially in a bone.
anus (ā'nŭs): the lower opening of the digestive tract, through which fecal matter is eliminated.
aorta (ā-ôr'tă): the main arterial trunk leaving the heart, and carrying blood to the various arteries throughout the body.
apex (ā'pĕks): the summit or extremity; the upper end of a lung or the heart.
aponcurosis (ăp-ŏ-nū-rō'sĭs): a broad, flat tendon; attachment of muscles.
apoplexy (ăp'ŏ-plĕk-sē): disabled by a stroke generally caused by rupture of blood vessels in the brain.
apparatus (ăp-ă-rā'tŭs): a collection of instruments or devices adapted for a special purpose.
apparent (â-pâr'ênt, â-păr'-): seeming; appearing to be like.
appendage (â-pĕn'dĕj): that which is attached to an organ, and is a part of it.
appendix (â-pĕn'dĭks): a small intestinal organ.
applicator (ăp'lĭ-kā-tẽr): an instrument for the application of remedies.
apposition (ăp-ŏ-zĭsh'ŭn): the act of fitting together; the state of being fitted together.
appropriate (ă-prō'prē-āt): suitable; fitting.
approximately (ă-prŏk'sĭ-māt-lē): about; nearly; closely.
aqueous (ā'kwē-ŭs): watery; pertaining to water.
araneous (â-rā'nē-ŭs): like a cobweb.
area (ā'rē-ă): an open space; a limited extent of surface.
areata, alopecia (ā-rē-ā'tă): baldness appearing in spots or patches.
areola (ă-rē'ŏ-lă): any small ring-like discoloration; the pigmented ring surrounding the nipple of the breast.
areolar tissue (tĭsh'ū): loose connective tissue with many interspaces.
argyria (är-jĭr'ē-ă): a form of discoloration of the skin produced by the prolonged administration of silver salts.
arnica (är'nĭ-kă): tincture; a preparation employed externally as an application to sprains and bruises.
aromatic (ăr-ŏ-mat'ĭk): pertaining to or containing aroma; fragrant.
arrector pili (â-rĕk'tôr pī'lī): plural of arrectores pilorum.
arnectores pilorum (â-rĕk-tō'rēz pĭ-lôr'ŭm): the minute involuntary muscle fibers in the skin inserted into the bases of the hair follicles.
arsenical compound (är-sĕn'ĭ-kâl kôm'-pound): a white poisonous powder, useful in the treatment of certain skin diseases; has a considerable caustic action on the skin.
art (ărt): skill; dexterity; an especial facility in performing any operation, intellectual or physical, acquired by experience or study; knack.
arterial (är-tē'rē'âl): pertaining to an artery.
arteriole (är-tē'rē-ôl): a minute artery; a terminal artery continuous with the capillary network.
arteriosclerosis (är-tē"rē-ŏ-sklĕ́-rō'sĭs): abnormal hardness and dryness of the arterial coats resulting from chronic inflammation.
artery (är'tẽr-ē): a vessel that conveys blood from the heart.
articular (är-tĭk'ū-lăr): pertaining to an articulation or joint.
articulation (är-tĭk-û-lā'shŭn): joint; a connection between two or more bones, whether or not allowing any movement between them.
artificial (är-tĭ-fĭsh'âl): not natural.
artificialis, acne (är-tĭ-fĭsh-âl'ĭs): pimples due to external irritants or drugs taken internally.

fāte, câre, ăm, finâl, ärm, ȧsk, sofă; ēve, évent, ĕnd, recênt, evẽr; īce, ĭll; ōld, ŏbey, ôrb, ŏdd, cônnect, sŏft, fōōd, fōŏt; ūse, ûrn, ŭp, circŭs

asbestos scalp pad (ăs-bĕs′tôs scălp-păd): a heat resisting scalp protector.
ascertain (ăs-ēr-tān′): to acquire an accurate knowledge of.
asepsis (ă-sĕp′sĭs): a condition in which pathogenic bacteria are absent.
aseptic (ă-sĕp′tĭk): free from pathogenic bacteria.
assimilate (â-sĭm′ĭ-lāt): to absorb; to incorporate into the body the digested food products.
assimilation (â-sĭm-ĭ-lā′shôn): the incorporation of materials, prepared by digestion from food, into the tissues of the body.
asteotosis (ăs-tē-â-tō′sĭs): a deficiency or absence of the sebaceous secretions.
astringent (ăs-trĭn′jênt): a substance or medicine that causes contraction of the tissues, and checks secretions.
athlete's foot (ăth′lēts foot): a fungus foot infection; epidermophytosis.
atmosphere (ăt′môs-fēr): the whole mass of air surrounding the earth.
atom (ăt′ûm): the part of an element incapable of further division; the smallest part capable of entering into the formation of a chemical compound, or uniting with another to form a molecule.
atrichia (ă-trĭk′ē-ă): absence of hair, congenital or acquired.
atrium (ăt′rē-ûm); pl. **atria** (-ă): the auricle of the heart.
atrophic (ă-trôf′ĭk): relating to atrophy.
atrophica, acne (ă-trôf′ĭ-kă): acne in which the lesions leave a slight amount of scarring.
atrophy (ăt′rō-fē): a wasting away of the tissues of a part or of the entire body from lack of nutrition.
attachment (â-tăch′mënt): that which is connected to.
attenuate (â-tĕn′û-āt): to make thin; to lessen the effect of an agent.
attolens (â-tŏl′ênz): a term applied to muscles that elevate.
attolens aurem (ô′rêm): muscle that elevates the ear.
attrahens (ăt′ră-hênz): a muscle that draws or pulls forward.
attrahens aurem (ô′rêm): a muscle which pulls the ear forward.
attune (ă-tūn′): to bring into harmony.
auditory (ô ′dĭ-tō-rē): eighth cranial nerve; controlling the sense of hearing.
auricle (ô′rĭ-k′l): the external ear; one of the upper cavities of the heart.
auriculo temporal (ô-rĭk′û-lō têm′pôr-âl): sensory nerve affecting the temple and pinna.
auricular (ô-rĭk′û-lăr): pertaining to the ear or cardiac auricle.
auto (ô′t ő): a prefix meaning self; of itself.
autoclave (ô′tō-klāv): an apparatus used to sterilize objects with steam under pressure.
autonomic; autonomous (ô-tŏn′ō-mĭ k; -mûs): independent in origin, action or function; self-governing.
autonomic nervous system (nûrv′ûs sĭs′tĕm): the sympathetic nervous system; controls the involuntary muscles.
axilla (ăk-sĭl′ă): the armpit.
axillary (ăk′sĭ-lā-rē): pertaining to the axilla, or armpit.
axon (ăk′sŏn): a long nerve fiber extending from the nerve cell.

B

bacillus (bă-sil′us); pl. **bacilli** (-ĭ): rod-like shaped bacterium.
back combing (băk kōm′ĭng): combing the short hair toward the scalp while the hair strand is held in a vertical position; also called teasing.
bacteria (băk-tē′rē-ă): microbes, or germs.
bacterial (băk-tē′rē-âl): pertaining to bacteria.

fāte, câre, ăm, finâl, ärm, ȧsk, sofă; ēve, évent, ĕnd, recênt, evẽr; īce, ĭll; ōld, ŏbey, ôrb, ŏdd, cônnect, sŏft, food, foot; ūse, ûrn, ŭp, circûs

bactericide (băk-tē′rĭ-sīd): an agent that destroys bacteria.
bacteriology (băk-tē-rē-ôl′ō-jē): the science which deals with bacteria.
bacterium (băk-tē′rē-ûm); pl. **bacteria** (-ă): unicellular vegetable microorganism.
bakelite shield (bāk′kê-līt shēld): a strong shield made of a substance of strong chemical resistance, used as a scalp protector.
baldness (bôld′nêss): deficiency of hair; hair loss].
balsam of Peru (bôl′sâm of pê-r$\overline{oo}$): a thick, dark brown oily fluid exuded from the cut bark of Toluifera pereirae; used as an antiseptic and astringent..
bang (băng): the front hair cut so as to fall over the forehead; often used in the plural, as to wear bangs.
barber (bär′bĕr): one whose occupation it is to shave or trim the beard, and to cut and dress the hair.
barber science (sī′êns): the study of the beard and hair, and its treatment.
barber's itch (bär′bĕrz ĭch): tinea sycosis; ringworm of the beard; chronic inflammation of the hair follicles.
barium sulphide (bā′rē-ûm sŭl′fīd): a yellowish powder which decomposes in water with the liberation of hydrogen sulphide gas; used in depilatory preparations.
basal (bās′âl): foundation; pertaining to or located at the base.
basal layer (lā′er): the layer of cells at base of epidermis closest to the dermis.
base (bās): the lower part or bottom; chief substance of a compound; an electropositive element that unites with an acid to form a salt.
basilica vein (bȧ-sĭl′ĭk vān): the vein of the upper arm.
basis (bā′sĭs): foundation; the principal component part of a thing.
battery (băt′ĕr-ē): an apparatus containing two or more cells, for generating electricity.
bayberry plant (bā′bĕr-ē plânt): the leaves of Myrcia acris yield oil of bay which is used to make bay rum.
bay rum (bā rŭm): after-shaving lotion; used as a tonic and astringent.
beautician (blū-tĭsh′ân): one skilled in the art of beautifying the personal appearance.
beauty culture (bū′tē kŭl′tur): the study and practice of the improvement of the appearance.
belch (bĕlch): to emit gas from the stomach through the mouth.
belladonna (bĕl-ȧ-dŏn′ă): a poisonous European plant, used for medicinal purposes.
beneficial (bĕn-ḗ-fĭsh′âl): conferring real improvement to a desired end.
benign (bḗ-nīn): mild in character.
benzine (bĕn′zēn): an inflammable liquid derived from petroleum and used as a cleansing fluid.
benzoin (bĕn′zō-ĭn, -zoin): a balsamic resin used as a stimulant, and also as a perfume.
beriberi (bĕr′ē-bĕr′ē): a deficiency disease due to lack of vitamins in the diet.
Bernay tablets (bŭr′nā tăb′lĕts): a trade name; special tablets dissolved in water to be used as an antiseptic.
bevel (bĕv′êl): to slope the edge of a surface.
bi (bī): a prefix denoting two, twice, double.
bicarbonate of soda (bī-kär′bôn-ât of sō′dă): baking soda; relieves burns, itching, urticarial lesions and insect bites; is often used in bath powders as an aid to cleansing oily skin. Adding baking soda to the water in which instruments are to be boiled will keep them bright.
biceps (bī′sĕps): having two heads; a muscle producing the contour of the front and inner side of the upper arm.

fāte, câre, ăm, finâl, ärm, ȧsk, sofă; ēve, ḗvent, ĕnd, recênt, evẽr; īce, ĭll; ōld, ṓbey, ôrb, ŏdd, cônnect, sŏft, f$\overline{oo}$d, f$\overbrace{oo}$t; ūse, ûrn, ŭp, circûs

bichloride (bī-klō′rīd): a compound having two parts or equivalents of chlorine to one of the other element.
bichromate (bī-krō′māt): a compound having two parts of chromic acid to one of the base.
bicipital (bī-sĭp′ĭ-tâl): pertaining to the biceps muscle.
bile (bīl): a yellowish or greenish viscid fluid secreted by the liver; an aid to digestion.
binding posts (bīn′dĭng pōsts): small metal posts in which are fitted the metal tips of the conducting cords.
biology (bī-ôl′ō-jē): the science of life and living things.
bipolar (bī-pō′lăr): having two poles.
birthmark (bûrth′märk): any mark which is present at birth, usually lasting; a form of nevus.
biterminal (bī-tûr′mī-nâl): two terminals or poles of an electric current.
blackhead (blăk′hĕd): a comedone; a plug of sebaceous matter.
bladder (blăd′ĕr): a sac for the holding of urine.
bleach (blēch): to whiten or lighten.
bleached hair (blēcht hâr): hair from which the color has been wholly or partially removed by means of a bleaching solution.
bleaching solution (blēch′ĭng sō-lū-shŭn): hydrogen peroxide with addition of ammonia.
bleb (blĕb): a blister of the skin filled with watery fluid.
blemish (blĕm′ĭsh): a mark, spot, or defect, marring the appearance.
blend (blĕnd): to form a uniform mixture.
blister (blĭs′tĕr): a vesicle; a collection of serous fluid causing a raised elevation of the skin.
blond; blonde (blond): a person of air complexion, with light hair and eyes.
blood (blŭd): the nutritive fluid circulating through the arteries and veins.
blood poison (poi′z'n): an infection which gets into the blood stream.
blood vascular system (văs′ku-lär sĭs′tĕm): comprised of structures (the heart, arteries, veins and capillaries) which distribute blood throughout the body.
blood vessel (vĕs′êl): an artery, vein or capillary.
blue light (bloo lit): a therapeutic lamp used to soothe the nerves and ease pain.
bluing rinse (bloo′ĭng rĭns): a solution used to neutralize the unbecoming yellowish tinge on gray or white hair.
blunt (blŭnt): having a thick or rounded edge or point.
B.N.A.: an abbreviation for Basle Anatomical Nomenclature; a list of anatomical terms adopted by the German Anatomical Society in 1895.
bob (bŏb): a short haircut for women and children.
boil (boil): a furuncle; a subcutaneous abscess which drains out onto the surface of the skin.
boiling point (boil′ĭng point): 212°F or 100°C., the temperature at which a liquid begins to boil.
bone (bōn): os; the hard tissue forming the framework of the body.
bookkeeping (book′kēp-ĭng): the practice of keeping systematic business records.
borax (bō′răks): sodium tetraborate; a white powder used as an antiseptic and cleansing agent.
boric acid (bō′rĭk ăs′ĭd): acidum boricum; used as an antiseptic dusting powder; in liquid form as an eye wash.
brachial (brā′kĭ-âl): pertaining to the arm.
brachial artery (är′tĕr-ĭ): the main artery of the upper arm.
brachioradialis (brā″kĭ-ō-rā-dĭ-ā′lĭs): a flexor muscle on the radial side of the forearm.
braid (brād): to weave, interlace, or entwine together.
brain (brān): that part of the central nervous system contained in the cranial cavity, and consisting of the cerebrum, the cerebellum, the pons, and the medulla oblongata.
brew (broo): to extract the active ingredients by boiling.

fāte, câre, ăm, finâl, ärm, ȧsk, sofă; ēve, évent, ĕnd, recênt, evẽr; īce, ĭll; ōld, ŏ́bey, ôrb, ŏdd, cônnect, sŏft, foōd, foŏt; ūse, ûrn, ŭp, circûs

brilliantine (brĭl-yân-tēn'): an oily composition that imparts luster to the hair.
bristle (brĭs'l): short, stiff hairs found on brushes.
brittle (brĭt''l): easily broken; fragile.
broken circuit (brō'k'n sûr'kĭt): interruption in the flow of the electric current.
bromide (brō'mīd): a compound used as sedatives to allay nervous excitement.
bromidrosis (brō-mĭ-drō'sĭs): perspiration which smells foul.
bromo-acid (brō-mō-ăs'ĭd): a soluble dye used to impart a red indelible color in lipsticks.
bronchial (brŏn'kē-âl): pertaining to the wind pipe.
bronchus (brŏn'kûs); pl., **bronchi** (-kĭ): The main branch of the wind pipe.
brow (brou): the forehead.
bruise (brōōz): to injure, as by a blow or collision, without laceration.
brunette (brōō-nĕt): a person having brown or olive skin, brown or black hair and eyes.
brush curl (brŭsh cûrl): to wind the hair into ringlets with the aid of a hair brush.
bucca (bŭk'ă): the hollow part of the cheek.
buccal nerve (bŭk'âl nûrv): a motor nerve affecting the buccinators and the orbicularis oris muscle.
buccinators (bŭk'sĭ-nā-têr): a thin, flat muscle of the cheek, shaped like a trumpet.
bulbous (bŭl'bûs): pertaining to, or like a bulb in shape or structure.
bulky (bŭl'kē): of great thickness or of great weight.
bulla (bōōl'ă, bŭl'ă): a large bleb or blister.
bundle (bŭn'd'l): a structure composed of a group of muscular or nerve fibers.

C

cachecticorum, acne (kă-kĕk-tĭ-kōr'-ûm): pimples occurring in patrons having anemia or some debilitating constitutional disease.
cadmium (kăd'mĭ-ŭm): a white metallic element whose compounds are sometimes used in metallic hair dyes.
calamine (kăl'ă-mīn; -mĭn): zinc carbonate; pinkish powder, employed as a dusting powder or lotion.
calamine lotion (lō'shŭn): zinc carbonate in alcohol used for the treatment of dermatitis in its various forms.
calcium (kăl'sē-ûm): a brilliant silvery-white metal; enters into the composition of bone.
caliber, caliber (kăl'ĭ-bĕr): the diameter of a tube, such as the esophagus or urethra.
callous, callus (kăl'ûs): skin which has become hardened;; thick-skinned.
calory, calorie (kăl'ō-rē): a unit of heat.
chamomile (kăm'ŏ-mĭl): an herb whose flowers are brewed like tea and used as a brightening rinse for blond hair.
camphor (kăm'fẽr): a mild cutaneous stimulant; it produces redness and warmth, and has a slightly anaesthetic and cooling effect.
canaliculus (kăn-ă-lĭk'ū-lūs): a small canal or groove.
cancellous (kăn'sê-lûs): having a porous or spongy structure.
cancer (kăn'sẽr): a malignant growth, especially one attended with great pain and ulceration.
caninus (kȧn-nīn'ûs): the levator anguli oris muscle which lifts the angle of the mouth.
canitics (kă-nĭt'ĭks): the science which treats of canities.
canities (kă-nĭsh'ĭ-ēz): grayness or whiteness of the hair.
canitics, accidental (ăk-sĭ-dĕn'tâl): grayness of hair caused by fright.
canities, congenital (kŏn-jĕn'ĭ-tăl): a type of gray hair transmitted by heredity as in albinism.

fāte, câre, ăm, finâl, ärm, ȧsk, sofă; ēve, évent, ĕnd, recênt, evẽr; īce, ĭll; ōld, ŏbey, ôrb, ŏdd, cônnect, sŏft, fōōd, fŏŏt; ūse, ûrn, ŭp, circŭs

canities, premature (prē-mă-tūr): grayness of hair at an early age.
canities, senile (sē'nīl,-nǐl): grayness of hair in old age.
cantharides (kăn-thăr'ĭ-dēz): a preparation of dried blister beetles, a powerful counter-irritant.
canthus (kăn'thŭs): the corner of each side of the eye where the upper and the lower lids meet.
cape (kāp): a sleeveless garment used to protect the patron's clothing during beauty treatments.
capillary (kăp'ĭ-là-rē): any one of the minute blood vessels which connect the arteries and veins; hair-like.
capillurgy (kăp-ĭ-lôr'jē): the art of destroying superfluous hair.
capitate (kăp'ĭ-tāt): the large bone of the wrist.
capsicum (kăp'sĭ-kŭm): pungent berries or peppers; a counter-irritant which reddens the skin.
capsule (kăp'sūl): a membrane or sac-like structure enclosing a part or an organ; a small sac or case to enclose powders or drugs of disagreeable taste.
caput (kā'pŭt): poss., **capitis** (kăp'ĭ-tĭs): pertaining to the head.
carbohydrate (kär-bō-hī'drāt): a substance containing carbon, hydrogen, and oxygen, the two latter in the proportion to form water; sugars, starches and cellulose belong to the class of carbohydrates.
carbolic acid (kär-bŏl'ĭk ăs'ĭd): phenol made from coal tar; a caustic and corrosive poison; used in dilute solution as an antiseptic.
carbon (kär'bŏn): coal; an elementary substance in nature which predominates in all organic compounds and occurs in three distinct forms: black lead, charcoal, and lampblack.
carbona (kär-bō'nă): a trade name; a cleaning fluid containing carbon tetrachloride which is sometimes used in giving a liquid dry shampoo.
carbon-arc lamp (kär'bŏnärk lămp): an instrument which produces ultraviolet rays.
carbon dioxide (di-ŏk'sīd): carbonic acid gas; product of the combustion of carbon with a free supply of air.
carbon monoxide (mŏn-ŏk'sīd): a colorless, odorless and poisonous gas; its toxic action being due to its strong affinity for hemoglobin.
carbonic acid (kär-bŏn'ĭk ăs'ĭd): an acid formed by the union of carbon dioxide and water.
carbuncle (kär'bŭn-k'l): a large circumscribed inflammation of the subcutaneous tissue, similar to a furuncle, but much more extensive.
carcinoma (kär-sĭ-nō'mă): cancer; a malignant new growth of epithelial or gland cells infiltrating the surrounding tissues.
cardiac (kär'dē-ăk): pertaining to the heart.
caries (kā'rĭ-ē z): tooth decay.
carotid (kă-rŏt'ĭd): the principal artery of the neck.
carpal (kär'pâl): pertaining to the wrist or carpus.
carpus (kär'pŭs): the wrist; the eight bones of the wrist.
cartilage (kär'tĭ-lăj): gristle; a non-vascular connective tissue softer than bone.
casein (kā'sḗ-ĭn): the protein in milk and the principal constituent of cheese.
castor oil (kăs'tēroil): an oil obtained from the castor bean.
castile soap (kăs'tēl sōp): a fine, hard, white soap containing olive oil and other oils; originally came from Castile, Spain.
catabolism (kă-tăb'ô-lĭz'm): chemical changes which involve the breaking down process within the cells.
cataphoresis (kă-tăf-ố-rē'sĭs): the process of forcing medicinal substances into the deeper tissues, using the galvanic current from the positive towards the negative pole.

fāte, câre, ăm, finâl, ärm, ȧsk, sofă; ēve, ĕ́vent, ĕnd, recênt, evẽr; īce, ĭll; ōld, ŏ́bey, ôrb, ŏdd, cônnect, sŏft, fōod, fŏŏt; ūse, ûrn, ŭp, circŭs

catarrh (kă-tär): an inflammatory affection of the mucous membrane, especially of the nose and air passages; chronic rhinitis.
cathode (kăth′ōd): the negative pole or electrode of a constant electric current.
cation (kăt′ĭ-ŏn): an ion carrying a charge of positive electricity; the element which, during electrolysis of a chemical compound, appears at the negative pole or cathode.
caustic (kôs′tĭk): an agent that burns and chars tissue.
cauterize (kô′tĕr-īz): to burn or sear with a caustic.
cautery (kô′tĕr-ē): an agent used for scarring or burning the skin or tissues by means of heat or of a caustic chemical.
cava (kā′vă): a vena cava; any external cavity or hollow of the body.
cavity (kăv′ĭ-tē): a hollow space.
cell (sĕl): a minute mass of protoplasm forming the structural unit of every organized body.
cellophane retention paper (sĕ l′ō-fān rḗ-tĕn′shŭn pā′pĕr): material used to wrap hair in permanent waving.
cellular (sĕl′û-lăr): consisting of or pertaining to cells.
cellulose (sĕl′û-lōs): a carbohydrate, such as vegetable fiber.
centigrade (sĕn′t ĭ-grād): consisting of 100 degrees; one hundredth part of a circle; of or pertaining to centigrade thermometer.
centrosome (sĕn′trṓ-sōm): a cellular body which controls the division of the cell.
cephalic vein (sḗ-făl′ĭk vān): the vein of the upper arm.
cerebellum (sĕr-ḗ-bĕl′ûm): the posterior and lower part of the brain.
cerebral (sĕr′ḗ-brăl): pertaining to the cerebrum.
cerebrospinal system (sêr-ē-brō-spī′nāl sĭs′tĕm): consists of the brain, spinal cord, spinal nerves, and the cranial nerves.
cerebrum (sĕr′ḗ-brûm): the superior and larger part of the brain.
cerumen (sḗ-roo′mĕ n): the earwax.
cervix (sûr′vĭks): the neck; any neck-like structure.
cervical (sûr′vĭ-kăl): pertaining to the neck.
chancre (shăn′kẽr): the primary lesion of syphilis.
characterize (kăr′âk-tē r-īz): to indicate, or describe the character of.
chafe (chāf): to rub and make warm; to excite heat by friction; to irritate.
chemical (kĕm′ĭ-kăl): relating to chemistry.
chemical dye remover (dī rē-moov′ẽr): a dye remover containing a chemical solvent.
chemism (kĕm′ĭz′m): chemical action or influence.
chemistry (kĕm′ĭs-trē): the science dealing with the composition of substances; the elements and their mutual reactions, and the phenomena resulting from the formation and decomposition of compounds.
chic (shēk): stylish, smart.
chignon (shē′nyôn): a knot or mass of hair.
chiropody (kī-rêp′ṓ-dĭ): the art of treating minor diseases of the hands and feet.
chloasma (klṓ-ăz′mă): large brown irregular patches on the skin, such as liver spots.
chlorazene (klō′ră-zēne): a trade term; a chemical used for preparing an antiseptic or disinfectant.
chloride (klō′rīd): a compound of chlorine with another element.
chlorine (klō′rĭn, -rēn): greenish yellow gas, with a disagreeable suffocating odor; used in combined form as a disinfectant and a bleaching agent.
chlorophyll (klō′rṓ-fĭl): the green coloring matter found in plants.

fāte, câre, ăm, finâl, ärm, ȧsk, sofă; ēve, ḗvent, ĕnd, recĕnt, evẽr; īce, ĭll; ōld, ṓbey, ôrb, ŏdd, cônnect, sŏft, food, foot; ūse, ûrn, ŭp, circŭs

chlorozol (klō′rō-zōl): a trade name; a special tablet used for preparing an antiseptic or disinfectant.

cholesterin; cholesterol (kō-lĕs′tẽr-ĭn; -ōl): a waxy alcohol found in animal tissues and their secretions; it is present in lanolin, and used as an emulsifier.

choroid (kō′roid): the middle coat of the eyeball.

chromosome (krō′mô-sōm): tiny dark-stained bodies found in the nucleus of the cell; transmits hereditary characteristics in cell division.

chromatin (krō′mă-tĭn): a substance found in the nucleus of a cell.

chromidrosis (krō-mī-drō′sĭs): the excretion of colored sweat.

chronic (krŏn′ĭk): long-continued; the reverse of acute.

chrysarobin (krĭs-ă-rō′bĭn): a powerful parasiticide; used in the treatment of various forms of tinea.

chuck (chŭk): to strike vigorously; a term used in massage.

chyle (kīl): a creamy fluid taken up by the lacteals from the intestine during digestion.

chyme (kīm): food reduced to a liquid form in the process of digestion.

cicatrisata, alopecia (sĭ-kă-trī-sä′tă, ăl-ō-pē′shē-ă): baldness in irregular spots or patches, due to atrophy of the skin in certain areas.

cicatrix (sī-kă′trĭks, sĭk′ă-trĭks); pl., **cicatrices** (s ĭ k-ă-tr ī ′s ē z): the skin or film which forms over a wound, later contracting to form a scar.

cilia (sĭl′ĭ-ă): the eyelashes; microscopic hair-like extensions which assist bacteria in locomotion.

circuit (sûr′kĭt): the path of an electric current.

circuit, broken (brō′kĕn): caused by anything which diverts the current from its regular circuit.

circuit, closed (klōz′d): a circuit in which a current is continually flowing.

circuit, complete (kŏm-plēt): the path of an electric current in actual operation.

circuit, ground (ground): electricity in which one pole is used to deliver current and the other pole is connected to a ground (waterpipe or radiator).

circuit, open (ō′pên): a circuit through which the flow of current is interrupted.

circuit, short (shôrt): caused by anything which diverts the current from its regular circuit.

circulation (sûr kû-lā′shûn): the passage of blood throughout the body.

circulation, general (jĕn′êr-âl): blood circulation from the heart throughout the body and back again.

circulation, pulmonary (pŭl′mō-nā-rē): blood circulation from the heart to the lungs and back to the heart.

circumscribed (sûr-kûm-skrīb′d′): enclosed within limits.

citric acid (sĭt′rĭk ăs′ĭd): acid found in the lemon, orange, grapefruit; used for making a lemon rinse.

clasp (klăsp): a catch or hook used to hold objects together; ornamented hair clasp to hold the hair together.

clavicle (klăv′ĭ-k′l): collar bone, joining the sternum and scapula.

clay (klā): an earthy substance containing kaolin, etc. and used for facial packs.

cleido (klī′dō): prefix meaning pertaining to the clavicle.

clicking (klĭk′ĭng): small sharp sounds made by gentle blows one upon another, such as are made by rapidly opening and closing the marcel waving irons.

clipless sachet (klĭp′lĕs săsh-ā′): a special sachet which does not require a metal clip and can be folded to form a perfect steam chamber.

clipping (klĭp′ĭng): the act of cutting split hair ends with the shears or the scissors; the operation of removing the hair by the use of hair clippers.

clog (klŏg): to obstruct; to hamper.

fāte, câre, ăm, finâl, ärm, ȧsk, sofȧ; ēve, évent, ĕnd, recênt, evẽr; īce, ĭll; ōld, ŏ́bey, ôrb, ŏdd, cônnect, sŏft, fōōd, fŏŏt; ūse, ûrn, ŭp, circûs

closed circuit (klōz'd sûr'kĭt): a continuous flow of the electric current.
clot (klŏt): a mass or lump of coagulated blood.
club cutting (klŭb kŭt'ĭng): cutting the hair straight off without thinning or slithering.
cluster (klŭs'tẽr): to gather in a group or groups.
coagulate (kō-ăg'ū-lāt): to clot; to convert a fluid into a soft jelly-like solid.
coalescence (kō-ă-lĕs'êns): to grow together; the union of two or more parts or things previously separate.
coccus (kŏk'ûs); pl., **cocci** (kŏk'sī): spherical cell bacterium.
coiffeur (kwä-fûr'): a male hairdresser.
coiffeuse (kwä-fûz'): a female hairdresser.
coiffure (kwä-fūr'): an arrangement or dressing of the hair.
coil (coil): to twist or wind spirally; a spiral of wire used to produce an electric current by induction.
cold waving (kōld wāv'ĭ ng): a system of permanent waving involving the use of chemicals rather than heat.
cold waving solution (sô-lū'shŭn): a chemical solution which acts to soften the hair in cold waving.
collapse (kô-lăps'): any abnormal sinking or closing of the walls of an organ.
collodion (kô-lō'dē-ûn): a thick liquid used to form an adhesive covering.
colloid (kŏl'oid): particles having a certain degree of fineness and possessing a sticky consistency.
color rinse (kŭl'ẽrrĭns): a rinse which gives a temporary tint to the hair.
coma (kō'mă): a state of profound unconsciousness from which one cannot be roused.
comb (kōm): an instrument used to dress, comb, and arrange the hair.
combustion (kŏm-bûs'chŭn): the rapid oxidation of any substance, accompanied by the production of heat and light.
comedo; comedone (kōm'ē-dō; -dŏn): blackhead; a worm-like mass in an obstructed sebaceous duct.
comedome extractor (ĕks'trăk'tẽr): an instrument used for the removal of blackheads.
communicable (kō-mū'nĭ-kă-b'l): able to be communicated; transferable.
commutator (kōm'ū-tā-tẽr): an instrument for automatically interrupting or reversing the flow of electricity.
compact (kôm'pĕkt): a handy container used in carrying facial makeup.
compact tissue (tĭsh'ū): a dense, hard type of bony tissue.
complete circuit (kŏm-plēlt' sûr'kĭ t): a continuous flow of current which operates the electrical device.
complexion (kôm-plĕk'shŭn): hue or general appearance of the skin, especially the face.
complexus muscle (kŏm-plĕk'sŭs mŭs"l): a broad muscle of the back of the neck.
component (kôm-pō'nênt): entering into the composition of a part of the whole; a constituent part; an ingredient.
composition (kŏm-pō-zĭsh'ûn): the quality of being put together.
compound (kŏm'pound): a substance formed by a chemical union of two or more elements, and different from any of them.
compound henna (hĕn'ă): Egyptian henna to which has been added one or more metallic preparations.
compressor (kôm-prĕs'ẽr): a muscle that presses; an instrument for applying pressure on a blood vessel to prevent loss of blood.
concave (kŭn'kāv): hollow and round.
concentrated (kŏn'sên-trāt-ĕd): condensed; increasing the strength by diminishing the bulk.

fāte, câre, ăm, finâl, ärm, ȧsk, sofȧ; ēve, ĕvent, ĕnd, recênt, evẽr; īce, ĭll; ōld, ŏbey, ôrb, ŏdd, cônnect, sŏft, fōod, fŏot; ūse, ûrn, ŭp, circŭs

concha (kŏn'kă): a structure comparable to a shell in shape, as the auricle or pinna of the ear or a turbinated bone in the nose.
concise (kôn-sīs'): brief and comprehensive.
condensation (kŏn-dĕn-sā'shŭn): a physical change whereby a gas is converted into a liquid.
conducting cords (kôn-dŭkt'ĭng kôrdz): insulated copper wires which convey the current from the wall plate to the patron and operator.
conductor (kôn-dŭk'tĕr): any substance which will attract or allow a current to flow through it easily.
condyle (kŏn'dīl): a rounded articular surface at the extremity of bone.
condyloid (kŏn'dĭ-loid): relating to or resembling a condyle.
congeal (kôn-jēl): to change from a fluid to a solid state.
congenital (kŏn-jĕn'ĭ-tâl): existing at birth; born with.
congestion (kŏn-jĕs'chŭn): overfullness of the capillary and other blood vessels in any locality or organ; local hyperemia.
connecting cords (kôn-ĕkt'ĭng kôrdz): the insulated strands of copper wires which join together the apparatus and the commercial electric current.
connective (kô-nĕk'tĭv): connecting; joining.
consistency (kŏn-sĭs'tĕn-sĭ): the degree of firmness or density.
constituent (kôn-stĭt'ū-ênt): that which composes; an essential part of.
constitutional (kŏn-stĭ-tū'shŭn-âl): belonging to or affecting the physical or vital powers of an individual.
constrict (kôn-strĭkt'): bind or press together.
constructive (kôn-strŭk'tĭv): building up; setting in order.
contact (kŏn'tăkt): bringing together so as to touch.
contagion (kôn-tā'jŭn): transmission of specific diseases by contact.
contagiosa, impetigo (kôn-t-jē-ō'să ĭm-pĕt-ĭ-gō): a form of impetigo marked by flat vesicles that first become pustular, then crusted.
contagious (kôn-tā'jŭs): transmittable by contact.
contagium, animatum (kôn-tā'jē-ûm ăn-ĭ-mā'tûm): any living or animal organism that causes the spread of an infectious disease.
contamination (kôn-tăm-ĭ-nā'shŭn): pollution; soiling with infectious matter.
contiguous (kôn-tĭg'ū-û s): in contact; touching; adjoining.
contour (kŏn'tōōr): the outline of a figure or body; **contour of the hair**: shape of the hair, straight or wavy.
contra (kŏn'tră): a prefix denoting against; opposite; contrary.
contract (kôn-trăkt'): to draw together; to acquire by contagion.
contractile (kôn-trăk'tĭl): having the property of contracting.
contractility (kôn-trăk-tĭl'ĭ-tē): the property of contracting or shortening, as in muscular stimulation.
contraction (kôn-trăk'shŭn): having power to become shorter; the act of shrinking, drawing together.
contrary (kŏn'trâ-rē): in opposition.
controller (kôn-trōl'ĕr): magnetic device for the regulation and control of an electric current.
convalesce (kŏn-vă-lĕs'): to recover health and strength gradually after illness.
converter (kôn-vûr'tĕr): an apparatus used to convert the direct current to alternating current.
convex (kŏn'vĕks): curving outward like the segment of a circle.
convolute (kŏn'vô-lūt): roll or wound together, one part upon another.
convulsion (kôn-vŭl'shŭn): a violent involuntary muscular contraction.

fāte, câre, ăm, finâl, ärm, ȧsk, sofă; ēve, évent, ĕnd, recênt, evẽr; īce, ĭll; ōld, óbey, ôrb, ŏdd, cônnect, sŏft, fōod, fŏot; ūse, ûrn, ŭp, circûs

copious (kō′pē-ûs): large in amount.
copper (kŏp′ẽr): a metallic element, being a good conductor of heat and electricity.
coracoid (kŏr′ă-koid): a projecting part of the shoulder blade.
core (kôr): the heart or most vital part of anything.
corium (kō′rē-ûm): the derma or true skin.
corkscrew curl (kôrk′skroo kûrl): strands of hair having the form of a corkscrew spiral.
corneum (kôr′nḗ-um): the horny layer of the epidermis.
cornification (kôr-nĭ-fĭ-kā′shûn): the process of becoming a horny substance or tissue; a callosity.
coronal suture (kŏr′ṓ-nâl sū′tûr): the line of junction of frontal bone with the two parietal bones of the skull.
coronary (kŏr′ṓ-nā-rē): relating to a crown; encircling.
coronoid (kŏr′ṓ-noid): crown-shaped, as the process of the large bone of the forearm or of the jaw.
corpus (kôr′pûs): a body; the human body.
corpuscle (kôr′pŭs-'l): a minute cell; a cell found in the blood.
corpuscles, red (rĕd): cells in blood whose function is to carry oxygen to the cells.
corpuscles, white (whīt): cells in the blood whose function is to destroy disease germs.
corrode (kô-rōd′): to diminish gradually by chemical action; to eat away gradually.
corrosive (kô-rô′sĭv): a substance that eats away or destroys.
corrosive sublimate (sŭb′lĭ māt): an antiseptic, similar to bichloride of mercury.
corrugations (kōr-oo-gā′shŭns): alternate ridges and furrows; wrinkles.
corrugator (kŏr′oo-gā-tĕr): a muscle that draws together the skin, causing it to wrinkle.
corrugator supercilii (sū-pẽr-sĭl′ē-ī): draws eyebrows inward and downward, thus causing vertical wrinkles at the root of the nose.
cortex (kôr′tĕks): the second layer of the hair.
cortical (kôr′tĭ-kăl): pertaining to the cortex.
cosmetic dermatology (kŏs-mĕt′ĭk dûr-mă-tŏl′ṓ-jē): a branch of dermatology devoted to improving the health and beauty of the kin and its appendages.
cosmetic therapy (thĕr′ă-pē): a term used by some State Boards to designate the practice of cosmetology.
cosmeticians (kŏz-mĕ-tĭsh′ânz): those professionally engaged in the art of improving the complexion, skin, and hair.
cosmetics (kŏz-mĕt′ĭks): any external application intended to beautify the complexion, skin, hair, or nails.
cosmetologist (kŏz-mḗ-tŏl′ḗ-jĭst): one skilled in the art of improving beauty.
cosmetology (kŏz-mḗ-tŏl′ō-jē): the treatise or science of beautifying and improving the complexion, skin, hair or nails.
costal (kŏs′tâl): pertaining to a rib.
costal breathing (brēth′ĭng): shallow breathing involving the use of the ribs.
counteract (koun-tẽr-ăkt′): to act in opposition to; to hinder, defeat.
counter-irritant (ĭr′ĭ-tânt): producing artificial irritation, designed to counteract a morbid condition.
cowlick (kou′lĭk): a tuft of hair forming a whorl.
cranial (krā′ne-âl): of or pertaining to the cranium.
cranium (krā′nē-ûm): the bones of the head excluding bones of the face; bony case for the brain.
cream (krēm): a semi-solid cosmetic.

fāte, câre, ăm, finâl, ärm, ȧsk, sofȧ; ēve, ĕ́vent, ĕnd, recênt, evẽr; īce, ĭll; ōld, ṓbey, ôrb, ŏdd, cônnect, sŏft, foo͞d, foo͝t; ūse, ûrn, ŭp, circûs

create (krē-āt'): to bring into being.
creosol (rē'ŏ-sōl): a colorless oily liquid resembling phenol.
creosote (krē'ŏ-sōt): an oily antiseptic liquid obtained from beechwood tar.
cresol (krē'sōl): a colorless, oily liquid or solid derived from coal tar and wood tar and used as a disinfectant.
crepe wool (krāp wo͞ol): wool made from sheep wool and used to confine hair ends in winding or to fill in for bullk.
crest (krĕst): a ridge, line or thin mark made by folding or doubling, as a crest between two waves, where one begins and the other ends.
criterion (krī-tē'rē-ūn): a standard of judging; rule; test.
croquignole (krō'kĭ-nōl): winding of the hair from ends to the scalp.
crown of the head (kroun): the top part of the head.
crucible (kro͞o'sĭ-b'l): a pot of clay or other material used for melting substances with great heat.
crude (kro͞od): in a natural or unrefined state; imperfect.
crust (krŭst): a scab.
crypt (krĭpt): a small sac or cavity.
cuneiform (kū'nē-ĭ-fôrm): wedge-shaped; a bone of the wrist, or carpus.
curd (kûrd): soap residue found on the hair after an unsatisfactory shampoo.
curd soap (sōp): a white soap of curdy texture, usually containing free alkali.
cure (kūr): to take care of; to heal.
curl (kûrl): a lock of hair that curves spirally; a ringlet.
curler (kûr'lĕr): that which curls anything.
curling (kûr'lĭng): a process of hair waving.
curling, brush (kûr'lĭng): a process of tightly winding a wet strand of hair around the index finger, brushing with a stiff brush, pinning to the scalp with wire pins, and drying with artificial heat.
curling, paper (pā'pẽr): a process of dividing hair into small strands to form flat ringlets held in place by means of a folded piece of paper, and heated between the prongs of pressing irons.
curling, pin (pĭn): the process of forming hair ringlets by winding the hair in a series of concentric circles, fasten in place with hair pins.
curling, poker (pō'kẽr): handing curls having a corkscrew effect; tendril curls.
curling, round: a process of twisting the hair tightly and evenly around a heated curling iron.
curly (kûr'lē): tending to curl; full of curves, twists, or ripples.
current, alternating; A.C. (kŭr'ênt, ăl-tẽr-nāt-ĭng): an interrupted current.
current, D'arsonval (d'-är'sôn-vâl): a high-frequency current of low voltage and high amperage.
current, direct; D.C. (dī-rĕkt'): an uninterrupted and even-flowing current.
current, electric (ē-lĕk'trĭk): electricity in motion, or moving within a conductor.
current, faradic (fâ-răd'ik): an induced interrupted current whose action is mechanical.
current, galvanic (găl-văn'ĭk): a direct constant current having a positive and negative pole and producing a chemical action.
current, high-frequency; Tesla (hī-frē-kwên-sē; tĕs'lă): an electric current of medium voltage and medium amperage.
current, sinusoidal (sīn-û-soi'dâl): an induced interrupted current somewhat similar to faradic current.
curriculum (kû-rĭk'ū-lŭm): the course of study in a school.
cutaneous (kū-tā'nē-ûs): pertaining to the skin.

fāte, câre, ăm, finâl, ärm, ȧsk, sofă; ēve, ĕvent, ĕnd, recênt, evẽr; īce, ĭll; ōld, ŏbey, ôrb, ŏdd, cônnect, sŏft, fo͞od, fo͝ot; ūse, ûrn, ŭp, circŭs

cuticle (kū'tĭ-k'l): the very thin outer layer of the skin or hair.
cutis (kū'tĭs): the derma or deeper layer of the skin.
cycle (sī'k'l): circle; a complete wave of an alternating current.
cylinder (sĭl'ĭn-dẽr): a long circular body, solid or hollow, uniform in diameter.
cylindrical (sĭ-lĭn'drĭ-kâl): pertaining to, or having the form of a cylinder.
cyst (sĭst): a closed abnormally developed sac containing fluid, semi-fluid or morbid matter.
cystine (sĭs'tĭn): a sulphur containing amino acid found in hair and nails.
cystoma (sĭs-tō'mă): a tumor containing cysts of pathogenic origin.
cytoplasm (sī'tŏ -plăz'm): the protoplasm of the cell body, exclusive of the nucleus.

D

dandruff (dăn'drŭf): pityriasis; scurf or scales formed in excess upon the scalp.
d'Arsonval current (d'-är'sôn-vâl kŭr'ênt): a high-frequency current of low voltage and high amperage; a bi-terminal current.
de (dē): a prefix denoting from; down or away.
debility (dē-bĭl'ĭ-tē): weakness; feebleness; loss of strength.
debris (dā-brē'; dā'brē): remains; rubbish.
decalvant (dḗ-kăl'vânt): removing the hair; making bald; destroying hair.
decomposition (dḗ-kōm-pṓ-zĭsh'ŭn): act or process of separating the constituent parts of.
defective (dḗ-fĕk'tĭv): imperfect; lacking in some physical quality.
deficiency (dḗ-fĭsh'ên-sē): a lacking; something wanting.
deformity (dḗ-fôr'mĭ-tē): abnormal shape of a part of the body.
degenerate (dḗ-jĕn'ẽr-āt): to pass to a lower level of mental or physical qualities.
deltoid (dĕl'toid): a muscle of the shoulder.
demarcation (dē-mär-kā'shên): a line setting bounds or limits.
dendrite (dĕn'drīt): a treelike branching of nerve fiber extending from a nerve cell.
dense (dĕns): close; thick; heavy.
dentifrice (dĕn'tĭ-frĭs): a powder, paste or liquid used to clean the teeth.
deodorant (dē-ō'dẽr-ânt): a substance that removes or conceals offensive odors.
deodorize (dē-ō'dẽr-īz): to free from odor.
depilation (dĕp-ĭ-lā'shŭn): removal of hair.
depilatory (dḗ-pĭl'ă-tō-rē): a substance, usually a caustic alkali, used to destroy the hair; having the power to remove hair.
depleted (dḗ-plēt'ĕd): exhausted; reduced.
deportment (dḗ-pōrt'mĕnt): manner of conduct or behavior.
depression (dḗ-prĕsh'ŭn): a hollow or sunken area.
depressor (dḗ-pres'ẽr): that which presses or draws down; a muscle that depresses.
depressor alae nasi (ā'lēnā'sī): depressor septi; a muscle which contracts the nostril.
depressor anguli oris (ăng'ā-lī ŏr'ĭs): a muscle that depresses the angle of the mouth.
depressor labii inferioris (lā'bē-ī ĭn-fē-rē-ôr'ĭs): quadratus labii inferioris; a muscle that depresses the lower lip.
derivative (dḗ-rĭv'ă-tĭv): that which is derived; anything obtained or deduced from another.
derma (dûr'mă): the true skin; the corium; the sensitive layer of the skin below the epidermis.
dermal (dûr'mâl): pertaining to the skin.
dermatician (dûr-mă-tĭsh'ân): one skilled in the treatment of the skin.
dermatitis (dûr-mă-tī'tĭs): inflammation of the skin.
dermatitis combustions (kōm-bŭs-tĭ-ō'nēs): a type of dermatitis produced by extreme heat.

fāte, câre, ăm, finâl, ärm, ȧsk, sofȧ; ēve, ĕ́vent, ĕnd, recênt, evẽr; īce, ĭll; ōld, ṓbey, ôrb, ŏdd, cônnect, sŏft, fo͞od, fo͝ot; ūse, ûrn, ŭp, circûs

18

dermatitis medicamentosa (mē-dĭk-a̍-mĕn-tō′să): a type of dermatitis caused by the internal use of medicines, such as bromides.
dermatitis seborrheica (sĕb-ô-rē′ĭ-că): a type of dermatitis found co-existing with seborrhea.
dermatitis venenata (vē-nĕ-na̍′tă): inflammation of the skin caused by the action of an irritant substance such as hair dye.
dermatologist (dûr-mă-tŏl′ô-jĭst): a specialist who understands the science of treating skin and its diseases.
dermatology (dûr-mă-tŏl′ō-jē): the science which treats of the skin and its diseases.
dermatosis (dûr-mă-tō′sĭs): any disease of the skin.
dermis, derma (dûr′mĭs, dûr′mă): the layer below the epidermis; the corium or true skin.
desiccation (dĕs-ĭ-kā′shŭn): the process of drying; application for drying up secretions.
desmology (dĕs-mŏl′ō-jē): the science of the ligaments.
desquammation (dĕs-kwä-mā′shŭn): scaling of the superficial epithelial cells of the skin.
destructive (dē-strŭk′tĭv): tending to destroy.
detergent (dē-tŭr′jênt): an agent that cleanses the skin.
deteriorate (dé-tē′ŕé-ŏ́-rā t): to make or to grow worse; to become impaired in quality; to degenerate.
deterrent (dē-tĕr′ênt): that which hinders or prevents.
detriment (dĕt′rĭ-mênt): that which injures; reduces in value; causes damage.
device (dé-vīs′): an invention or contrivance of a simple nature for a particular use and purpose.
devitalize (dē-vī′tâl-īz): to destroy vitality; to destroy the life of.
dexterity (dĕks-tĕr′ĭ-tē): skill and ease in using the hands; expertness in manual acts.
di (dī): a prefix denoting two-fold; double; twice; separation or reversal.
dia (dī′ă): a prefix denoting through; apart; asunder; between.
diagnosis (dī-ăg-nō′sĭs): the recognition of a disease from is symptoms.
diagram (dī′ă-grăm): a figure for ascertaining or exhibiting certain relations between objects under discussion.
dialysis (dī-ăl′ĭ-sĭs): the process of separating different substances in solution by diffusion through a moist membrane or septum; separation.
diaphragm (dī′ă-frăm): a muscular wall which separates the thorax from the abdomen.
diathermy (dī′ă-thûr-mē): an instrument capable of generating a high-frequency current and elevating of temperature in the deep tissues.
dichromate, bichromate (dī-krō′măt; bī -): noting a salt having two parts equivalents of chromic acid to one of the base.
diet (dī′ĕt): a course of food selected with reference to a particular state of health.
diffuse (dĭ-fūz′): to pour out; to spread in every way; to operate.
diffusion (dĭ-fū′zhŭn): a spreading out; dialysis.
digest (dī-jĕst′): to prepare for absorption.
digestion (dī-jĕs′chŭn): the process of converting food into a form which can be readily absorbed by the body.
digital (dĭj′ĭ-tâl): pertaining to the fingers or toes.
digitalis (dĭj-ĭ-tā′lĭs): a drug used as a stimulant.
digits (dĭg′ĭts): fingers or toes.
digitus demonstrativus (dĭj′ĭ-tûs dé-mŏn′stră-tē′vûs): index finger.
digitus medicus (mĕd′ĭ-kûs): the ring finger.
digitus medius (mē′dē-ûs): the middle finger.
digitus minimus (min′ĭ-mûs): the little finger.

fāte, câre, ăm, finâl, ärm, a̍sk, sofă; ēve, évent, ĕnd, recênt, evēr; īce, ĭll; ōld, óbey, ôrb, ŏdd, cônnect, sŏft, foo̅d, foŏt; ūse, ûrn, ŭp, circûs

dilatator, dilator (dī-lāt′ă-tēr; dī-; dī-lā′tēr; dī-): that which expands or enlarges; an instrument for stretching a cavity or an opening.
dilate (dī-lāt; dī-lāt′): to enlarge ; to expand.
dilator (dī-lā′tēr): that which expands or enlarges.
dilator naris anterior (nā′rĭs ăn-tē′rē-ēr): a muscle which dilates the nostril.
dilute (dī-lūt′; dī-): to make thinner by mixing, especially with water.
dimethylglyoxime (dī-měth′′ĭl-glī′ôk-sīm): a compound used in ash testing of dyed hair.
diminish (dĭ-mĭn′ĭsh): to make smaller or less; to reduce.
dimple (dĭm′p'l): a slight natural depression in the skin of the body, especially on the cheek or chin.
dip (dĭp): to slope, turn or hang down as in hair waving.
diphtheria (dĭp-thē′rē-ă): an infectious disease in which the air passages, and especially the throat, become coated with false membrane, caused by a specific bacillus.
diplococcus (dĭ-plŏ-kŏk′ûs): bacteria exhibiting pairs.
direct current (dī-rěkt′ kŭr′ênt): a current constant in direction, in counter distinction to an alternating current.
dis (dĭs): a prefix denoting apart; away; asunder; between.
disc (dĭsk): a circular plate or surface.
discharge (dĭs-chärj′): to set free; to remove the contents or load; the escape or flowing away of the contents of a cavity.
discharger (dĭs-chärj′ēr): an instrument for setting free electricity.
disconnect (dĭs-kô-někt′): to sever or interrupt.
discretion (dĭs-krěsh′ûn): good judgment.
disease (dĭ-zēz): a pathologic condition of any part or organ of the body, or of the mind.
disease carrier (kăr′ĭ-ēr): a healthy person capable of transmitting disease germs to another person.
disinfect (dĭs-ĭn-fěkt′): to free from infection.
disinfect (dĭs-ĭn-fěk′tânt): an agent used for destroying germs.
disintegrate (dĭs-ĭn′tê-grāt): to separate or decompose into its component parts; to reduce to fragments or powder.
dislocate (dĭs′lô-kāt): to displace, as a bone, from its natural position.
dispensary (dĭs-pěn′sȧ-rī): a place where medicines or other supplies are prepared and dispensed.
dissect (dī-sěkt′): to divide into separate parts, as an animal or plant, for examination; to analyze.
dissolve (dĭ-zŏlv): to make a solution of; to break up.
distal (dĭs′tâl): farthest from the center or median line.
distill (dĭs-tĭl′): to extract the essence or active principle of a substance.
distillation (dĭs-tĭ-lā′shûn): the process of distilling.
distinctive (dĭs-tĭnk′tĭv): marking a difference or distinction; characteristic outstanding.
distributive (dĭs-trĭb′ū-tĭv): tending to divide among several or many.
dormant (dôr′mânt): inactive; asleep.
dorsal (dôr′sâl): pertaining to the back.
dorsal artery of the foot (är′tēr-ē): a vessel which supplies blood to the back of the foot.
dowager's hump (dou′ȧ-jēr): a bony prominence at the back of the neck.
drab (drăb): a yellowish gray color.
dry cell (drī sěl): a metallic cup which generates electricity by chemical action.
dry cleanser (klěn′zēr): an agent such as benzene or orris root powder used to cleanse the hair without the use of soap and water.

fāte, câre, ăm, finâl, ärm, ȧsk, sofȧ; ēve, ėvent, ěnd, recênt, evēr; īce, ĭll; ōld, ŏbey, ôrb, ŏdd, cônnect, sŏft, fōod, fŏot; ūse, ûrn, ŭp, circûs

duct (dŭkt): a passage or canal for fluids.
duodenum (dū-ŏ́-dē'nûm): the part of the small intestines just below the stomach.
durability (dū-răbĭl'ĭ-tē): the power of lasting.
dye (dī): to stain or color.
dye remover (rĕ́-mo͞ov'ẽr): a chemical liquid used to remove old dye from the hair.
dynamo (dī'nȧ-m ō): a machine for changing mechanical energy into electrical power.

E

ease (ēz): relief from labor or effort; freedom from pain, trouble, or annoyance.
ectal (ĕk'tâl): external; outer.
ecto (ĕk'tŏ): a prefix denoting without; outside; external.
ectodermic (ĕk-tō-dûr'mĭk): pertaining to the outer layer of cells formed from the inner cell mass in the embryonic cell.
eczema (ĕk'zē-mă): an inflammatory itching disease of the skin.
edema; oedema (ĕ-dē'mă): an abnormal accumulation of clear watery fluid in the lymph spaces of the tissues; dropsy; hydrops.
efferent (ĕf'ĕr-ênt): conveying outward, as efferent nerves conveying impulses away from the central nervous system.
effete (ĕ-fēt'): worn out; incapable of further vital use; exhausted of energy.
efficacious (ĕf-ĭ-kā'shus): possessing the quality of being effective.
efficiency (ĕ-fĭsh'ên-sē): usefulness; quality or degree of being able to produce results; economic productivity.
efficient (ĕ-fĭsh'ênt): characterized by energetic and useful activity.
effile (ĕ-fīl-ĕ'): French term meaning tapered or thinned out, as in shaping a coiffure.
effilate (ĕf'ĭ-lāt): to cut the hair strand by a sliding movement of the scissors.
effileing (ĕ-fīl'ĭng): slithering; the tapering of hair to graduated lengths.
effleurage (ĕ-flû-rȧzh'): a stroking movement in massage.
effluvium (ĕ-flo͞o'vē-ûm): a bad odor; spark discharge from a high frequency current.
effusion (ĕ-fū'shûn): to pour out; the escape of fluid from the blood vessels or lymphatics into the tissue or cavity.
Egyptian henna (ê-jĭp'shân hĕn'ă): a pure vegetable hair dye.
elastic (ê-lăs'tĭk): returning to the original form after being stretched; having ability to stretch.
elasticity (ē-lăs'tĭs'ĭ-tē): the quality of being elastic.
electrical (ē-lĕk'trĭ-kâl): consisting of, containing, producing, or operated by electricity.
electric current (ē-lĕk'trĭk kŭr'ênt): electricity in motion through a conductor.
electric heater (ē-lĕk'trĭk hē'tẽr): as used in permanent waving, a name for a heating device connected to a permanent wave machine.
electricity (ē-lĕk-trĭs'ĭ-tē): a form of energy, which when in motion, exhibits magnetic, chemical or thermal effects.
electricity, animal (ân'ĭ-mâl): the free electricity in the body.
electricity, chemical (kĕm'ĭ-kâl): a kind of electricity which is generated by chemical action in a galvanic cell.
electricity, faradic (fă-răd'ĭk): a kind of electricity produced by the action of a magnetic field in an induction coil.

fāte, câre, ăm, finâl, ärm, ȧsk, sofă; ēve, ĕ́vent, ĕnd, recênt, evẽr; īce, ĭll; ōld, ŏ́bey, ôrb, ŏdd, cônnect, sŏft, fo͞od, fo͝ot; ūse, ûrn, ŭp, circûs

electricity, frictional (frĭk′shûn-âl): a kind of electricity produced by rubbing certain objects together.
electricity, galvanic (găl-văn′ĭk): a kind of electricity which is generated by chemical action in a galvanic cell.
electricity, high-frequency (hī-frē′kwên-sē): a kind of electricity having extremely rapid vibrations, 10,000 cycles or more per second.
electricity, induced or inductive (ĭn-dūst or ĭn-dŭk′tĭv): a kind of electricity produced by proximity to an electrified body.
electricity, magnetic (măg-nĕt′ĭk): a kind of electricity developed by bringing a conductor near the poles of a magnet.
electricity, sinusoidal (sī-nûs-oid′âl): an alternating induced electric current which resembles the faradic current.
electricity, static (stĕt′ĭk): frictional electricity.
electricity, voltaic (vōl-tā′ik): galvanic or chemical electricity.
electrification (ē-lĕk″trĭ-fĭ-kā′shûn): the application of electricity to the body by holding an electrode in the hand and charging the body with electricity.
electro-coagulation (é-lĕk′trō-kŏ̆-ăg′ū-lā-shûn): a process employing high-frequency current to removed excess hair from the body.
electrode (ē-lĕk′trōd): a pole of an electric cell; an applicator for directing the use of electricity on a patron.
electrologist (ē-lĕk-tr ō l′ ô -jĭst): proposed term for a person versed in electrology, and who may, in addition, be skilled in applying the science.
electrology (ē-lĕk-trŏl′ō-jē): science in relation to electricity.
electrolysis (ē-lĕk-trŏl′ĭ-sĭs): decomposition of a chemical compound or body tissues by means of electricity.
electrolyte (ē-lĕk′trô-līte): any compound which, in solution, conducts a current of electricity and is decomposed by it.
electrolytic (ē-lĕk-trô-lĭt′ĭk): pertaining to electrolysis.
electrolytic cup (ē-lĕk-trô-lĭt′ĭk kŭp): an appliance used to cleanse the skin, before giving a massage.
electromagnet (ē-lĕk″trô-măg′nĕt): a mass of soft iron surrounded by a coil of wire; a current passing through the wire will make the iron core magnetic.
electrometer (ē-lĕk-trŏm′ê-tĕr): an instrument which indicates the presence of electricity.
electromotive force (ē-lĕk-trô-mō′tĭv fôrs): the force which by reason of difference in potential, produces electrical currents.
electron (ē-lĕk′trōn): an extremely minute corpuscle or charge of negative electricity, the smallest known to exist.
electrophobia (ē-lĕk-trô-tō′bē-ă): a morbid fear of electricity.
electropositive (ē-lĕk″trô-pŏz′ĭ-tĭv): relating to or charged with positive electricity.
electrotherapeutics (ē-lek-trô-thĕr-ă-pū′tĭks): the treatment of disease with electricity.
element (ĕl′ē-mĕnt): a simple substance, one which is incapable of being split up into other substances.
elementary (ĕl-ê-mĕn′tă-rē): introductory; the first principle of any study.
elimination (ê-lĭm-ĭ-nā′shûn): act of expelling or excreting.
elongate (ê-lŏn′gāte): to extend; to lengthen; to stretch out.
emaciation (é-mā″shē-ā′shûn): make lean; loss of the fat and fullness of the flesh of the body; leanness.
embellish (ĕm-bĕl′ĭsh): to make beautiful or decorate.
embryo (ĕm′brē-ō): in the first stages of development; a bud.

fāte, câre, ăm, finâl, ärm, ȧsk, sofă; ēve, évent, ĕnd, recênt, evẽr; īce, ĭll; ōld, ŏ́bey, ôrb, ŏdd, cônnect, sŏft, fo͞od, fo͝ot; ūse, ûrn, ŭp, circûs

embryology (ĕm-brē-ŏl′ō-jē): science dealing with the development of the embryo.
embryonic (ĕm-brē-ŏn′ĭk): of or pertaining to an organism in the early stages of development.
emesis (ĕm′ĕ́-sĭs): the act of vomiting.
eminence (ĕm′ĭ-nêns): prominence; a circumscribed area raised above the general level of the surrounding surface.
emollient (ē-mŏl′yênt): an agent that softens or soothes the surface of the skin.
emotion (ĕ́-mō′shûn): mental excitement.
emulsifier (ē-mŭl′sĭ-fī-ĕ̃r): an agent used to make an emulsion.
emulsion (ē-mŭl′shûn): a milky fluid obtained by suspending oil in water.
enamel (ĕn-ăm′êl): gloss; polish.
endo (ĕn′dṍ): a prefix denoting inner; within.
endocrine (ĕn′dō-krĭn): any internal secretion or hormone.
endosteum (ĕn-dŏs′tĕ́-ûm): the membrane covering the inner surface of bone in the medullary cavity.
endothelial (ĕn-dṍ-thē-lē-âl): a thin lining of the interior of the heart, blood vessels, lymphatics, etc.
energy (ĕn′ĕ̃r-jē): power or capacity for performing work.
enervate (ĕn′ĕ̃r-vāt; ĕ́-nûr′vāt): to weaken.
enteric (ĕn-tĕr′ĭk): pertaining to the intestinal tract.
environment (ĕn-vī′rûn-mênt): the surrounding conditions.
enzyme (ĕn′zīm): a substance which induces a chemical change in other substances, without undergoing any change itself.
eosin (ē′ṍ-sĭn): a synthetic organic dye used in lipstick to impart a bluish-red tint to the lips.
epi (ĕp′ĭ): a prefix denoting upon; beside.
epicranium (ĕp-ĭ-krā′nī-ūm): the structure covering the cranium.
epicranius (ĕp-ĭ-krā′nē-ûs): the occipito-frontalis; the scalp muscle.
epidemic (ĕp-ĭ-dĕm′ĭk): common to many people; a prevailing disease.
epidermal (ĕp-ĭ-dûr′mâl): pertaining to or arising from the outer layer of the skin.
epidermis (ĕp-ĭ-dûr′mĭs): the outer epithelial portion of the skin.
epilation (ĕp-ĭ-lā′shûn): the removal of hair by the roots.
epilepsy (ĕp-ĭ-lĕp′sē): a chronic nervous affection characterized by sudden loss of consciousness with general tonic and clonic convulsions.
epileptic (ĕp-ĭ-lĕp′tĭk): one affected by epilepsy.
epithelial (ĕp-ĭ-thē′lē-âl): relating to or consisting of epithelium.
epithelioma (ĕp-ĭ-thē″lē-ō′mă): a malignant growth consisting of epithelial cells; skin tumor.
epithelium (ĕp-ĭ-thē′-ûm): a cellular tissue or membrane, with little intercellular substance, covering a free surface or lining a cavity.
eponychium (ĕp-ṍ-nīk′ē-ûm): the extension of cuticle at base of nail.
equipment (ĕ́-kwĭp′mênt): supplies needed for service.
eradication (ĕ́-răd-ĭ-kā′shûn): act of plucking by the roots; to destroy utterly.
erector (ĕ́-rĕk′tĕ̃r): an elevating muscle.
erosion (ĕ́-rō′zhûn): the eating away; corrosion.
eructation (ē-rŭk-tā′shûn): the elimination of gas from the stomach through the mouth.
eruption (ē-rŭp′shûn): a visible lesion of the skin due to disease, marked by redness or popular condition, or both.
erysipelas (ĕr-ĭ-sĭp′ĕ́-lâs): an acute infectious disease accompanied by a diffused inflammation of the skin and mucous membrane.
erythema (ĕr-ĭ-thē′mă): a superficial blush or redness of the skin.

fāte, câre, ăm, finâl, ärm, ȧsk, sofă; ēve, ĕ́vent, ĕnd, recênt, evẽr; īce, ĭll; ōld, ṓbey, ôrb, ŏdd, cônnect, sŏft, fo͞od, fo͝ot; ūse, ûrn, ŭp, circŭs

erythrasma (ĕr-i-thră z'mă): an eruption of reddish brown patches, in the axillae and groins especially due to the presence of a fungus.
erythrocyte (ĕ-rĭth'rṓ-sīt): a red blood cell; red corpuscle.
eschar (ĕs'kȧr): a dry slough, crust, or scab following a burn.
esophagus; oesophagus (ê-sof'ă-gôs): the canal leading from the pharynx to the stomach.
essential oil (ĕ-sĕn'shâl oil): natural or synthetic product having a fragrant odor and used in the making of perfumes.
esthetic; aesthetic (ĕs-thĕt'ĭk): relating to sensation, either mental or physical.
ether (ē'thĕr): a substance obtained from distilling alcohol with sulphuric acid; used as an anaesthetic.
ethics (ĕth'ĭks): principles of good character and proper conduct.
ethmoid (ĕth'moid): resembling a sieve; a bone forming part of the walls of the nasal cavity.
etiology (ĕ-tē-ŏl'ṓ-jē): the science of the causes of disease.
evaporation (ê-văp-ṓ-rā'shŭn): change from liquid to vapor form.
evolution (ĕv-ô-lū'shŭn): the process of developing from a simple to a complex form.
ex (ĕks): a prefix denoting out of; from; away from;
exaggerate (ĕg-zăj'ĕr-ăt): to enlarge or increase beyond the normal.
excitation (ĕk-sī-tā'shŭn): the act of stimulating or irritating.
excoriation (ĕks-kō-rē-ā'shŭn): act of stripping or wearing off the skin; an abrasion.
excrescence (ĕks-krĕs'ĕns): a disfiguring outgrowth.
excretion (ĕks-krē'shŭn): that which is thrown off or eliminated from the body.
excretory (ĕks'krḗ-tṓ-rē): pertaining to or serving for excretion.
exercise (ĕk'sẽr-sīz): a putting into action, use or practice; exertion for the sake of improvement.
exfoliation (ĕks-fō-lē-ā'shŭn): the process of throwing off scales from the skin as in dandruff.
exhalation (ĕks-hȧ-lā'shŭn): the act of breathing outward.
exhaustion (ĕg-z ô s'chŭn): loss of vital and nervous power from fatigue or protracted disease.
expansion (ĕks-jăn'shŏn): distention; dilation or swelling.
expert (ĕks'pûrt): an experienced person; one who has special knowledge or skill in a particular subject.
exposure (ĕks-pō'shûr): act of being open to view; unprotected, as from the weather.
extensibility (ĕks-tĕn-sĭ-bĭl'ĭ-tĭ): capable of being extended or stretched.
extensor (ĕks-tĕn'sôr): a muscle which serves to extend or straighten out a limb or part.
exterior (ĕks-tē'rē-ẽr): outside.
external (ĕks-tûr'nâl): pertaining to the outside.
externus (ĕks-tûr'nŭs): external; pertaining to the outside.
extract (ĕks'trăkt): a solid obtained by evaporating a solution of a drug.
extreme (ĕks-trēm'): to a very great or to the greatest degree; to the farthest point.
extremity (ĕks-trĕm'ĭ-tē): the distant end or part of any organ; a hand or foot.
exudation (ĕks-û-dā'shŭn): act of discharging from a body through pores or incisions as sweat, moisture or other liquid; oozing out.
eye (ī): organ of vision.
eyeball (ī'bôl): the globe of the eye.
eyebrow (ī'brou): the hair, skin, and tissue above the eye.
eyelashes (ī'lĕsh-ês): the hair of the eyelids.
eyelid (ī'lĭd): the protective covering of the eyeball.
eye shadow (ī'shăd"ō): a cosmetic applied on the eyelids to accentuate their brilliance.

fāte, câre, ăm, finâl, ärm, ȧsk, sofă; ēve, évent, ĕnd, recênt, evẽr; īce, ĭll; ōld, ṓbey, ôrb, ŏdd, cônnect, sŏft, fōod, fŏot; ūse, ûrn, ŭp, circûs

F

facial (fā'shâl): pertaining to the face; the seventh cranial nerve.
Fahrenheit (fä'rên-hīt): pertaining to the Fahrenheit thermometer or scale; water freezes at 32°F and boils at 212°F.
faradic current (fă-răd'ĭk kŭr'ênt): relating to an induced interrupted current of electricity.
faradism (făr'ă-dĭz'm): a form of electrical treatment used for stimulating activity of the tissues.
fascia (făsh'ē-ă): a sheet of connective tissue covering, supporting, or binding together internal parts of the body.
fascial (făsh'ē-âl): relating to a fascia.
fascicle (făs'ĭ-k'l): a small band or a bundle of muscle or nerve fibers.
fasciculus (fâ-sĭk'û-lûs): a fascicle.
fat (făt): a greasy soft-solid material found in animal tissue.
fatigue (fă-tēg'): body or mental exhaustion.
favus (fā'v û s): a contagious parasitic disease of the skin, with crusts.
feather edge (fĕth'ẽr ĕj): a very thin fringe of hair resembling the edge of a feather.
fecal (fē'kâl): relating to the matter discharged from the bowel during defecation.
felon (fĕl'ûn): paronychia of the nail.
felt protector (fĕlt prô-tĕk'tẽr): a felt disk or rectangle used to protect the scalp from heat and fluid in permanent waving.
fertilization (fûr'tĭ-lī-zā-'shûn): the union of the male and female reproductive cells.
fermentation (fûr-mĕn-tā'shûn): a chemical decomposition of organic compounds into more simple compounds, brought about by the action of an enzyme.
fetid (fĕt'ĭd; fē'tĭd): having a foul smell; stinking.
fever (fē'vẽr): rise of body temperature.
fever blister (blĭs'tẽr): an acute skin disease characterized by the presence of vesicles over an inflammatory base; herpes simplex.
fiber; fibre (fī'bẽr): a slender thread or filament; thread-like in structure.
fiber rod (rŏd): a rod composed of fibrous material, not metal.
fibrin (fī'brĭn): the active agent in coagulation of the blood.
fibrinogen (fī'brĭn'ô-jĕn): a substance capable of producing fibrin.
fibroma (fī-brō'mă): a tumor composed mainly of fibrous or fully developed connective tissue.
fibrous (fī'brûs): containing, consisting of, or like fibers.
fibula (fĭb'û-là): the slender bone at the outer part of the leg.
filament (fĭl'ă-mênt): a thread-like structure.
file (fīl): a hardened steel instrument having cutting ridges, for the removal of fine shavings; nail file, used to remove portion of the free edge of the nail.
film (fĭlm): a membranous covering, causing opacity; thin skin.
filter (fĭl'tẽr): anything porous through which liquid is pass4ed to cleanse or strain it.
finesse (fĭ-nĕs'): delicate skill.
finger (fĭn'gẽr): one of the digits of the hand.
finishing cream (fĭn'ĭsh-ĭng krēm): a special cream used before applying make-up.
fish-kettle sterilizer (fĭsh-kĕt'l stĕr'ĭ-lī-zẽr): a special container used to dip objects into a disinfectant solution.
fission (fĭsh'ŏn): reproduction of bacteria by cellular division.
fissure (fĭsh'ûr): a narrow opening made by separation of parts; a furrow; a slit.
fixative (fĭk'sa-tĭv): a hair dressing used to keep hair in place; in cold waving, it stops the chemical action of the cold waving solution and sets or hardens the hair.
flabby (flăb'ē): lacking firmness; flaccid.

fāte, câre, ăm, finâl, ärm, àsk, sofă; ēve, évent, ĕnd, recênt, evẽr; īce, ĭll; ōld, ŏbey, ôrb, ŏdd, cônnect, sŏft, fōōd, fŏŏt; ūse, ûrn, ŭp, circûs

flaccid (flăk′sĭd): flabby; relaxed; being without bone.
flagella (flă-jĕl′ă): slender whip-like processes which permit locomotion in certain bacteria.
flannel (flăn′êl): a strip of flannel is used in permanent waving, as a cover for the curl to be steamed; it helps to retain moisture and prevents burning the hair.
flat winding (flăt wīn′dĭng): winding the hair on a rod without twisting.
flatter (flăt′ẽr): to beguile; soothe; to charm.
flexible (flĕk′sĭ-b′l): that which may be bent; pliable; not stiff.
flexor (flĕk′sôr): a muscle that bends or flexes a part or a joint.
florid (flŏr′ĭd): flushed with red.
fluctuate (fluk′tû-āt): to roll back and forth; to cause to move as a wave.
fluid (flōō′ĭd): a non-solid substance, liquid or gas.
foam (fōm): white bubbles forming on the surface of a liquid as a result of mixing or decomposition.
foil (foil): a sheet of metal (such as aluminum or tin) used in the construction of the permanent wave sachet or pad.
follicle (fŏl′ĭ-k′l): a small secretory cavity or sac; the depression in the skin containing the hair root.
folliculitis (fŏ-lĭk-û-lī′tĭs): an inflammation of any follicle.
folliculose (fŏ-lĭk′ū-lōs): full of follicles.
folliculosis (fŏ-lĭk-ū-lō′sĭs): a disease in which there is excessive development of the follicles.
food (fōōd): nutriment; material capable of being utilized for the growth and the repair of the tissues.
foramen (fô-rā′mĕn): a passage or opening through a bone or membrane.
forceps (fōr′sĕps): pincers or pliers for extracting, especially for delicate operations.
formaldehyde (for-măl′dê-hīd): a pungent gas possessing powerful disinfectant properties.
formalin (fôr′mă-lĭn): a 37% to 40% solution of formaldehyde.
formula (fôr′mă-lă): a prescribed method or rule; a recipe or prescription.
fossa (fŏs′ă); pl., **fossae** (-ē): a depression, furrow or sinus, below the level of the surface of a part.
foundation (foun-dā′shûn): the lowest and supporting layer of a structure.
fragilitas (fră-jĭl′ĭ′tăs): brittleness.
fraud (frôd): deceit; trickery.
fraudulent claim (frôd′û-lênt clăm): characterized by, founded on, or obtained by fraud.
frayed (frād): worn away by friction or use.
freckle (frĕk″l): a yellow or brown spot on the skin; lentigo.
free edge (frē ĕj): part of the nail body extending over the finger tip.
frequency (frē′kwên-sē): the number of complete cycles of current produced by an alternating current generator per second. Standard frequencies are 25 and 60 cycles per second.
friction (frĭk′shûn): the resistance encountered in rubbing one body on another.
frontal (frŭn′tâl): in front; relating to the forehead; the bone of the forehead.
frontalis (frŏn-tă′lĭs): anterior portion of the epicranium; muscle of the scalp.
fulguration (fŭl-gû-rā′shûn): act of flashing or of sparking with special electrode and high frequency current, in treating malignant tumors.
fuller's earth (fōōl′ẽrz ûrth): a soapy clay often used as a foundation for packs and masks.
fulling (fōōl′ĭng): a massage movement in which the limb is rolled back and forth between the hands.
full twist (fōōl twĭst): a rope-like winding of the hair on the rod in spiral permanent waving.
fume (fūm): a vaporous or odorous smoke.

fāte, câre, ăm, finâl, ärm, ȧsk, sofȧ; ēve, év́ent, ĕnd, recênt, evẽr; īce, ĭll; ōld, ȯbey, ôrb, ŏdd, cônnect, sŏft, fōōd, fōŏt; ūse, ûrn, ŭp, circûs

fumigate (fū'mĭ-gāt): disinfect by the action of smoke or fumes.
function (fŭnk'shôn): a normal or special action of a part.
fundamental (fŭn-dă-mĕn'tâl): essential; basic rule or principle.
fundus (fŭn'dŭs): the bottom or lowest part of a sac or hollow organ.
fungus (fŭn'gŭs): a vegetable parasite; a spongy growth of diseased tissue on the body.
funny bone (fŭn'ē bōn): the bone on the inner side of the forearm; the ulna; a tingling sensation is felt when the nerve is struck.
furfurol (fûr'fû-rol): a colorless aromatic fluid obtained from the distillation of bran with dilute sulphuric acid.
furrow (fŭr'ō): a groove; wrinkle.
furuncle (fū-rŭn'k'l): a boil.
fuscin (fŭs'ĭn): the black pigment of the retina.
fuse (fūz): to liquefy by heat; a special device which prevents excesive current from passing through a circuit.

G

galea (gā'lê-ă): a form of head-bandage; headache extending all over the head; the aponeurotic portion of the occipito-frontalis muscle.
galvanic current (găl-văn'ĭk kŭr'rent): a direct constant and silent current having a positive and a negative pole; named for Galvani (1737-1798).
galvanism (găl'vă-nĭz'm): a constant current of electricity the action of which is chemical.
ganglion (găn'glē-ôn); pl., **ganglia** (-ă): subcutaneous tumors; bundles of nerve cells in the brain, in organs of special sense, or forming units of the sympathetic nervous system; circumscribed cystic swellings connected with tendon sheaths.
gangrene (găn-grēn'): the dying of tissue due to interference with local nutrition.
gasoline (găs'ô-lēn): an inflammable liquid used as a cleansing fluid.
gastric (găs'trĭk): pertaining to the stomach.
gastric juice (jōōs): the digestive fluid secreted by the glands of the stomach.
gastrocnemiuis muscle (găs-trōk-nē'mĭ-ŭs mŭs'l): the largest and most superficial muscle of the calf of the leg.
gastro-intestinal (găs-trô-ĭn-tĕs'tĭ-nâl): pertaining to both the stomach and the intestines.
gauze (gôz): a thin open-meshed cloth used for dressings.
gelatin (jĕlă-tĭn): jelly-like substance; glutinous matter obtained from animal tissues by prolonged boiling.
general system, blood (jĕn'ēr-âl sĭs'tĕm): blood circulation from the heart throughout the body and back again.
generator (jĕn'ēr-ā-tēr): a machine for changing mechanical energy into electrical energy; a dynamo.
genesiology (jē-nē'sē-ŏl'ô-jē): the science of reproduction.
gentian violet jelly (jĕn'shăn vī'ô-lĕt jĕl'ĭ): an antiseptic used in the first aid treatment of a scalp burn.
genus (jē'nŭs): the knee; kind; order.
germ (jûrm): a bacillus; a microbe; an embryo in its early stages.
germicidal (jûr-mĭ-sī'dâl): destructive to germs.
germicide (jûr'mĭ-sīd): any chemical, especially a solution that will destroy germs.
germination (jûr-mĭ-nā'shŭn): the formation of an embryo from an impregnated ovum; the first act of growth in a germ, seed or bud.

fāte, câre, ăm, finâl, ärm, ȧsk, sofȧ; ēve, évent, ĕnd, recênt, evẽr; īce, ĭll; ōld, ŏbey, ôrb, ŏdd, cônnect, sŏft, fōōd, fŏŏt; ūse, ûrn, ŭp, circŭs

germinative (jûr′mĭ-nâ-tĭv): having power to grow or develop.
germinative layer (lā′ẽr): stratum germinativum; the inner layer of the epidermis resting on the corium.
germitabs (jûr′mĭ-tăbs): a trade name; special tablets, which, when dissolved in water, form an antiseptic solution.
glabrous (glā′brŭs): smooth; without hair.
gland (glănd): a secretory organ of the body.
glandular (glăn′dû-lăr): pertaining to a gland.
glint (glĭnt): brightness; luster; shine.
globule (glōb′ūl): a small round body.
glossa (glŏs′ă): tongue; lingua.
glossy (glŏs′ē): smooth and shining; highly polished.
glossopharyngeal (glŏs-ô-fâ-rĭn′jê-âl): pertaining to the tongue and pharynx; the ninth cranial nerve.
glycerin; glycerine (glĭs′ẽr-ĭn): sweet oily fluid, used as an application for roughened and chapped skin; also used as a solvent.
glycogen (glī′kô-jĕn): animal starch.
goiter (goi′tẽr): enlargement of the thyroid gland.
gonads (gŏn′ăds): essential sexual glands; ovaries and testes.
gonococcus (gŏn-ō-kŏk′ŭs); pl., **gonococci** (-s ē): the germ causing gonorrhea.
gonorrhea (gŏn-ō-rē′ă): a contagious venereal disease.
gracious (grā′shŭs): kindly, pleasant.
graduation (grăd-ū-ā′shŭn): regular progress, step by step.
granular layer (grăn′û-lăr lā′ẽr): the stratum granulosum of the skin.
granules (grăn′ūlz): small grains; small pills.
granulosum (grăn′ū-lōs′ûm): granular layer of the epidermis.
great auricular (grāt ô-rĭk′û-lăr): a nerve affecting the face, ear, neck, and parotid gland.
greater multangular (mŭl-tăn′gû-lăr): trapezium; bone of the wrist.
greater occipital (grăt′ẽr ôk-sĭp′ĭ-tâl): sensory and motor nerve affecting the splenius, complexus, and scalp.
gristle (grĭs″l): cartilage.
groom (groom): to make neat or tidy.
groove (groov): of a marcel iron, the long hollow part of the iron into which the rod fits.
ground wire (ground wīr): a wire which connects an electric current to a ground (waterpipe or radiator).
gumma (gŭm′ă): the gummy tumor in the tertiary stage of syphilis.
guttate (gŭt′āt): drop-like in form, characterizing certain cutaneous lesions.

H

habit (hăb′ĭt): an acquired tendency to repetition.
hacking (hăk′ĭng): a chopping stroke made with the edge of the hand in massage.
hair (hâr): pilus; a slender thread-like outgrowth on the body of animals.
hair, superfluous (sŭ-pûr′floo-ŭs): unwanted hair found on the face of women and girls.
hair bobbing (bŏb′ĭng): the term commonly applied to the cutting of women's and children's hair.
hair bulb (bŭlb): the lower extremity of the hair.

fāte, câre, ăm, finâl, ärm, ȧsk, sofă; ēve, ĕvent, ĕnd, recênt, evẽr; īce, ĭll; ōld, ŏbey, ôrb, ŏdd, cônnect, sŏft, food, foot; ūse, ûrn, ŭp, circŭs

hair clipping (klĭp'ĭng): removing the hair by the use of hair clippers; removing split hair ends of the hair with the scissors.
haircutting (hâr'kŭt-ĭng): shortening and thinning of the hair, and molding the hair into a becoming style; hair shaping.
hair dressing (hār drĕs'ĭng): art of arranging the hair into various becoming shapes or styles.
hair dyeing (dī'ĭng): to give the hair new and permanent color by impregnating it with a coloring agent.
hair follicle (fŏl'ĭ-k'l): the depression in the skin containing the root of the hair.
hairline (hâr'līn): the edge of the scalp at the brow where the hair growth of the head begins.
hair papilla (hâr pă-pĭl'ă): a small cone-shaped elevation at the bottom of the hair follicle.
hair piece (pēs): curl, braid or other hair section worn over the hair.
hair pressing (prĕs'ĭng): a method of straightening curly or kinky hair by means of a heated iron or comb.
hair pressing oil (oil): an oily or waxy mixture used in hair pressing.
hair restorer (rē-stōr'ĕr): a preparation containing a metallic dye.
hair root (root): that part of the hair contained within the follicle.
hair shaft (shăft): the portion of the hair which projects beyond the skin.
hair straightener (strāt'n-ĕr): a physical or chemical agent used in straightening kinky or over-curly hair.
hair test (tĕst): a sampling of how the hair will react to a particular treatment.
hair tint (tĭnt): to give a coloring to the hair; color or shade of hair.
hair trim (trĭm): trimming; cutting the hair lightly over the already existing formed lines.
half twist (hăf twĭst): a term used in spiral permanent waving to designate a type of winding, flat on one side of the rod and twisted on the other side in each revolution.
halitosis (hăl″ĭ-tō'sĭs): offensive odor from the mouth; foul breath.
hamamelis (hăm-ă-mē'lĭs): a shrub of eastern North America; witch-hazel is an extract of this plant, and is used as an astringent.
hamate (hā'māt): hooked; unciform; a bone of the wrist.
hanging curls (hăng'ĭng kŭrlz): curls suspended from the head with a downward slope or inclination.
hangnail (hăng'nāl): a tearing up of a strip of epidermis at the side of the nail; agnail
hard water (härd wô'tĕr): water containing certain minerals; does not lather with soap.
Haversian canals (hâ-vûr'shăn): small channels through which the blood vessels divide in the bone.
heal (hēl): to cure.
health (hĕlth): state of being hale or sound in body and mind.
heart (härt): a hollow muscular organ which, by contracting rhythmically keeps up the circulation of the blood.
heating coil (hēt coil): an electric coil which heats the air in a hair dryer.
heat regulation (hēt rĕg-û-lā'shŭn): temperature controlled.
helical (hĕl-ĭ-kâl): shaped like a spiral.
heliotherapy (hē-lĭ-ô-thĕr'á-pĭ): the use of sun rays to treat disease.
hemal; haemel (hē'mâl): relating to the blood or blood vessels.
hematidrosis; hemidrosis (hĕm″ă-tī-drō'sĭs, hĕm-ī-drō'sĭs): the excretion of sweat stained with blood or blood pigment.
hematocyte (hĕ'mă-tô-sīt): a blood corpuscle.
hemi (hĕm'ĭ): a prefix signifying half.
hemoglobin; haemoglobin (hē″mô-glō'bĭn): the coloring matter of the blood.

fāte, câre, ăm, finâl, ärm, ȧsk, sofă; ēve, évent, ĕnd, recĕnt, evẽr; īce, ĭll; ōld, ŏbey, ôrb, ŏdd, cônnect, sŏft, food, foot; ūse, ûrn, ŭp, circûs

hemorrhage (hĕm'ô-râj): bleeding; a flow of blood, especially when profuse.
henna (hĕn'ă): the leaves of an Asiatic thorny tree or shrub used as a dye, imparting a reddish tint; it is also used as a cosmetic.
henna, compound (kŏm'pound): Egyptian henna to which has been added one or more metallic preparations.
henna, white (whīt): a mixture of magnesium carbonate, peroxide and ammonia used in giving a bleach retouch.
hereditary (hê-rĕd'ĭ-tâ-rē): descending from ancestor to heir.
heredity (hê-rĕd'ĭ-tĭ): the transfer of qualities or disease from parents to offspring.
herpes (hûr'pēz): an inflammatory disease of the skin having small vesicles in clusters.
herpes simplex (sĭm'plĕks): fever blister; cold sore.
hidrosis (hī-drō'sĭs): abnormally profuse sweating.
high-frequency, Tesla (hī-frē'kwĕn-sē): violet ray; an electric current of medium voltage and medium amperage.
hirsute (hûr'sūĭt; hēr-sūt'): hairy; having coarse, long hair; shaggy.
histologists (hĭs-tŏl'ô-jĭsts): experts in the science of histology.
histology (hĭs-tŏl'ô-je): the science of the minute structure of organic tissues; microscopic anatomy.
hives (hīvz): urticarial; a skin eruption.
honey (hŭn'ē): mel; the product of the honey bee.
horizontal (hŏr-ĭ-zŏn'tâl): parallel to the horizon; level.
hormone (hôr'mōn): a chemical substance formed in one organ or part of the body and carried in the blood to another organ or part which it stimulates to functional activity or secretion.
horny (hôr'nē): composed of or resembling horns; hard.
humerus (hū'mēr-ûs): the bone of the upper part of the arm.
humidity (hû-mĭd'ĭ-tĭ): moisture; dampness.
hyaline (hī'ā-lĭn): transparent like glass.
hydrate (hī'drāt): a compound formed by the union of water with some other substance.
hydration (hī-drā'shûn): the chemical union of a substance with water.
hydro (hī'drô): a prefix denoting water; hydrogen.
hydro-carbon (hī-drô -kär'bôn): charcoal; any compound composed only of hydrogen and carbon.
hydrochloric acid (hī"-drô-klō'rĭk ă-s'ĭd): a compound of hydrogen and chlorine.
hydrocyst (hīd'rō-sĭst): a cyst containing a water-like liquid.
hydrocystoma (hīd-rō-sĭs-tō'mă): a variety of sudamina appearing on the face, especially of women in middle and advanced life.
hydrofluoric acid (hī"drô-floo-ŏr'ĭk ăs'ĭd): a compound of hydrogen and fluorine.
hydrogen (hī'drô-jên): a colorless, odorless and tasteless gaseous inflammable element, lighter than any other known substance.
hydrogen peroxide (pēr-ŏk'sīd): a powerful oxidizing agent; in liquid form is used as an antiseptic.
hydrolysis (hī-drŏl'ĭ-sĭs): chemical decomposition involving the addition of water.
hydroscope (hī"drŏ-skōp): hygroscope; water clock.
hydrotherapeutics (hī'drŏthēr-ȧ-pū'tĭks): treating disease by baths and mineral waters.
hygiene (hī-jēn): the science of preserving health.
hygroscopic (hī-grŏ'skŏp'ĭk): readily absorbing and retaining moisture.
hyoid (hī'oid): the "u" shaped bone at the base of the tongue.
hyper (hī'pēr): a prefix denoting excessive; above normal; above; beyond.

fāte, câre, ăm, finâl, ärm, ȧsk, sofȧ; ēve, évent, ĕnd, recênt, evẽr; īce, ĭll; ōld, ŏbey, ôrb, ŏdd, cônnect, sŏft, fo͞od, fo͝ot; ūse, ûrn, ŭp, circŭs

hyperacidity (hī″pĕr-ă-sĭd′ĭ-tē): an excess of acidity.
hyperemia (hi″pĕr-ē′mē-ă): the presence of an excessive quantity of blood in a part of the body; congestion.
hyperhidrosis, hyperhidrosis (hī″pĕr-ĭ-drō′sĭs): excessive sweating.
hyperostosis (hī-pĕr-ŏs-tō′sĭs): general hypertrophy of bone tissues.
hyperplasia (hī-pĕr-plā′zhē-ă; -zē-ă): an increase in number of the individual tissue elements, excluding tumor formations, whereby the bulk of the part or organ is increased.
hypersecretion (hī″pĕr-sê-krē′shŭn): excessive secretion.
hypertrichosis; hypertricosis (hī″pĕr-trĭ-kō′sĭs): a condition of excessive development or abnormal growth of the hair; superfluous hair.
hypertrophica (hī″pĕr-trŏf′ĭ-kă): a form of acne in which the lesions leave conspicuous pits and scars upon healing.
hypertrophy (hī″pĕr-trō′fē): abnormal increase in the size or a part of an organ; overgrowth.
hypo (hī′pō): a prefix denoting under; beneath; lower state of oxidation.
hypodermic (hī″pō-dûr′mĭk): beneath the skin; a liquid injection into the subcutaneous tissues.
hypoglossal (hi″pô-glŏs′âl): under the tongue; the twelfth cranial nerve.
hyponychium (hi″pô-nīk′ē-ûm): the extension of the skin underneath the free edge of the nail.
hypothenar (hī-pŏth′ê-năr): the fleshy eminence on the palm of the hand over the metacarpal bone at the base of the fingers.
hypothesis (hī-pŏth′ê-sĭs): a specific or detailed statement of a topic of discourse; a theory assumed as true.
hysteria (hĭs-tē′rĭ-ȧ): a nervous disorder peculiar to women.

I

ichthyosis (ĭk-thē-ō′sĭs): a skin disease in which the skin becomes rough with diminished sweat and sebaceous secretion; fish skin disease.
ide (īd): a word termination forming names of compounds, such as chlorides.
identical (ĭ-dĕn-tĭ-kâl): exactly alike.
idiosyncrasy (ĭd-e-ô-sĭn′kră-sē): an individual characteristic or peculiarity; a susceptibility, peculiar to the individual due to the action of certain drugs, articles of diet, etc.
illicit (ĭ-lĭs′ĭt): not allowed; improper.
imbecile (ĭm′bê-sĭl): mentally deficient; a weak minded person.
imbibition (ĭm-bĭ-bĭsh′ŭn): the act of sucking up moisture.
imbrication (ĭm-brĭ-kâ′shŭn): overlapping of the edges like that of the shingles.
imbrications of hair: tiny overlapping scales found on the hair cuticle.
immerse (ĭ-mûrs′): to plunge into; dip; submerge in a liquid.
immiscible (ĭ-mĭs′ĭ-b′l): a liquid that will not mix with another liquid.
immune (ĭ-mūn′): safe from attack; protected by vaccination.
immunity (ĭ-mūn′ĭ-tē): freedom from or resistant to disease.
impermeable (ĭm-pūr′mê-ă-b′l): impenetrable; not permitting passage.
impervious (ĭm-pûr′vē-ûs): impenetrable; especially passage of liquids.
impetigo (ĭm-pĕ́-tī′gō): an eruption of pustules, which soon rupture or become crusted, occurring chiefly on the face around the mouth and the nostrils.
impetigo contagiosa (kôn-tā″jē-ō′să): scrumpox; a contagious disease, characterized by an eruption of flat vesicles which may develop into pustules.
implement (ĭm′plê-mênt): an instrument or tool used by man to accomplish a given work.
impregnate (ĭm-prĕg′nāt): to mix with an active agent.
in (ĭn): a prefix denoting not; negative; within; inside.

fāte, câre, ăm, finâl, ärm, ȧsk, sofă; ēve, évent, ĕnd, recênt, evẽr; īce, ĭll; ōld, ȯbey, ôrb, ŏdd, cônnect, sŏft, fo͞od, fo͝ot; ūse, ûrn, ŭp, circŭs

incision (ĭn-sĭzh'ûn): a cut; a division of the soft parts made with a knife.
incandescent (ĭn-kăn-dĕs'ĕnt): giving forth light and heat.
incisor teeth (ĭn-sī'zẽr; -sẽr tēth): the four anterior teeth in each jaw.
inclined (ĭn-klīnd'): bowed forward; bent.
incubation (ĭn-kû-bā'shŭn): the period of a disease between the implanting of the contagion and the development of the symptoms.
indemnity (ĭn-dĕm'nĭ-tē): compensation for loss.
indent (ĭn-dĕnt'): a cut in a margin.
index (ĭn'dĕks): the forefinger; the pointing finger.
indigo (ĭn'dĭ-go): a blue dyestuff.
indispensable (ĭn-dĭs-pĕn'să-b'l): absolutely necessary.
individually (ĭn-dĭ-vĭd'ŭ-ăl-ē): each by itself.
induction (ĭn-dŭk'shŭn): the transfer of electricity from a current to a magnetized object.
indurate, acne (ĭn-dû-ră'tă): deeply seated popular eruptions with hard tubercular lesions.
induration (ĭn-d û -rā'sh û n): the process or act of hardening; a spot or area of hardened tissue.
inefficiency (ĭn"ĕ-fĭsh'ên-sē): quality, state or fact of being incapable.
inert (ĭn-ûrt): inactive.
infect (ĭn-fĕkt): to cause infection.
infection (ĭn-fek'shŭn): the invasion of the body tissues by disease germs.
infection, general (jĕn'ẽr-êl): the result of the disease germs gaining entrance into the blood stream and thereby circulating throughout the entire body.
infection, local (lō'kâl): confined to only certain portions of the body, such as an abscess.
infectious (ĭn-fĕk'shûs): capable of spreading infection.
inferior (ĭn-fē'rē-ẽr): situated lower down, or nearer the bottom or base.
inferioris (ĭn-fē"rē-ŏr'ĭs): below; lower.
infiltration (ĭn-f ĭ l-trā'sh û n): the act of passing one substance into another.
inflammation (ĭn-flâ-mā'shŭn): the reaction of the body to irritation with accompanying redness, pain, heat, and swelling.
influenza (ĭn-flo͞o-ĕn'ză): a contagious epidemic catarrhal fever, with great prostration an varying symptoms; grippe.
infra (ĭn'fră): a prefix denoting below; lower.
infra-mandibular (ĭn"fră-măn-dĭb'û-lăr): below the lower jaw.
infra-mental (mĕn'tâl): below the chin.
infra-orbital (ôr'bĭ-tâl): below the orbit; in the floor of the orbit; a sensory and motor nerve affecting the cheek muscles, nose, and upper lip.
infra-red (ĭn"fră-rĕd'): pertaining to that part of the spectrum lying outside of the visible spectrum and below the red rays.
infra-trochlear (trŏk'lē-ăr): sensory nerve affecting the lacrimal sac, the skin of the nose and the inner muscle of the eye.
ingestion (ĭn-jĕs'chŭn): the act of taking substances, especially food, into the body.
ingredient (ĭn-grē'dē-ênt): any constituent part of a compound.
ingrown hair (ĭn'grōn hâr): a wild hair that has grown underneath the skin, thereby causing an infection.
ingrown nail (ĭn'grōn nāl): the growth of the nail into the flesh instead of toward the tip of the finger or toe, thereby causing an infection.
inhalation (ĭn-hă-lā'shûn): the inbreathing of air or other vapors.
inhibition (ĭn-hĭ-bĭsh'ûn): the diminution or arrest of the function in an organ.

fāte, câre, ăm, finâl, ärm, ȧsk, sofă; ēve, évent, ĕnd, recênt, evẽr; īce, ĭll; ōld, ŏ́bey, ôrb, ŏdd, cônnect, sŏft, fo͞od, fo͝ot; ūse, ûrn, ŭp, circûs

innervation (ĭn-ẽr-vā′shûn): distribution of the nerves in a part.
innominate veins (ĭ-nŏm′ĭ-nât vāns): veins of the neck.
inoculation (ĭn-ŏk-û-lā′shûn): the process by which protective agents are introduced into the body.
inorganic (ĭn-ôr-găn′ĭk): composed of matter not relating to living organisms.
insanitary; unsanitary (ĭn-săn′i-tā-rē; ŭn-): not sanitary or healthful; injurious to health; unclean.
insanity (ĭn-săn′ĭ-tĭ): unsoundness or derangement of mind.
insertion (ĭn-sûr′shûn): act of inserting; that which is set in.
insidious (ĭn-sĭd′ē-ûs): treacherous; hidden or stealthy.
insolation (ĭn-sō-lā′shûn): exposure to the rays of the sun; sunstroke.
insoluble (ĭn-sŏl′ū-b′l): incapable of being dissolved or very difficult to dissolve.
instantaneous (ĭn-stăn-tā′nē-ûs): acting immediately.
insulation (ĭn-sû-lā′shûn): the non-conducting substance by which electricity or heat is prevented from escaping.
insulator (ĭn′sū-lā-tẽr): a non-conducting material or substance. Materials used to cover electric wires.
insulin (ĭn′sŭ-lĭn): a hormone which regulates carbohydrate metabolism.
insurance (ĭn-shoor′ăns): protection against loss, damage or injury.
insure (ĭn-shoor′): to make sure or secure.
integument (ĭn-tĕg′û-mênt): a covering, especially the skin.
inter (ĭn′tẽr): a prefix denoting amid; between; among.
intercellular (ĭn-tẽr-sĕl′ū-lăr): between or among cells.
interior (ĭn-tē′rē-ẽr): inside.
intermediate (ĭn-tẽr-mē′dē-ăt): between two extremes.
intermittent heat (ĭn-tẽr-mĭt′ênt hēt): interrupted heating period; electric current turned on and off during the steaming period.
internal (ĭn-tûr′nâl): pertaining to the inside; inner part.
internus (ĭn-tûr′nûs): internal; pertaining to the inside.
interosseous (ĭn-tẽr-ŏs′ĕ-ûs): lying between or connecting bones.
interstice (ĭn-tûr′stĭs): a small gap or hole in the substance of an organ or a tissue; pore.
interval (ĭn′tẽr-vâl): a time or space between two periods or objects.
intestinal (ĭn-tĕs′tĭ-nâl): pertaining or relating to the intestines.
intestine (ĭn-tĕs′tĭn): the digestive tube from the stomach to the anus.
intolerance (ĭn-tŏl′ẽr-âns): quality or state of being unable to endure, especially refusal to allow others the enjoyment of their opinions.
invasion (ĭn-va′zhûn): the beginning of a disease.
inversion (ĭn-vûr′shûn): the act of turning inward.
involution (ĭn-vṓ-lū′shûn): that in which anything is folded or wrapped; the return of an enlarged part or organ to its normal size.
involuntary muscles (mŭs″ls-z): function without the action of the will.
iodine (ī′ṓ-dīn; -dĭn): a non-metallic element used as an antiseptic for cuts, bruises, etc.
iodoform (ī-ō′dô-fôrm): a yellow crystalline compound formed by the action of iodine on alcohol and potash; a valuable antiseptic for wounds and sores.
ion (ī′ŏn): an atom or group of atoms carrying an electric charge.
ionization (ī-ŏn-ī-zā′shûn): the separating of a substance into ions.
iontophoresis (ī-ŏn-tō-fṓ-rē′sĭs): the introduction of ions into the body by the electric current.
iridescence (ĭr-i-dĕs′êns): the rainbow-like play of colors, as in mother of pearl.

fāte, câre, ăm, finâl, ärm,ȧsk, sofȧ; ēve, évent, ĕnd, recênt, evẽr; īce, ĭll; ōld, ṓbey, ôrb, ŏdd, cônnect, sŏft, fōōd, fŏŏt; ūse, ûrn, ŭp, circûs

iris (ī′ris): the colored muscular disk-like diaphragm of the eye which regulates the pupil or opening in the center.
iron (ī′ûrn): ferrum; a metallic element.
irradiation (ĭ-rā″dĭ-ā′shŭn): the process of exposing an object to the natural or artificial sunlight.
irregularity (ĭ-rĕg′-ū-lăr-tē): quality or state of being uneven or not uniform.
irreparable (ĭ-rep′ă-ră-b′l): damaged beyond repair.
irritability (ĭr-ĭ-tȧ-bĭl′ĭ-ĭ): readily excited or stimulated.
irritant (ĭr′ĭ-tȧnt): causing irritation; an irritating agent; a stimulus.
itinerant beauty operator (ī-tin′ĕr-ânt bū′tē ŏp′ĕr-ā-tĕr): an operator who does work from house to house.
ive (īv): a word termination signifying relating or belonging to, such as active.
ize (īz): a word termination forming transitive verbs, such as sterilize.

J

jaundice (jôn′dĭs): a morbid condition, characterized by yellowness of the eyes, skin and urine, constipation, loss of appetite, and general languor.
jowl (jōl): the hanging part of a double chin.
joint (joint): a connection between two or more bones.
jugular (jŭ′gū-lăr): pertaining to the neck or throat; the large vein in the neck.

K

kaolin; kaoline (kā′ô-lĭn; kä-): fuller's earth; porcelain clay; employed occasionally as a dusting powder, but chiefly in the form of a poultice with glycerine (mud pack).
karaya gum (kă-ră′ă-gŭm): Indian gum; a gum obtained in India and Africa from the trees of the genus Sterculia; used to make mucilages and wave set preparations.
keloid (kē′loid): a skin disease marked by whitish indurated patches surrounded by a pinkish or purplish border; a fibrous growth arising from irritation and usually from a scar.
keratoma (kĕr-ă-tō′mă): a callosity; a horny tumor; an acquired thickened patch of the epidermis.
keratosa, acne (kĕr-ă-tō ′să): horny plugs projecting from the hair follicles, accompanied by inflammation.
keratosis (kĕr-ă-tō′sĭs): any disease of the epidermis, especially one marked by the presence of circumscribed overgrowths of the horny layer; callous or keratoma.
key (kē): in permanent waving, a device used to tighten the hair wound on the rod.
kidney (kĭd′nē): a glandular organ which excretes urine.
kilowatt (kĭl′ô-wŏt): one thousand watts of electricity.
kinky (kĭnk′ĭ): very curly hair.
knead (nēd): to work and press with the hands as in massage.
knowledge (nŏl′ĕj): instruction; learning; practical skill.
kohl (kōl; kō″l): a preparation used to darken the edges of the eyelids.
kolsterol (kōl′stê-rōl): a trade name; a prepared germicide.

fāte, câre, ăm, finâl, ärm, ȧsk, sofă; ēve, ĕvent, ĕnd, recênt, evẽr; īce, ĭll; ōld, ŏbey, ôrb, ŏdd, cônnect, sŏft, fōōd, fŏŏt; ūse, ûrn, ŭp, circûs

L

labial (lā′bē-ăl): pertaining to the lips'
labii (lā′bē-ī): of or pertaining to the lip
labium (lā′bē-ûm); pl., **labia** (-ă): lip
laboratory (lăb′ô-ră-tô-rē): a room containing apparatus for conducting experiments
laceration (lăs′ĕr-ā′shûn): a tear of the skin or tissues
lachrymal; lacrimal (lăk′rĭ-mâl): pertaining to tears or weeping; bone at the front of the orbits
lacquer, nail (lăk′ĕr nāl): a thick liquid which forms a glossy film on the nail.
lacteals (lăk′tḗ-âlz): any one of the lymphatics of the small intestines that take up the chyle.
lacuna (lă-kū′nă): a small cavity or hollow space; a gap or defect.
lamina (lăm′ĭ-nă): a thin layer or scale.
lamp black (lămp blăk): a fine black substance, almost pure carbon, made by burning coal oils in an atmosphere deficient in oxygen.
lanolin (lân′ô-lĭn): purified wool fat.
languor (lăn′gĕr): not inclined to take bodily exercise; dullness; lack of vigor.
lanugo (lă-nū′gō): the fine hair which covers most of the body.
larkspur (lärk′spûr): the seeds of the Delphinium plant; its tincture is used to treat head lice.
laryngeal (là-rĭn′jê-ăl): pertaining to the larynx.
laryngitis (là-rĭn-jī′tĭs): inflammation of the larynx.
larynx (lăr′ĭnks): the upper part of the trachea or wind pipe; the organ of voice production.
lateral (lăt′ĕr-âl): on the side.
lather (lăth′ĕr): froth made by mixing soap and water.
latissimus dorsi (là-tĭs′ĭ-mŭs dôr′sī): a broad, flat superficial muscle of the back.
laxative (lăk′sà-tĭv): a medicinal agent which relieves constipation
layer cutting (lā′ĕr kŭt′ĭng): shortening the hair into many thin layers.
lecithin (lĕs′ĭ-thĭn): a yellowish-brown waxy solid occurring in various animal and vegetable tissues; used as an emulsifier.
legislation (lĕj-ĭs-lā′shŭn): the making of laws by an authority.
legitimate (lḗ-jĭt′ĭ-mât): real; genuine; lawful.
lemon rinse (lĕm′ûn rĭns): a product containing lemon juice or citric acid; used to lighten the color of the hair.
lentigo (lĕn-tī′gō); pl., **lentigines** (lĕn-tĭ-jī′nēz): a freckle; circumscribed spot or pigmentation in the skin.
lepothrix (lĕp′ō-thrĭks): a bacterial infection resulting in dry and scaly hair.
lesion (lē′zhûn): a structural tissue change caused by injury or disease.
lesser multangular (lĕs′ĕr mŭl-tăn′gū-làr): trapezoid; bone of the wrist.
lesser occipital (lĕs′ĕr ŏk-sĭp′ĭ-tâl): the nerve supplying muscles at the back of the ear.
leuco (lū′kô): a prefix denoting white; colorless.
leucocyte (lū′kô-sīt): a white corpuscle; white blood cell.
leukoderma (lū′kô-dûr′mă): abnormal white patches on the skin; absence of pigment in the skin.
leukonychia (lū′kôn-ĭk′ē-ă): a whitish discoloration of nails; white spots.
levator (lê-vā′tôr): a muscle that elevates a part.
levator anguli oris (âng′ū-lī ŏr′ĭs): caninus; muscle that raises the angle of the mouth and draws it in.
levator labii superioris (lā′bē-ī sû-pē-ŏr′ĭs): quadratus labii superioris; muscle that elevates upper lip and dilates the nostrils.
levator palpebrae (păl′pê-brē): muscle that raises upper eyelid.

fāte, câre, ăm, finâl, ärm, àsk, sofă; ēve, ḗvent, ĕnd, recênt, evẽr; īce, ĭll; ōld, ỏbey, ôrb, ŏdd, cônnect, sŏft, fōod, fŏŏt; ūse, ûrn, ŭp, circûs

liability insurance (lī-ă-bĭl′ĭ-tē ĭn-shoo′âns): the act or system of insuring against personal damage.
lichen (lī′kên): a dry, popular eruption of the skin.
ligament (lĭg′ă-mênt): a tough band of fibrous tissue, serving to connect bones, or to hold an orgn in place.
ligation (lī-gā′shŭn): the operation of tying together, especially an artery.
light therapy (līt thĕr′ă-pē): the application of light rays for treatment of diseases.
lime (līm): a white powder containing calcium oxide.
limp (lĭmp): weak; lacking firmness or strength.
linear (lĭn′ē-ăr): composed of lines; straight.
lingual (lĭn′gwăl): shaped like or pertaining to the tongue.
liniment (lĭn′ĭ-mênt): a liquid intended for application to the skin by gentle friction.
linseed (lĭn′sēd): the dried seeds of flax; contains a mucilage which is used as an emollient in hand preparations.
lipomatodes (lĭ-pō-mȧ-tō′dēs): a birth mark of a fatty nature.
liquefy (lĭk′wḗ-fī): to reduce to the liquid state said of both solids and gases.
liquid (lĭ′kwĭd): flowing like water; a fluid that is not solid or gaseous.
liquor cresolis compound (lĭk′ĕr krē-sōl′ĭs kŏm′pound): a powerful germicide.
listerine (lĭs-tẽr-ēn): a trade name; a mild antiseptic in liquid form.
litmus paper (lĭt′mûs pāpẽr): a blue coloring matter that is reddened by acids and turned blue again by alkalies.
liver (lĭ′vẽr): an internal organ which secretes bile for digestion.
liver spots (lĭv′ẽr spŏts): the lesions of chloasma.
lobe (lōb): a branch extending from a body; ear lobe.
lock-jaw (lŏk′jôw): tetanus; specifically trismus; a firm closing of the jaw due to tonic spasm of the muscles of mastication.
locomotion (lō-kô-mō′shŭn): animal movement.
logical (lŏj′ĭ-kâl): the result of correct reasoning; correct thinking.
lotion (lō′shûn): a liquid solution used for bathing the skin.
louse (lous); pl., **lice** (līs): pediculus; an animal parasite infesting the hairs of the head.
lubricant (lū′brĭ-kânt): anything that makes things smooth and slippery, such as oil.
lucid (lū′sĭd): clear; distinct; marked by mental clarity.
lucidum (lū′sĭ-dûm): the clear layer of the epidermis.
luminous (lū′mĭ-nŭs): full of light; brilliant.
lunate (lū′nāt): crescent-shaped.
lunate bone (bōn): semi-lunar; a bone of the wrist.
lung (lŭng): one of the two organs of respiration.
lunula (lū′nū-lă): the half-moon-shaped area at the base of the nail.
lustre (lŭs′têr): glossy; shining.
lusterless lŭs′têr-lĕs): without brightness; dull.
luxuriant (lŭks-ū′rē-ânt): very abundant; strong vigorous growth.
lymph (lĭmf): a clear yellowish or light straw colored fluid, which circulates in the lymph spaces. or lymphatics of the body.
lymphatic (lĭm-făt′ĭk): pertaining to, containing or conveying lymph.
lymphatic system (sĭs′tĕm): consists of lymph flowing through the lymph spaces, lymph vessels, lacteals, and lymph nodes or glands.
Lysol (lī′sōl): a trade name; a disinfectant and antiseptic; a mixture of soaps and phenols.

fāte, câre, ăm, finâl, ärm, ȧsk, sofă; ēve, ḗvent, ĕnd, recênt, evẽr; īce, ĭll; ōld, ȯbey, ôrb, ŏdd, cônnect, sŏft, food, foot; ūse, ûrn, ŭp, circûs

M

machineless (mă-shēn′lĕss): without a machine; heated by chemicals.
macroscopic (măk′-rô-skŏp-ĭk): visible to the unaided eye.
macula (măk′û-lă); pl., **maculae** (-le): a spot or discoloration level with skin; a freckle; macule.
madarosis (măd-ă-rō′sĭs): loss of the eyelashes or eyebrows.
magnesia (măg-nā′zhē-ă; -zhă): a fine white odorless powder of an earthy taste, insoluble in water, antacid and laxative
magnet (măg′nĕt): a body having the power to attract iron bodies.
magnetize (măg′nĕt-īz): convert into a magnet; to communicate magnetic properties to.
magnify (măg′nĭ-fī): to increase the size or importance of.
magnum (măg′nûm): largest bone of the wrist.
major (mā′jĕr): greater; larger; most important.
makeup (māk′ŭp): the way in which one is dressed, painted, etc., for a part.
mal (măl): a prefix denoting ill; evil.
malaise (mȧ-lâz′; măl′āz): discomfort; an indefinite feeling of bodily uneasiness.
malar (mā′lăr): of or pertaining to the cheek; the cheek bone.
malassimilation (măl-â-sĭm-ĭ-lā′shûn): faulty or incomplete assimilation.
malformation (măl-fôr-mā′shûn): an abnormal shape or structure; badly formed.
malignant (mă-lĭg′nânt): resistant to treatment; growing worse; occurring in severe form; a tumor recurring after removal.
malingerer (mȧ-lĭn′gĕr-ĕr): one who falsifies illness or inability.
malnutrition (măl-nū-trĭsh′ûn): poor nutrition resulting from malassimilation.
malpighian (măl-pĭg′ê-ân): stratum nucosum; the deeper portion of the epidermis.
mammal (măm′ăl): a warm-blooded animal who nourishes its young with milk.
management (măn′āj-mênt): directing; carrying on; control.
mandible (măn′dĭ-b′l): the lower jaw bone.
mandibular (măn′dĭb′ū-lăr): pertaining to the lower jaw.
mandibular nerve (nûrv): the fifth cranial nerve which supplies the muscles and skin of the lower part of the face
manicure (măn′ĭ-kūr): the artful care of the hands and nails.
manicurist (măn′ĭ-kūr-ĭst): one who professionally attends to the care of the hands and nails.
manipulation (mă-nĭp-ū-lā′shûn): act or process of treating, working or operating with the hands or by mechanical means, especially with skill.
mantilla (măn-tĭl′ȧ): a Spanish veil which covers the head and falls down upon the shoulders.
mantle (măn′t′l): nail mantle, the fold of the skin into which the nail root is lodged.
manus (mā′nûs); pl., **mani** (-nī): the hand.
marcel wave (mär-sĕl′wäv): resembling a perfect natural wave, produced by means of a heated iron; originated by Francois Marcel, a French hairdresser.
marrow (măr′ō): a soft fatty substance filling the cavities of bone.
mascara (măs-kă′ră): a preparation used to darken the eyelashes.
mask (mȧsk): a special cosmetic formula used to beautify the face.
massage (mă-säzh): manipulation of the body by rubbing, pinching, kneading, tapping, etc., to increase metabolism, promote absorption, relieve pain, etc.
masseter (mă-sē′tĕr): a chewer; one of the muscles of the jaw used in mastication.
masseur (mă-sûr′): a man who practices massage.
masseuse (mă-sûz′): a woman who practices massage.
mastication (măs-tĭ-kā′shûn): the act of chewing.
mastoid (măs′toid): breast shaped; relating to the mastoid process.

fāte, câre, ăm, finâl, ärm, ȧsk, sofȧ; ēve, évent, ĕnd, recênt, evêr; īce, ĭll; ōld, ŏbey, ôrb, ŏdd, cônnect, sŏft, fōod, fŏŏt; ūse, ûrn, ŭp, circûs

mastoid process (prŏs'ĕs): a conical nipple-like projection of the temporal bone.
materia medica (mă-tĕ'rē-ă mĕd'ĭ-kă): the branch of medical science treating of drugs.
matrix (mā'trĭks): the formative portion of a nail or a tooth; the intercellular substance of a tissue.
matter (măt'ẽr): pus; a substance that occupies space and has weight.
matured (mă-tūrd'): fully developed; completely worked out.
maxilla (măk-sĭl'ă): jaw bone.
maxilla, inferior (ĭn-fē'rē-ẽr): lower jaw bone or mandible.
maxilla, superior (sû-pē'rē-ẽr): upper jaw bone.
maxillary (măk'sĭ-lā-rē): pertaining to the jaws.
maximum (măk'si-mum): the greatest or highest degree or amount of anything.
measles (mē'z'lz): an acute contagious respiratory disease marked by fever and other constitutional disturbances, usually in children.
meatus (mē-ā'tûs): passage or channel of the ear.
mechanical (mē-kăn'ĭ-kâl): relating to a machine; performed by means of some apparatus not manual.
mechanism (mĕk'ă-nĭs'm): mechanical construction; parts of a machine.
mechanotherapy (mĕk-à-nō-thēr'à-pĭ): the treatment of disease by special machines which bring about forced movements of the body.
medial; median (mē'dē-âl; -ân): pertaining to the middle.
medicament (mē-dĭk'ă-mênt): a medicinal application; a remedy.
medicamentosus (mē-dĭk"ă-mên-tō'-sûs): dermatitis; a term characterizing an eruption caused by a drug.
medication (mĕd-ĭ-kā'shûn): the act of treating disease with drugs.
medicine (mĕd'ĭ-sĭn): a drug; the art of preventing or curing disease.
medius (mē'-dē-ûs): the middle finger.
medulla (më-dŭl'ă): the marrow in the various bone cavities; the pith of the hair.
medulla oblongata (ŏb-lŏn-gā'tă): the lowest, or posterior, part of the brain, continuous with the spinal cord.
medullary (mĕd'û-lā-rē): pertaining to the marrow, or medulla.
medullary space (spās): the cavity through the shaft of the bones.
mega (mĕg'ă): a prefix denoting great; extended; powerful; a million.
megascopic (mĕg-ă-skŏp'ĭk): enlarged; magnified.
mel (mĕl): honey.
melanin (mĕl'ă-nĭn): the dark or black pigment in the epidermis and hair, and in the choroid or coat of the eye.
membrane (mĕm'brān): a thin sheet or layer of pliable tissue, serving as a covering.
menopause (mĕn'ō-pôz): the physiological cessation of menstruation.
menstruation (mĕn-strōō-ă-shŭn): the periodic discharge of blood from the female sex organ.
mental (mĕn'tâl): pertaining to the mind; pertaining to the chin.
mental nerve (nûrv): a nerve which supplies the skin of the lower lip and chin.
mentalis (mĕn-tā'lĭs): the muscle that elevates the lower lip, and raises and wrinkles the skin of the chin.
menthol (mĕn'thōl): peppermint camphor; often employed for its marked cooling effect.
menthyl salicylate (mĕn'thĭl să-lĭs'ĭ-lāt): an organic compound which is used as a filtering agent in subburn preventives; produces an even tan by removing the majority of the ultraviolet rays.
mentum (mĕn'tûm); pl., **menti** (-i): of or pertaining to the chin.

fāte, câre, ăm, finăl, ärm, ȧsk, sofă; ēve, ĕvent, ĕnd, recênt, evẽr; īce, ĭll; ōld, ŏbey, ôrb, ŏdd, cônnect, sŏft, fōōd, fŏŏt; ūse, ûrn, ŭp, circûs

mercurochrome (mẽr-kū′rṓ-krōm): a trade name; ;a germicide.
mercury bichloride (mûr′kū-rē bī-klō′rīd): a powerful germicide, poisonous and also corrosive to metal.
mercury cyanide (sī′ă-nīd): a powerful germicide, very poisonous.
meso (mĕs′ṓ): a prefix denoting in the middle; intermediate.
mesoblast (mĕs′ṓ-blĕst): middle germinal layer of the embryo.
mesodermic (mĕs′-ō-dûr′mĭk): relating to the mesoderm, the middle layer of the skin.
meta (mĕt′ă): a prefix signifying over; beyond; among.
metabolism (mĕ-tăb′ō-lĭz′m): the constructive and destructive life process of the cell.
metacarpus (mĕt-ă-kär′pûs): the bones of the palm of the hand.
metatarsus (mĕt-ȧ-tär′sŭs): the bones which comprise the instep of the foot.
metal curler (mĕt′âl kûr′lẽr): a metal device upon which the hair is rolled while wet, to make curls.
metallic (mė-tăl′ĭk): relating to, or resembling metal.
metal salts (mĕt′âl sôlts): a compound of a base and an acid.
metamorphosis (mĕt-ȧ-môr′fō-sĭs): structural change
meter (mē′tẽr): an instrument used for measuring; a measure of length, the basis of the metric system.
methyl salicylate (mĕth′ĭl să-lĭs′ī-lāt): the chief constituent of oil of wintergreen.
meticulosis (mē-tĭk′ū-lŭs): unduly careful of small details.
metric (mĕt′rĭk): pertaining to the meter as a standard of measurement.
mica (mīkă): a mineral occurring in the form of thin, shining plates.
micro (mī′krō): a prefix denoting very small; slight; millionth part of.
microbe (mī′krōb): a micro-organsism; a minute one-celled animal or vegetable bacterium.
micrococcus (mī-krō-kŏk′ûs): a minute bacterial cell having a spherical shape.
micron (mī′krŏn): a colloid particle visible under the microscope; one millionth of a meter.
micro-organism (mī-krō-ôr′gân-ĭz′m): microscopic plant or animal cell; a bacterium.
microscope (mī′krō-skōp): an instrument for making enlarged views of minute objects.
microspira (mī-krō-spī′ră): pathogenic bacteria which causes cholera.
mid (mĭd): a prefix denoting the middle part.
midway (mĭd-wā′): halfway.
milliampere (mĭl′-ē-ăm-pâr): one thousandth of an ampere.
milliamperemeter (-mē′tẽr): an electrical instrument which registers the amount of current required for a given treatment.
miliaria (mĭl-ē-ā′rē-ă): an eruption of minute vesicles due to retention of fluid at the mouths of the sweat glands.
miliaria rubra (rōob′ră): prickly heat; burning and itching usually caused by exposure to excessive heat.
miliary fever (mĭl′ē-ă-rē fē′vẽr): sweating sickness; an infectious disease characterized by fever profuse sweating, and sudamina.
milium (mĭl′ē-ûm); pl., **milia** (-ă): a small whitish pimple due to a retention of sebum, beneath the epidermis; a whitehead.
millimeter (mĭl′ĭ-mē-têr): one thousandth of a meter.
mineral (mĭn′ẽr-âl): any inorganic material found in the earth's crust.
mineral salts (sôlts): salts derived from an inorganic chemical compound.
minor (mī′nẽr): lesser; contrary to greater.
minute (mī-nūt′): very small; tiny.
miscible (mĭs′ĭ-b′l): the property of certain liquids to mix with each other in equal proportions.

mitosis (mī-tō'sĭs): indirect nuclear division, the usual process of cell reproduction of the human tissues.
mobility (mō-bĭl'ĭ-tĭ): being easily moved.
modality (mō-dăl'ĭ-tē): any condition influencing or modifying drug action or electricity.
mode (mōd): fashion; way; style.
modification (mŏd-ĭ-fĭ-kā'shŭn): the result of slight change in form.
modified swirl (mŏd'ĭ-fīd swûrl): the back of the head waved on a slant, waves not connected symmetrically.
mold; mould (mōld): to form into a particular shape.
mole (mōl): a small brownish spot on the skin.
molecule (mŏl'ĕ-kūl): the smallest possible unit of existence of any substance.
monilethrix (mŏ-nĭl'ĕ-thrĭks): beaded hair; a condition in which the hairs show a series of constrictions, giving the appearance of a string of fusiform beads.
mono (mŏn'ō): a prefix denoting unit singly.
monoterminal (mŏn-ŏ-tûr'mĭ-nâl): one terminal of an alternating current.
morbid (môr'bĭd): diseased.
mordant (môr'dânt): a substance, such as alum, used to make fast a dye.
motile (mō'tĭl): having the power of movement, as certain bacteria.
motor (mō'tẽr): moving or causing motion.
motor nerves(nûrvz): carry impulses from nerve centers to muscles for certain motions.
motor oculi (ŏk'ū-lī): third cranial nerve; the nerve controlling most of the eye muscles.
mould (mōld): to conform to a given shape.
mucosa (mû-kō'să): mucous membrane.
mucosum, stratum (mû-kō'sûm strā-tûm): mucous or Malpighian layer of the epidermis; a deeper portion of the skin.
mucous membrane (mū'kûs mĕm'brân): a membrane secreting mucus, which lines passages and cavities communicating with exterior.
mucus (mū'kûs): the clear viscid secretion of mucous membrane.
mug (mŭg): a cup used for shaving purposes.
mumps (mŭmps): a specific infectious disorder characterized by an inflammation of the parotid and other salivary glands.
muscle (mŭs"l: the contractile tissue of the body by which movement is accomplished.
muscle curl (kûrl): shaped like a muscle shell; larger at the head and tapering toward the end, hanging at an angle.
muscle oil (oil): an oil, vegetable or mineral, in which eithr lecithin or cholesterin is dissolved; used in conjunction with massage to relieve fatigue and sore muscles.
muscle strapping (străp'ĭng): a heavy massage treatment used to reduce fatty deposits.
muscle tone (tōn): the normal degree of tension in a healthy muscle.
myelin (mī'e-lĭn): a white substance forming the covering for certain nerve fibers.
mylohyoid (mī-lô-hī'oid): relating to the molar teeth, or posterior portion of the lower jaw, and to the hyoid bone.
myocardium (mī-ō-kär'dē-ûm): the muscular substance of the heart.
myology (mī-ŏl'ô-jē): the science of the function, structure, and diseases of muscles.

N

naevus; nevus (nē'vûs); pl. **naevi; nevi** (vī): a birthmark; a congenital skin blemish.
nail (nāl): unguis; the horny protective plate located at the end of the finger or toe.
nail-bed (bĕd): that portion of the skin on which the body of the nail rests.

fāte, câre, ăm, finâl, ärm, åsk, sofă; ēve, ĕvent, ĕnd, recênt, evẽr; īce, ĭll; ōld, ŏbey, ôrb, ŏdd, cônnect, sŏft, fo͞od, fo͝ot; ūse, ûrn, ŭp, circûs

nail-body (bŏd'ē): the horny nail blade resting upon the nail-bed.
nail-fold (fōld): nail-wall.
nail-grooves (grōōvz): the furrows between the nail-walls and the nail-bed.
nail matrix (mā'trĭks): the portion of the nail-bed extending beneath the nail-root.
nail-root (rōōt): located at the base of the nail, imbedded underneath the skin.
nail-wall (wôl): cuticle covering the sides and base of the nail body.
nape (nāp): the back part of the neck.
narcotic (när-kŏt'ĭk): a drug, which in moderate doses relieves pain, but in large doses produces stupor and convulsions.
naris (nā'rĭs); pl., **nares** (-rēz): a nostril.
nasal (nā'zâl): pertaining to the nose.
nasalis (nā-sā'lĭs): a muscle of the nose.
nasitis (nâ-sī'tĭs): rhinitis; inflammation of the nasal mucous membrane of the nose.
nasociliary (nā-zô-sĭl'yă-rē): a nerve affecting the mucous membrane of the nose.
nasus (nā'sûs); pl., **nasi-** (-si): the nose.
natural neckline (năt'û-râl nêk-līn): not in a definite outline, retaining the natural tendency of hair growth.
nausea (nô'shê-ă): sickness of the stomach; with a desire to vomit.
navicular (nă-vĭk'û-lăr): boat-shaped; a bone of the wrist.
neck duster (nĕk dŭs'tĕr): a brush used to brush the hair from the neck after cutting; in most states its use is prohibited because it is not sanitary.
neckline (nĕk'līn): in hair cutting, where the hair growth of the head ends and the neck begins;; hair line.
necrosis (nĕk-rō'sĭs): the death of cells surrounded by living tissue.
negative (nĕg'ă-tĭv): the opposite of positive; expressing denial.
negative pole, N. (pōl N): the pole from which negative current flows.
negative terminal (tûr'mĭ-nâl): the end of the conducting circuit of the electric current manifesting alkaline reaction; the zinc plate in a battery.
neoplasm (nē'ō-plăz'm): a new growth or turnor.
nerve (nûrv): a whitish cord, made up of bundles of nerve fibers, through which impulses are transmitted.
nerve papillae (pă-pĭl'ē): a bundle of nerve tissue in the true skin.
nervous (nûr'vûs): easily excited.
Nettle rash (nĕt'l răsh): a skin eruption caused by the sting from the nettle plant.
network (nĕt'wûrk): any system of lines crossing each other at certain intervals.
neuralgia (nū-răl'jē-ă): a severe pain along the course of a nerve.
neurasthenia (nû-răs-thē'nē-ă): nerve tire; nervous exhaustion.
neuritis (nû-rī'tis): inflammation of nerves, marked by neuralgia.
neurology (nū-rōl'ô-jē): the science of the structure, function, and pathology of the nervous system.
neuron (nū'rŏn): the unit of the nervous system, consisting of the nerve cell and its various processes.
neurosis (nû-rō'sĭs): a functional nervous disorder.
neutral (nū'trâl): exhibiting no positive properties; indifferent; in chemistru, neither acid nor alkaline.
neutralization (nū-trâl-ĭ-zā'shûn): the rendering ineffective of any action or process; a chemical reaction between an acid and a base.
neutralizer (nū'trâl-īz-ēr): an agent capable of neutralizing another substance.

fāte, câre, ăm, finâl, ärm, ȧsk, sofă; ēve, ĕ́vent, ĕnd, recênt, evēr; īce, ĭll; ōld, ŏ́bey, ôrb, ŏdd, cônnect, sŏft, fōōd, fŏŏt; ūse, ûrn, ŭp, circûs

nevus (nē'vŭs): a birthmark.
nicotine (nĭk-ō-tēn'): a poisonous alkaloid in tobacco.
nimble (nĭm'b'l): light and quick in motion.
nit (nĭt): the egg of a louse, usually attached to a hair.
nitric acid (nī'trĭk ăs'ĭd): concentrated acid employed as a caustic for the removal of warts.
nitro-celluose (nī-trô-sĕl'û-lōs): pyroxylin; gun cotton; a granulaar, yellowish mass formed in the chemical reaction between cellulose and nitric acid; used in nail polishes.
nitrogen (nī'trô-jĕn): a colorless gaseous element, tasteless and odorless found in air and living tissue.
nitrous (nī'trŭs): designating a compound of nitrogen in the lower valence.
node (nôd): a knot or knob; a circumscribed swelling; a knuckle or ringer joint.
nodosa (nô-dōs'ă): having nodes or knot-like swellings.
nodule (nŏd'ūl): a small node.
non (nŏn): a prefix denoting not.
non-conductor (nŏn-kôn-dŭk'tẽr): any substance that resists the passage of electricity, light, or heat towards or through it.
non-pathogenic (nŏn-păth-ô-jĕn'ĭk): non-disease producing; growth promoting.
non-striated (strī'āt-ĕd): involuntary muscle function without the action of the will; consists of spindle-shaped cells without striations; smooth muscle.
non-vascular (văs'kû-lăr): not supplied with blood vessels.
normal (nŏr'mâl): regular; natural.
nose (nōz): the organ of smell.
nostril (nŏs'trĭl): an external opening of the nose.
nourish (nŭr'ĭsh): to feed; to furnish with whatever promotes growth.
nourishment (nŭr'ĭsh-mênt): anything which nourishes; ;nutriment; food.
noxious (nŏk'shŭs): harmful; poisonous.
nozzle (nŏz'l): the projecting end.
nucleus (nū'klê-ûs); pl., **nuclei** (-ī): the active center of cells.
nude (nūd): naked; bare; unclothed.
nutriment (nū'trĭ-mênt): that which nourishes; food.
nutrient (nū'trē-ênt): nutritious; a food constituent.
nutrition (nū-trĭsh'ûn) the process of nourishment.
nutritious (nū-trĭsh'ûs): yielding nourishment.
nutritive (nū'trĭ-tĭv): pertaining to nutrition.

O

obese (ȯ-bēs'): extremely fat.
objective (ôb-jĕk'tĭv): a goal; aim; existing independently of mind.
objective symptom (sĭmp'tûm): symptom that can be seen, as in pimples, pustules, etc.
oblique (ŏb-lēk'; -lik); **obliquis** (-ūs): slanting or inclined.
oblongata (ŏ b-lōn-gā'tă): medulla oblongata; the lowest part of the btain near the spinal cord.
obnoxious odor (ôb-nŏk'shŭs ō'-dẽr): offensive; hateful.
observation (ŏb-zẽr-vā'shûn): respectful attention; act of observing; also the information or record so obtained.
obsolete (ŏb'-sô-lēt): old; gone out of date.
occipital (ŏk-sĭp'ĭ-tâl): pertaining to the back part of the head; the bone which forms the back and lower part of the cranium.
occipital nerve (nûrv): a nerve which supplies the occipito-frontalis muscle.

fāte, câre, ăm, finâl, ärm, ȧsk, sofȧ; ēve, ėvent, ĕnd, recênt, evẽr; īce, ĭll; ōld, ȯbey, ôrb, ŏdd, cônnect, sŏft, fōod, fŏŏt; ūse, ûrn, ŭp, circûs

occipito-frontalis (ŏk-sĭp′ĭ-tō-frŏn-tā′lĭs): epicranius; the scalp muscle.
occiput (ŏk′sĭ-pŭt): the back of the head.
occupational disease (ŏk-û-pā′shŭn-âl dĭ-zēz′): due to certain kinds of employment, such as coming into contact with chemicals, dyes, etc.
ocular (ŏk′û-lăr): pertaining to the eye; the eyepiece of a microscope; the lenses at the upper end of the microscope.
oculist (ŏk′û-lĭst): a specialist in diseases of the eyes.
oculomotor (ŏk″û-lô-mō′tĕr): third cranial nerve; controlling the motion of the eye.
oculus (ŏk′û-lûs); pl., **oculi** (-lī): the eye.
odor (ō′dĕr): scent; smell.
offensive (ŏ-fĕn′sĭv): giving offense, disagreeable; obnoxious; distasteful.
ohm (ōm): a unit of measurement used to denote the amount of resistance in an electrical system or device.
Ohm's Law (ōmz lô): the simple statement that the current in an electric circuit is equal to the pressure divided by the resistance.
oil (oil): a greasy liquid.
ointment (oint′mênt): a fatty, medicated mixture used externally.
ol (ôl): a word ending denoting that the name of the substance to which the ending is added, belongs to the series of alcohols, or hydroxyl derivatives, such as carbonol, glycerol.
oleaginous (ō-lê-aj′ĭ-nûs): oily; greasy.
olecranon (ō-lê-krā′nŏn): tip of the elbow; the prominent curved upper extremity of the ulna.
oleum (ō′lê-ûm); pl., **olea** (ă): oil.
olfactory (ŏl-făk′tô-rē): relating to the sense of smell; first cranial nerve, the special nerve of smell.
oma (ō′mă): a word ending properly added to words derived from Greek roots, denoting a tumor, such as cystoma.
omohyoid (ō-mô-hī′oid): connected with the hyoid and scapula bones.
onychatrophia (ŏn-ĭ-kă-trō′fê-ă): atrophy of the nails.
onychauxis (ōn-ĭ-kôk′sĭs): enlargement of the nails.
onychia (ô-nĭk′ē-ă): inflammation of the matrix of the nail with pus formation and shedding of the nail.
onycho (ôn′ĭ-kô): a prefix meaning relating to the nails.
onychoclasis (ŏn-ĭ-kô-klā′sĭs): breaking of the nail.
onychocryptosis (ŏn-ĭ-kô-krĭp-tō′sĭs): ingrowing nail.
onychogryposis (ŏn-ĭ-kô-grī-pō′sĭs): denotes enlargement with increased curvature of the nail.
onycholysis (ŏn-ĭ-kôl′ĭ-sĭs): loosening of the nail without shedding.
onychomycosis (ŏn-ĭ-kô-mī-kō′sĭs): refers to any parasitic disease of the nails.
onychophagy (ŏn-ĭ-kŏf′ă-jē): the morbid habit of eating or biting the nails.
onychophosis (ŏn-ĭ-kŏf-ō′sĭs): growth of horny epithelium in the nail-bed.
onychophyma (ŏn-ĭ-kŏf-ī′mă): a morbid degeneration of the nail.
onychoptosis (ŏ n-ĭ-kô-kŏp-tō′sĭs): falling off of the nails.
onychorrhexis (ŏn-ĭ-kô-rĕk′sĭs): abnormal brittleness of the nails with splitting of the free edge.
onychosis; onychonosus (ŏn-ĭ-kô′sĭs; ŏn-ĭ-kő-nō′sûs): any disease of the nails.
onyx (ő′-nĭks): a nail of the fingers or toes.
onyxis (ô-nĭk′sĭs): ingrowing of the nails.
opacity (ô-păs′ĭ-tĭ): the quality of being shaded or obscure.
opaque (ő-pāk′): not transparent to light.
operative (ŏp′ĕr-â-tĭv): relating to, or affected by means of an operation; active, effective.

fāte, câre, ăm, finâl, ärm, ȧsk, sofȧ; ēve, évent, ĕnd, recênt, evẽr; īce, ĭll; ōld, ŏbey, ôrb, ŏdd, cônnect, sŏft, fo͞od, fo͝ot; ūse, ûrn, ŭp, circŭs

operator (ŏp'ẽr-â-tẽr): one who is able to perform correctly any service rendered professionally in the care of the face, hair, etc.
ophthalmic (ŏp-thăl'mĭk): pertaining to the eye.
opsonin (ŏp'sô-nĭn): a blood constituent which renders invading germs more susceptible to the action of white blood cells.
optic (ŏp'tĭk): second cranial nerve; the nerve of sight; pertaining to the eye, or to vision
optional (ŏp'shûn-âl): left to one's discretion or choice; not compulsory.
optician (ŏp'tĭsh'ân): a maker of optical instruments pursuant to an oculist's prescription.
optimistic (ŏp'tĭ-mĭs'tĭk): hoping for the best.
orangewood stick (ŏr'ĕnj-wōod stĭk): a stick made of orangewood used in manicuring the nails.
optometrist (ŏp-tŏm'ế-trĭst): a trained person who fits glasses to correct visual defects.
orbicular (ŏr-bĭk'ū-lăr): circular; a muscle whose fibers are circularly arranged.
orbicularis oris (ŏr-bĭk-ū-lă'rĭs ō'rĭs): orbicular muscle; muscle of the mouth.
orbicularis palpebral (păl'pế-brăl): a muscle of the eyelid.
orbit (ôr'bit): the bony cavity of the eyeball; the eye-socket.
orbital (ôr'bĭ-tâl): pertaining to the orbits.
orbital nerve (nûrv): a sensory nerve supplying the temple and cheek.
organ (ôr'gân): any part of the body exercising a specific function.
organic (ŏr-gân'ĭk): relating to an organ; pertaining to substances derived from living organisms.
organism (ŏr'gân-ĭz'm): any living being, either animal or vegetable.
orifice (ŏr'ĭ-fĭs): a mouth; an opening.
origin (ŏr'ĭ-jĭn): the beginning; the starting point of a nerve; the place of attachment of a muscle to a bone.
originate (ŏ-rĭj'ĭ-nāt): to produce as new.
oris (ŏ'rĭs): pertaining to the mouth; an opening.
orris root (or'is-rōot): a special powder used to give a dry shampoo.
os (ŏs): a bone.
oscillation (ŏs'ĭ-lā'shûn): movement like a pendulum; a swinging or vibration.
osis (ŏ'sĭs): a word ending denoting an abnormal or a diseased condition.
os magnum (ŏs măg'nûm): bone in the lower rfow of the carpus.
osmidrosis (ŏs-mĭ-drō'sĭs; ŏz): bromidrosis; foul smelling perspiration.
osmosis (ŏs-mō'sĭs; ŏz): the passage of fluids and solutions through a membrane or other porous substance.
osseous; osseus (ŏs'ê-ûs): bony.
osteology (ŏs-tế-ŏl'ố-jē): science of the anatomy structure and function of bones.
ottoman (ŏt'ố-mån): foot pedal of a chair.
Oudin current (ōō'dĭn kŭr'rênt): high frequency current of high voltage and low amperage.
ounce (ouns): a unit of measure of weight; one-sixteenth of a pound.
ovarian (ố-vā'rē-ân): relating to the ovary.
ovary (ō-vă'rē): one of the two reproductive glands in the female, containing the ova or germ cells.
overlap (ō-vẽr-lăp'): to lie or be folded partly upon.
ovular (ō'vū-lăr): egg-like in shape; pertaining to the ovum, or egg.
oxidation (ŏk-sĭ-dā'shûn): the act of combining oxygen with another substance, with or without generation.
oxide (ŏk'sīd): a compound of oxygen with another element or radical.

fāte, câre, ăm, finâl, ärm, ȧsk, sofă; ēve, évent, ĕnd, recênt, evẽr; īce, ĭll; ōld, ốbey, ôrb, ŏdd, cônnect, sŏft, fōod, fŏŏt; ūse, ûrn, ŭp, circûs

oxidize (ŏk'sĭ-dīz): the process of combining oxygen with another substance.
oxygen (ŏk'sĭ-jên): a gaseous element, essential to animal and plant life.
oxygenation (ŏk"sĭ-jê-nā'shûn): saturation with oxygen, noting especially the aeration of the blood in the lungs.
ozone (ō'zōn): a form of oxygen used as a disinfectant.

P

pack (păk): a special cosmetic formula used to beautify the face.
palate (păl'ăt): the roof of the mouth and the floor of the nose.
palatine bones (bōnz): situated at the back part of the nasal fossae.
palmar (păl'măr): referring to the palm of the hand.
palpebral (păl'pê-bră); pl. **palpebrae** (-brē): eyelids.
palpebrarum (păl-pê-bră'rûm): of or pertaining to the eyelids.
panacea (păn-ă-sê'ă): a remedy that is claimed to be curative for all diseases; a universal remedy.
pancreas (păn'crê-ăs): a gland connected with the digestive tract.
panicula (pă-nĭk'û-lă): a swelling or a tumor.
panidrosis (păn-ĭ-drō'sĭs): general perspiration.
paper curl (pā'pêr kûrl): a curl rolled up on a stick encased in a triangle of special paper and pinched with a warm iron.
papilla (pă-pĭl'ă): a small, nipple-like process.
papilla, hair (hăr): a small cone-shaped elevation at the bottom of the hair follicle in the dermis.
papillary (păp'ĭ-lâ-rē; pă-pĭl'ă-rē): relating to, resembling, or provided with papillae.
papillary layer (lā'ẽr): the outer layer of the dermis.
papilloma (păp-ĭ-lō'mă); pl. **papillomata** (păp-i-lo-mātă): an epithelial tumor formed by hypertrophy of the papillae of the skin.
papular (păp'ū-lăr): characterized by papules.
papule (păp'ûl): a pimple; a small, circumscribed elevation on the skin containing no fluid.
papulous (păp'û-lûs): covered with papulae or pimples.
para (pă'ră): a prefix denoting alongside of; beyond; beside, against; near.
paraffin (păr'â-fĭn): a white mineral wax consisting of hydrocarbons and extracted from petroleum.
paralysis (pă-răl'ĭ-sĭs): loss of physical or mental functions through nerve injury or disease.
para-phenylene-diamine (păr-ă-fēn-ĭ-lēn-dĭ-âm'ĭn; dī'ă-mēn): an aniline derivative used in hair dyeing.
parasite (păr'ă-sīt): a vegetable or animal organism which lives on or in another organism, and draws its nourishment therefrom.
parasiticide (păr-ă-sīt'ĭ-sīd): a substance that destroys parasites.
parathyroid (păr-ă-thī'roid): a endocrine gland located near the thyroid.
parchment paper (pärch'mĕnt pā'pêr): thin paper used to wrap hair in permanent waving.
parietal (pă-rīê-tâl): pertaining to the wall of a cavity; a bone at the side of the head.
paronychia (păr-ô-nīk'ē-ă): felon; an inflammation of the tissues surrounding the nail.
parotid (păr-ô-tĭd): near the ear; a gland near the ear.
patch test (păch tĕst): a skin test used to determine individual reaction to a chemical substance
patella (pȧ-tĕl'ȧ): a flat movable bone forming the front part of the knee.
pathogenic (păth-ő-jĕn'ĭk): causing disease; disease producing.
pathological (păth-ő-lôj'ĭ-kâl): relating to pathology; morbid; diseased.

fāte, câre, ăm, finâl, ärm, ȧsk, sofă; ēve, évent, ĕnd, recênt, evẽr; īce, ĭll; ōld, őbey, ôrb, ŏdd, cônnect, sŏft, fo͞od, fo͝ot; ūse, ûrn, ŭp, circûs

pathology (păth-ŏl'ṓ-jē): the science which treats or modifications of the functions and changes in structure caused by disease.

patron (pâ'trŭn): the person to whom service is rendered.

patter (pât'ẽr): a mechanical device used during muscle strapping treatments.

pectoralis (pĕk-tṓ-rā'lĭs): a muscle of the breast.

pediculosis (pĕ-dĭk″ū-lō'sĭs): lousiness; state of being infected with pediculi or lice.

pediculosis capitis (kăp'ĭ-tĭs): lousiness of the hair of the head.

pediculous (pḗ-dĭk'ū-lûs): infested by pediculi; lousy.

pedicure (pĕd'ĭ-kūr): the care of the feet and toe nails.

pelada (pĕ-lā'dă): a disease of the hair causing circumscribed patches of baldness; alopecia areata.

pelage (pĕl'ăj): the hair covering of the body of man and the lower animals.

pellagra (pĕ-lăg'ră): a skin affection manifesting digestive disturbances, followed by scaling or peeling of the skin, and nervous symptoms.

pellicle (pĕl'ĭ-k'l): thin skin; cuticle.

penetrate (pĕn'ḗ-trāt): to pierce; to pass into the deeper tissues.

pepsin (pĕp'sĭn): an enzyme which digests protein.

per (pĕr): a prefix denoting through.

percussion (pĕr-kŭsh'ûn): a form of massage consisting of repeated blows or taps of varying force.

perforate (pûr'fṓ-rāt): to pierce with holes.

perfume (pûr-fūm'; pĕr-fūm'): a fluid preparation, as of the essence of flowers, used for scenting.

pH: symbol for hydrogen; ion concentration; the relative degree of acidity or alkalinity.

peri (pĕr'ĭ-): a prefix denoting about; near; around.

pericardium (pĕr-ĭ-kär'dē-ûm): the membranous sac around the heart.

perionychium (pĕr-ĭ-ô-nĭk'ĭ-ûm): the epidermis about the nail.

periosteum (pĕr-ĭ-ôs'tê-ûm): the fibrous membrane covering the surface of the bones.

peripheral system (pê-rif'ẽr-âl sis'tĕm): consists of the nerve endings in the skin and sense organs.

periphery (pê-rĭf'ẽr-ē): the outer part or surface.

peristalsis (pêr-ĭ-stăl'sĭs): muscular movements of the digestive tract.

permalite (pûr'mâ-līt): a trade name; a light for drying the permanent wave after the wave has been set.

permanent wave, cold (pûr'mă-nĕnt wāv, kōld): a system of permanent waving employing chemicals rather than heat.

permanent wave, heat: accomplished by changing the hair structure from an ordinary and natural straightness to one of permanent curliness or waviness.

permanent wave, pin curl (pĭn kûrl): a cold or heatless permanent in which the hair is set n pin curls insteadof being rolled on curlers.

permeable (pûr'mê-â-b'l): permitting the passage of liquids.

peroneus muscle (pêr-ō-nẽ-ŭs mŭs'l): one of several muscles of the lower leg.

peroneal nerve (pĕr-ō-nē'ăl nŭrv): a nerve which supplies the lower leg and foot.

peroxide (pêr-ŏk'sīd): an oxide with the highest amount of oxygen.

peroxide of hydrogen (hī'drô-jên): a powerful oxidizing agent; in liquid solutions is used as an antiseptic.

peroxide rinse (rĭns): it is used to lighten the color of the hair.

perpendicular (pûr-pên-dĭk'û-lăr): being perfectly upright.

personality (pûr-sŭn-ăl'ĭ-tĭ): the sum total of physical and mental qualities in a person.

fāte, câre, ăm, finâl, ärm, ȧsk, sofă; ēve, ĕvent, ĕnd, recênt, evẽr; īce, ĭll; ōld, ṓbey, ôrb, ŏdd, cônnect, sŏft, fo͞od, fo͝ot; ūse, ûrn, ŭp, circŭs

personality bob (pûr′sŭn-ăl′ĭ-tĭ bŏb): a type of bob which constitutes distinction of individuality.
perspiration (pûr′spĭ-rā′shŭn): sweat; the fluid excreted from the sweat glands of the skin.
pessimistic (pĕs-ĭ-mĭs′tĭk): hoping for the worst.
petrissage (pĕt-rĭ-säj′): the kneading movement in massage,
petrolatum (pĕt-rô-lā′tûm): petroleum jelly; Vaseline; a purified, yellow mixture of semi-solid hydrocarbons obtained from petroleum.
petroleum (pḗ-trō′lê-ûm): an oily liquid coming from the earth and consisting of a mixture of hydrocarbons.
petrous (pĕt′rûs): of stony hardness.
phagocyte (făg′ṍ-sīt): a cell possessing the property of ingesting bacteria, particles, and other cells.
phalangette; phalanget (fă-lăn′jĕt): the last phalanx or terminal bone of a finger or toe.
phalanx (fā′lănks); pl., **phalanges** (fă-lăn′jēz): the long bone of the finger or toe.
pharmacologist (fär-mă-kŏl′ṍ-jĭst): one versed in the science of the nature and properties of drugs.
pharynx (făr′ĭnks): the upper portion of the digestive tube, behind the nose and mouth.
phenol (fē′nōl): carbolic acid; caustic poison; in dilute solution is used as an antiseptic and disinfectant.
phenomenon (fê-nŏm′ê-nŏn): observing facts or events that which appeals to one as strange or unusual.
phobia (fō′bĭ-ȧ): a morbid fear of anything.
phoresis (fô-rē′sĭs): the process of introducing solutions into the tissues through the skin by the use of galvanic current.
phosphoric (fŏs-fôr′ĭk): pertaining to compounds containing phosphorus.
phosphorus (fŏs′fôr-ûs): an element found in the bones, muscles, and the nerves.
phototherapy (fō-tō-thĕr′ă-pĭ): the application of light for the treatment of disease.
phyma (fī′mă); pl., **phymata** (fī′mă-tă): a circumscribed swelling one the skin larger than a tubercle.
physic (fĭz′ĭk): a medicine, especially a laxative; drugs in general.
physical (fĭz′ĭ-kâl): relating to the body, as distinguished from the mind.
physics (fĭz′ĭks): the branch of science that deals with matter and motion and comprises the study of light, heat, electricity, sound, and mechanics.
physiology (fĭz-ē-ŏl′ô-jē): the science of the functions of living things.
physio therapy (fĭz′ē-ō thĕr′ă-pē): the use of natural forces such as light, heat, air, water, and exercise in the treatment of disease.
picric acid (pĭk′rĭk ăs′ĭd): an organic acid used as an antiseptic.
pigment (pĭg′mênt): any organic coloring matter, as that of the red blood cells, of the hair, skin, iris, etc.
pigmentation (pĭg″mên-tā′shûn): the deposition of pigment in the skin or tissues.
pilary (pī′lă-rē): pertaining to hair.
pilocarpine (pī-lô-kär′pĭn; -pēn): an alkaloid obtained from the leaves of pilocarpus; stimulates the tissues and increases secretion of the glands.
pilose (pī′lōs): covered with hair.
pilosebaceous (pī″lô-sê-bā′shûs): pertaining to the hair follicles and the sebaceous glands.
pilus (pī′lûs); p., **pili** (-lī): hair.
pimple (pĭm′p′l): any small pointed elevation of the skin; a papule or small pustle.
pin curl permanent (pĭn kûrl pûr′mă-nênt): a cold or heatless permanent in which the hair is set in pin curls instead of being rolled on curlers; basic curl permanent; foundation curl.
pineal (pĭn′ḗ-âl): a ductless gland located in the region of the brain.

fāte, câre, ăm, finâl, ärm, ȧsk, sofă; ēve, ḗvent, ĕnd, recênt, evẽr; īce, ĭll; ōld, ṍbey, ôrb, ŏdd, cônnect, sŏft, fōod, fŏŏt; ūse, ûrn, ŭp, circûs

pinna (pĭn′ă): wing; the external ear, exclusive of meatus.
pipette (pī-pĕt′): a slender tube for measuring liquids.
pisiform (pī′sĭ-fôrm): pea-shaped; a bone of the wrist.
pit (pĭt): a surface depression or hollow.
pith (pĭth): the marrow of bones; the center of the hair.
pituitary (pĭ-tū′ĭ-tĕr-ē): a ductless gland located at the bass of the brain.
pityriasis (pĭt-ĭ-rī′ă-sĭs): dandruff; an inflammation of the skin characterized by the formation and flaking of the fine branny scales.
pityriasis capitis (kăp′ĭ-tĭs): a scale inflammation marked by dry dandruff or branny exfoliation.
pityriasis pilaris (pī-lă′rĭs): characterized by an eruption of papules surrounding the hair follicles, each papule pierced by a hair, and tipped with a horny plug or scale.
pityriasis steatoides (stē-ă-toy′dēz): a scalp inflammation marked by fatty type of dandruff characterized by yellowish to brownish waxy scales or crusts on the scalp.
pityroid (pĭt′ĭ-roid): branny.
plantar artery (plăn′tar är′tĕr-ē): a blood vessel which extends across the sole and around the toes of the foot.
plasma (plâz′mă): the fluid part of the blood and lymph.
plasticizer (plăs′tĭ-sī-zĕr): a compound which keeps a substance soft and thick as in nail polishes.
plastic surgeon (plăs′tĭk sûr′jŭn): a surgeon who builds up or molds tissue or repairs physical skin defects.
platelets (plāt′lĕts): blood cells which aid in the formation of clots.
platinum nail polish (plāt′ĭ-nŭm nāl pŏl′ĭsh): a liquid nail enamel, silver white in appearance.
platinum rinse (rĭns): used on extremely light hair to give it a beautiful white blonde effect.
platysma (plă-tĭz′mă): a broad thin muscle of the neck.
pledget (plĕj′ĕt): a compress or small flat mass of lint, absorbent cotton, or the like.
plexus (plĕk′sûs): a network of nerves or veins.
pluck (plŭk): to pull with sudden force.
pneumogastric (nū-mô-găs′trĭk): relating to the lungs and stomach.
pneumogastric nerve (nûrv): vagus nerve; tenth cranial nerve.
pneumonia (nū-mŏ′nē-ă): inflammation of the lungs.
podiatrist (pō′dĭ-â-trĭst): one who treats disease of the feet.
point (point): a sharp end or apex; an abscess, the wall of which becomes thin and is about to break.
poise (poiz): the manner in which the head or body is carried.
poison (poi′z′n): a substance, which when taken internally is injurious to health, or dangerous to life.
poison ivy (ī′vĭ): a harmful plant which is poisonous to the touch.
poisoning, blood (poi′z′n-ĭng, blŭd): a diseased condition due to the presence of germs or harmful substances in the blood.
polarity (pô-lăr′ĭ-tē): the property of having two opposite poles, as that possessed by a magnet or galvanic current.
poliosis (pŏl-ē-ō′sĭs): a condition characterized by absence of pigment in the hair.
pollex (pŏl-eks): the thumb.
poly (pō′lĭ): a prefix denoting many; much.
pomade (pô-mâd′; -mäd′): a medicated ointment for the hair.
pomphus (pŏm′fus): a whitish or pinkish elevation of the skin; a wheal.
pore (pôr): a small opening of the sweat glands of the skin.
porous (pō′rûs): full of pores.

fāte, câre, ăm, finâl, ärm, àsk, sofă; ēve, évent, ĕnd, recênt, evẽr; īce, ĭll; ōld, ŏbey, ôrb, ŏdd, cônnect, sŏft, fōod, fŏot; ūse, ûrn, ŭp, circûs

portability (pôr-tă-bĭl′ĭ-tē): quality or state of being easily carried about.
portable (pōr′tà-b′l): easily carried.
positive (pŏz′ĭ-tĭv): affirmative; not negative; the presence of abnormal condition; having a relative high potential in electricity.
positive pole, P. or + (pōl): the pole from which positive electricity flows.
positive terminal (tûr′mĭ-nâl): the end of a conducting circuit manifesting acid reaction; the carbon plate in a battery.
post (pōst): a prefix denoting back; after.
posterior (pŏs-tē′rē-ēr): situated behind; coming after or behind.
posterior auricular (ô-rĭk′û-lăr): a nerve which supplies muscles in the posterior surface of the ear.
postiche (pôs-tēsh): artificial hair piece; curls, braids, or other extra hair piece used in creating coiffures.
posture (pŏs′tûr): the position of the body as a whole.
potassium (pô-tăs′ē-ûm): an element, the salts of which are used in medicine.
potassium hydroxide (hī-drŏk′s-īd): a powerful alkali, used in the manufacture of soft soaps.
potassium permanganate (pēr-măn′gă-nāt): a salt of permanganate acid; used as an antiseptic and deodorant.
potential (pô-těn′shâl): indicting possibility; tension in an electrical source enabling it to do work under suitable conditions.
pouch (pouch): a cyst or sac containing fluid.
poultice (pōl′tĭs): a medicinal preparation used as a local stimulant on the skin.
powder (pou′dĕr): a dry mass of extremely fine particles.
precaution (prê-kô′shûn): to warn or advise beforehand.
precipitation (prê-sĭp-ĭ-tā′shûn): the formation of an insoluble substance which settles out as a result of a chemical reaction between substances in solution.
predicament (prê-dĭk′ă-měnt): condition; especially unpleasant, unfortunate, or trying position.
predisposition (prē-dĭs-pô-zĭsh′ûn): a condition of special susceptibility to disease; allergy.
pregnant (prĕg′nânt): a female bearing a child.
prehension (prḗ-hěn′shûn): grasping; taking hold of, as in eating.
preliminary (prḗ-lĭm′ĭ-nâ-rē): introductory; preparatory.
premature (prē′mă-tūr): happening before the usual time.
presenilis (prē-sê-nĭl′ĭs): prematurely old.
pressing (prĕs′ĭng): a method of straigtening over-curly or kinky hair with a heated comb or iron.
preventive (prê-věn′tĭv): a prophylactic; warding off disease.
primary (prī′mă-rē): first; primitive.
prism (prĭz′m): a transparent solid with triangular ends and two converging sides it breaks up white light into its component colors.
procerus (prṓ-sē′rûs): pyramidalis nasi muscle.
process (prŏ′sĕss): a course of development; a projecting part.
profession (prô-fĕsh′ûn): vocation; those engaged in work which requires special knowledge to serve the public in a particular art.
profuse (prṓ-fūs): to spend too liberally; abundant.
prognosis (prŏg-nô-sĭs): the foretelling of the probable course of a disease.
progressive dyes (prṓ-grĕs′ĭv dīz): hair restorers requiring time to oxidize; color develops gradually.
proliferate (prô-lĭf′ĕr-āt): to grow by reproduction of similar forms.
prominences (prŏm′ĭ-nên-sēz): projections.

fāte, câre, ăm, finâl, ärm, àsk, sofă; ēve, ĕ́vent, ĕnd, recênt, evẽr; īce, ĭll; ōld, ṓbey, ôrb, ŏdd, cônnect, sŏft, fōod, fŏot; ūse, ûrn, ŭp, circŭs

pronate (prō′nāt): to bend forward.
prong (prŏng): the round rod of the marcel iron.
prophylactic (prō-fĭ-lăk′tĭk): preventing disease; relating to prophylaxis.
prophylaxis (prō-fĭ-lăk′sĭs): prevention of disease.
proportion (prṓ-pōr′shûn): comparative relation of one thing to another.
prostration (prŏs-trā′shûn): the state of being weak or destroyed.
protection (prô-tĕk′shûn): the act of shielding from injury.
protein (prō′tê-ĭn): a complex organic substance present in all living tissues, both animal and vegetable, necessary in the diet.
protoplasm (prō′tṓ-plăz′m): the material basis of life; a substance found in all living things.
protozoa (prō′tṓ-zō′ă): subkingdom of animals, including all the uni-cellular animall organisms.
protrude (prṓ-trōōd′): to project; to push forward or outward.
proximal (prŏk′sĭ-măl): nearest.
pruritus (prōō-rī′tŭs): itching; a symptom of various skin and scalp diseases.
psoriasis (sô-rī′ă-sĭs): a skin disease with circumscribed red patches, covered with adherent white scales.
psychic (sī′kĭk): relating to the mind.
psychology (sī-kŏl′ô-jē): the science of the mind and its operations.
pterygium (tê-rĭj′ē-ûm): a forward growth of the eponychium with adherence to the surface of the nail.
pterygoid (tĕr′ĭ-goid): wing-shaped.
pterygoideus (tĕr-ĭ-goid′ê-ûs): internus and externus muscle between mandible and cheek bone, draws mandible forward.
ptomaine (tō′mā-ĭn; -ēn): a poison produced during the decomposition of dead animal or vegetable matter.
ptyalin (tī′ă-lĭn): a starch splitting enzyme found in the saliva.
puberty (pū′bĕr-tē): the period of life in which the organs of reproduction are developed.
pull burn (pōōl bûrn): scalp irritation resulting from pulling the hair during permanent waving.
pulmonary (pŭl′mṓ-nā-rē): relating to the lungs.
pulmonary circulation (sûr-kū-lā′shûn): blood circulation from heart to lungs and back to heart.
pulse (pŭls): stroke; the rhythmical dilation of an artery, produced by the increased volume of blood that is thrown into the vessel by the contraction of the heart.
pumice (pŭm′ĭs): hardened volcanic glass froth, white or gray in color, used for polishing in manicuring; called also pumice stone.
punctata, acne (pŭnk-tā′tă): a form of acne in which the lesions are pointed papules with a comedone in the center.
pungent (pŭn′jĕnt): producing a sharp sensation; painful; caustic.
purgative (pûr′gă-tĭv): an agent causing active movement of the bowels.
pupil (pū′pĭl): a small opening in the iris of the eye through which light enters.
purification (pū-rĭ-fĭ-kā′shûn): the act of cleaning or removing foreign matter.
purpura (pûr′pū-ră): a disease characterized by the formation of purple patches on the skin and the mucous membrane.
pus (pŭs): a fluid product of inflammation, consisting of a liquid containing leucocytes and the debris of dead cells and tissue elements.
pusher (pōōh′ēr): a steel instrument used to loosen the cuticle from the nail.
push wave (pōōsh wăv): a wave which is pushed into place with the hands.
postulation (pŭs-tû-lā′shûn): the formation or the presence of pustules.

fāte, câre, ăm, finâl, ärm, ȧsk, sofȧ; ēve, ĕvent, ĕnd, recênt, evẽr; īce, ĭll; ōld, ṓbey, ôrb, ŏdd, cônnect, sŏft, fōod, fŏot; ūse, ûrn, ŭp, circûs

pustule (pūs'tūl): an inflamed pimple containing pus.
pustulosa acne (pŭs-tū-lō'să): a form of acne characterized by pustules.
putrefaction (pū-trê-făk'shŭn): decomposition; decay; the splitting up of the molecule of a protein into less complex substances.
pyloric (pĭ-lŏr'ĭk): pertaining to an opening found between the stomach and small intestine.
pyogenic (pī-ó-jĕn'ĭk): pus forming.
pyosis (pī-ō-sĭs): the formation of pus.
pyramidal (pĭ-răm'ĭ-dăl): shaped like a pyramid; relating to the pyramidal bone.
pyramidal bone (bōn): the wedge-shaped bone of the carpus.
pyramidalis nasi (pĭ-răm-ĭ-dā'lĭs nā'sī): pocerus; muscle of the nose.
pyro (pī'rō): a prefix denoting fire; prepared by fire.
pyrogallic acid (pī-rô-găl'ĭk ăs'ĭd): pyrogallol.
pyrogallol (pī-rô-găl'ŏl;-ōl): a substance obtained from gallic acid by the action of heat, employed externally in the treatment of psoriasis, ringworm, and other skin affections.
pyrogenic (pī-rô-jĕn'ĭk): producing fever.

Q

quadratus (kwod-rā'tûs): a square-shaped muscle; a muscle of the lower jaw.
quadratur labii superioris (lā'bē-īsû-pē'rē-ŏr'ĭs): a muscle of the upper lip.
quality (kwŏl'ĭ-tī): distinctive kind, trait, or character.
quarantine (kwŏr'ân-tēn): the isolation of a person to prevent spread of a contagious disease.
quince seed (kwĭns sēd): the dried seeds of Pyrus Cydonia which yield a mucilage used in the making of hand lotions.
quinine (kwī'nīn; kwĭ-nēn): enters into the composition of many hair lotions in small quantities; its effect is slightly antiseptic.

R

rabies (rā'bēz): an acute infectious disease of dogs, wolves, and other animals, corresponding to hydrophobia in human beings.
race (rās): a family, people or nation having a common ancestor.
radical (răd'ĭ-kăl): in chemistry, a group of atoms behaving like a single atom.
radial artery (rā'dĭ-ăl är'tĕr-ē): a blood vessel which supplies the lower arm and hand.
radial nerve (nûrv): a nerve which affects the arm and hand.
radiation (rā-dĭ-ā'shŭn): the process of giving off light or heat rays.
radius (rā'dē-ûs): the outer and smaller bone of the forearm.
ramus (rā'mûs): a branch of an artery, vein, or nerve.
rash (răsh): a skin eruption having little or no elevation.
rat-tail comb (răt-tāl kōm): a comb having a thick handle and used to push a wave in place.
ray (rā): a beam or light or heat.
re (rē): a prefix denoting back to the original or former state or position.
reaction (rē-ăk'shŭn): a response.
reagent (rê-ā'jĕnt): any substance used in detecting, examining, or measuring other substances.
receptacle (rē-sĕp'tâ-k'l): a utensil used for storage.
recondition treatment (rē-k û n-d ĭ sh' û n trēt'mênt): a treatment to bring the hair back to a healthy condition; an oil treatment.

fāte, câre, ăm, finâl, ärm, ȧsk, sofã; ēve, évent, ĕnd, recênt, evẽr; īce, ĭll; ōld, óbey, ôrb, ŏdd, cônnect, sŏft, fo͞od, fo͝ot; ūse, ûrn, ŭp, circûs

rectifier (rĕk′tĭ-fī-ẽr): an apparatus to change an alternating current of electricity into a direct current.
rectum (rĕk′tûm): the terminal portion of the digestive tube.
rectus (rĕk′tûs): in a straight line; the name of small muscles of the eye.
recuperate (rê-kû′pẽr-āt): to recover health or strength.
red corpuscle (rêd kôr′pŭs-'l): red blood cell.
reddish cast (rĕd′ish kȧst): a tinge of red.
reflex (rē′flĕks): an involuntary nerve reaction.
rejuvenate (rê-jōō′vê-nāt): to make young or vigorous again.
relapse (rê-lăps): a slipping back, especially to a former bad condition.
relaxation (rē-lăk-sȧ′shûn): the act of being loose and less tense.
renal (rē′nâl): relating to a kidney.
reproductive (rē-prô-dŭk′tĭv): pertaining to reproduction or the process by which plants and animals give rise to offspring.
research (rê-sûrch): a careful search for facts or principles.
residue (rĕz′ĭ-dū): that which remains after a part is taken; remainder.
resilient (rê-zĭl′ĭ-ĕnt): elastic.
resistance (rê-zĭs′tȧns): opposition; act or capacity of striving against defeat; in electricity the opposition of a substance to the passage hrough it of an electric current.
respiration (rĕs-pĭ-rā′shûn): the act of breathing; the process of inhaling air into the lungs and expelling it
respiratory system (rê-spĭr′ȧ-tô-rē sĭs′tĕm): consists of the nose, pharynx, larynx, bronchi, and lungs which assist in breathing.
resorcin (rĕz-ôr′sin): resorcinal.
resorcinal (rĕz-ôr′sĭ-nâl): chiefly used as an external antiseptic in psoriasis, eczema, seborrhea, and ringworm.
restorative (rḗ-stôr′ȧ-tĭv): a food or medicine which helps to regain normal health and vigor.
restore (rḗ-stōr): to bring back to former strength;; repair; rebuild.
retard (rḗ-tärd′): to hinder or delay.
rete (rē-tḗ): any interlacing of either blood vessels or nerves.
reticular (rê-tĭk′û-lăr): having form of a network.
reticular layer (lā′ẽr): the inner layer of the corium.
retina (rĕt′ĭ-nă): the sensitive membrane of the eye which receives the image formed by the lens.
retinitis (rĕ-tĭn-ī′tĭs): inflammation of the retina.
retouch (rē′-tŭch): application of hair dye to new growth of hair.
retrahens aurem (rē′trȧ-hĕnz ôr′êm): a muscle back of the ear.
revivification (rĕ-vĭv-ĭ-fı-kā′shûn): to cause to revive or restore.
revolution (rĕv-ô-lū′shŭn): progressive motion of a body around a center.
rewave (rē′wāv): a permanent wave given to hair which still retains some of the former permanent.
rhagades (răg′ȧ-dēz): cracks, fissures or chaps on the skin.
rheostat (rē-ō-stăt): a resistance coil; an instrument used to regulate the strength of an electric current.
rheumatism (rōō-mă-tĭz′m): a painful disease of the muscles and joints, accompanied by swelling and stiffness.
rhinitis (rī-nī′tĭs): inflammation of the nasal mucous membrane.
rhythm (rĭth′m): regular recurring movements.

fāte, câre, ăm, finȧl, ärm, ȧsk, sofă; ēve, ḗvent, ĕnd, recênt, evẽr; īce, ĭll; ōld, ṍbey, ôrb, ŏdd, cônnect, sŏft, fōod, fŏŏt; ūse, ûrn, ŭp, circûs

rickets (rĭk′ĕts): a disease of childhood, due chiefly to deficient nutrition, in which the bones become soft and cause deformity.
rickettsia (rĭk-ĕt′sĭ-ä): a type of pathogenic microorganism, capable of producing disease.
ridge (rĭj): crest of a wave.
ringed hair (rĭngd hâr): a variety of canities in which the hair appears white or colored in rings.
ringlet (rĭng′lĕt): a curl of hair.
ringworm (rĭng′wûrm): a vegetable parasitic disease of the skin and its appendages which appears in circular lesions and is contagious.
rinse (rĭns): to cleanse with a second or repeated application of water after washing; a prepared rinse water.
risorius (rĭ-zôr′ē-ûs): muscle at the side of the mouth.
rod (rŏd): the round solid prong of a waving iron; a slender bar on which hair is wound for curling or permanent waving.
rolling (rōl′ĭng): a massage movement in which the tissues are pressed and twisted.
root (ro͞ot): in anatomy the base; the foundation or beginning of any part.
rosacea, acne (rô-zā′shē-ă): an eruption on the cheeks and nose.
rotate (rō′tāt): to turn; to revolve.
rouge (ro͞ozh): a cosmetic to color the skin pink or red.
ruffing (rŭf′ĭng): back combing; teasing.
round curling (round kûrl-ĭng): process of winding the hair tightly and evenly around a heated curling iron.

S

Sabouraud Rousseau (sä′bo͞o-rōro͞o′-sō): a discoverer of a 24-hour skin test used in hair dyeing to determine whether or not a patron can tolerate an aniline derivative hair dye.
saccular (săk′ū-lăr): shaped like a sac.
sachet (sȧ-shā′): shaped like a sac.
sage tea rinse (sāj tē rĭns): given to darken the hair.
salicylic acid (săl-ĭ-sĭl′ĭk ăs′ĭd): white crystalline acid; it is used as an antiseptic in treating rheumatism.
saline (sā′līn): salty; containing salt.
saliva (să-lī′vă): the secretion of the salivary glands; spittle.
salivary gland (săl′ĭ-vă-rē glănd): the gland in the mouth secreting spittle.
sallow (săl′ō): having a yellowish color; of a pale, sickly color.
salt (sôlt): the union of a base with an acid, used to season food.
saturate (săt′ū-rāt): to cause to become soaked or completely penetrated; that which has absorbed all that it can hold.
scab (skăb): a crust formed on the surface of a sore.
scabies (skā′bĭ-ēz): a skin diseases caused by an animal, parasite, attended with intense itching; the itch.
scale (skāl): any thin plate of horny epidermis; regular markings used as a standard in measuring and weighing.
scalp (skălp): the skin covering of the cranium.
scalpial (skăl′pē-âl): the technical term for general all around treatment of the scalp.
scaphoid bone (skăf′oid bōn): the boat-shaped bone of the tarsus and the carpus.
scapula (skăp′ū-lă): the shoulder blade; a large flat triangular bone of the shoulder.
scar (skär): a mark remaining after a wound has healed.

fāte, câre, ăm, finâl, ärm, ȧsk, sofȧ; ēve, ĕvent, ĕnd, recĕnt, evẽr; īce, ĭll; ōld, ŏbey, ôrb, ŏdd, cônnect, sŏft, fo͞od, fo͝ot; ūse, ûrn, ŭp, circûs

scarf skin (skärf ĭn): epidermis.
scarlet fever (skär'lĕt fē'vẽr): a contagious disease accompanied by fever and scarlet eruption
sciatica (sī-ăt'ĭ-kă): a painful inflammation of the sciatic nerve running down the back of the leg.
science (sī'êns): knowledge duly arranged and systematized.
scientific (sī-ên-tĭf'ĭk): pertaining to, or used in science.
sclerosis(sklĕr-ō'sĭs): hardening of tissue as a result of chronic inflammation.
scrum-pox (skrŭm'pŏks): impetigo contagiosa.
scrupulous (skroo'pû-lûs): careful; cautious.
sculpture curl (skŭlp'tūr kûrl): a curl placed close to the head, to appear as if it were carved.
scurf (skûrf): thin dry scales or scabs on the body, especially on the scalp; dandruff.
sebaceous (sêbā'shûs): oily; fatty.
sebaceous cyst (sĭst): a distended oily or fatty follicle or sac.
sebaceous glands (glăndz): oil glands of the skin.
seborrhea (sĕb-ô-rē'ă): over-action of the sebaceous glands.
seborrhea capitis (kăp'ĭ-tĭs): seborrhea of the scal, commonly called dandruff; pityriasis.
seborrhea oleosa(ō-lē-ō'să): excessive oiliness of the skin, particularly the forehead and nose.
seborrhea sicca (sĭk'ă): an accumulation on the scalp, of greasy scales or crusts, due to over-action of the sebaceous glands; dandruff or pityriasis.
seborrheic (sĕb-ô-rē'ĭk): seborrheal; pertaining to the over-action of the sebaceous glands.
seborrheic alopecia (ăl-ô-pē'shē-ă): baldness caused by diseased sebaceous glands.
sebum (sē'bŭm): the fatty or oil secretions of the sebaceous glands.
secondary (sĕk'ûn-dâ-rē): second in order.
secretion (sê-krē'shûn): a product manufactured by a gland for a special purpose.
secretory (sê-krē'tô-rē): relating to secretion or the secretions.
sectioning (sĕk'shûn-ĭng): dividing the hair into separate parts.
sedative (sĕd'ă-tĭv): tending to quiet or allay nervous excitement.
sedentary (sĕd'ên-tâ-rē): occupied in sitting; settled; inactive.
seep (sēp): to ooze out slowly.
segment (sĕg'mênt): to divide and re-divide into minute equal parts.
selector switch (sĕ-lĕk'tẽr swĭch): an apparatus used to select the kind of current desired for a treatment.
semilunar bone (sĕm-ĭ-lū'năr bōn): a crescent-shaped bone of the wrist.
senility (sê-nĭlĭ-tē): quality or state of being old.
sensation (sĕn-sā'shûn): a feeling or impression arising as the result of the stimulation of an afferent nerve.
sensitive (sĕn'sĭ-tĭv): easily affected by outside influences.
sensory (sĕn'sô-rē): relating to or pertaining to sensation.
sensory nerve (nûrv): afferent nerve; a nerve carrying sensations.
sentient (sĕn'shĭ-ênt): sensitive; capable of sensation.
sepsis (sĕp'sĭs): the presence of various pus forming and other pathogenic organisms, or their toxins, in the blood or tissues; septicemia.
septal artery (sĕp'tâl är'tẽr-ē): supplies the nostrils.
septic (sĕp'tĭk): relating to or caused by sepsis.
septicemia (sēp'tĭ-sē-mē-ă): the condition which exists when the pathogenic bacteria enter the bloodstream and circulate through the body, causing a general infection.
septum (sĕp'tûm): a dividing wall; a partition.
serous (sē'rûs): relating to, or containing serum.

fāte, câre, ăm, finâl, ärm,ȧsk, sofă; ēve, évent, ĕnd, recênt, evẽr; īce, ĭll; ōld, ŏbey, ôrb, ŏdd, cônnect, sŏft, food, foot; ūse, ûrn, ŭp, circŭs

serratus (sē-rā′tŭs): a muscle of the chest assisting in breathing and in raising the arm.
serum (sē′rŭm): the fluid portion of the blood obtained after coagulation; an antitoxin as prepared for therapeutic use.
sewage (sū′āj): the waste mater, solid and liquid, passing through a sewer.
shadow weaving (shăd′ō wāv′ĭng): a very soft wave for resistant hair which does not readily take finger waving.
shaft (shăft): slender stem-like structure; the long slender part of the hair above the scalp.
shampoo (shăm-pōō′): to subject the scalp and hair to washing and rubbing with some cleansing agent such as soap and water.
sheath (shēth): a covering enclosing or surrounding some organ.
sheen (shēn): gloss; brightness.
shingling (shĭng′lĭng′): cutting the hair close to the nape of the neck and gradually longer toward the crown.
shock (shŏk): a marked lowering of the vital activities from an injury or operation; a blow to the feelings.
short circuit (shôrt sûr′kĭt): to shut or break off an electric current before it has completed its course.
siccant; siccative (sĭ′kănt; sĭk′ă-tĭv): drying; tending to make dry.
silica (sĭl′ĭ-kă): dioxide of silicon used in the making of glass.
silicon (sĭl′ĭ-kŏn): a very abundant non-metallic element.
silver dye (sĭl′vẽr dī): a hair restorer, containing a silver salt used as a dye.
simplex (sĭm′plĕks): common; simple.
simplex, acne (ăk′nē): common pimple.
Singeing (sĭnj′ĭng): process of lightly burning hair ends with a lighted wax taper.
sinus (sī′nŭs): a cavity or depression; a hollow in bone or other tissue.
sinusoid (sī′nŭs-oid): resembling a sinu; a blood space in certain organs, as the liver, pancreas, etc.
sinusoidal current (sī-nŭs-oid′âl kûr′ênt): an induced interrupted current similar to faradic current.
skeletal muscles (skĕl′é-tâl mŭs′l′z): muscles connected to the skeleton.
skeleton (skĕl′é-tŭn): the bony framework of the body.
skin (skĭn): the external covering of the body.
skull (skŭl): the bony case or the framework of the head.
slake (slāk): to become mixed with water in chemical combination.
sleek (slēk): to render smooth, soft, and glossy.
slip (slĭp): a smooth and slippery feeling imparted by talc to face powder.
slithering (slĭth′ẽr-ĭng): tapering the hair to graduated lengths with scissors.
slough (slŭf): to separate as dead matter from living tissues; to discard.
small pox (smôl pŏks): a contagious skin disease resulting in the production of pock marks.
smaller occipital (smôl′ẽr ŏk-sĭp′ĭ-tâl): sensory nerve affecting skin behind the ear.
snarls (snarlz): tangles, as of hair.
soap (sōp): compound of fatty acid with an alkaline base.
soapless shampoo (sōp′lĕs shăm-pōō′): a shampoo made with sulfonated oil, alcohol, mineral oil and water; this type of shampoo does not foam and is usually slightly acid in reaction.
socket (sŏk′ĕt): a cavity in which a movable part is inserted.
sodium (sō′dē-ŭm): a metallic element of the alkaline group.
sodium bicarbonate (bī-kär′bôn-āt): baking soda: bicarbonate of soda; it relieves burns, bites; is often used in bath powders as an aid to cleansing oily skin.

fāte, câre, ăm, finâl, ärm, ȧsk, sofă; ēve, évent, ĕnd, recênt, evẽr; īce, ĭll; ōld, ȯbey, ôrb, ŏdd, cônnect, sŏft, fōōd, fŏŏt; ūse, ûrn, ŭp, circûs

sodium carbonate (kär′bôn-āt): washing soda; used to prevent corrosion of metallic instruments when added to boiling water.
sodium hydroxide (hī-drŏk′sīd): powerful alkali used in the manufacture of hard soaps.
sodium thiosulphat (thī-ō-sŭl′fât): it is used in solutions for impetiginous conditions and parasitic alopecias of the beard.
soft water (sŏft wô′tẽr): water which readily lathers with soap.
solar (sō′lẽr): pertaining to the sun.
solarium (sô-lă′rē-ûm): a sun parlor.
sole (sōl): the plantar surface of the foot.
soluble (sŏl′û-b′l): capable of being dissolved.
solution (sō-lū′shûn): the act or process by which a substance is absorbed into a liquid.
solvent (sŏl′vĕnt): an agent capable of dissolving substances.
somnolence (sŏm′nō-lêns): sleepiness; drowsiness.
sparsely (spärs′lē): pertaining to the hair, thinly scattered.
spatula (spăt′ū-lă): a flexible, knife-like implement for handling creams and drugs, etc.
specialist (spĕsh′ă-lĭst): one who devotes himself to some special branch of learning, art, or business.
specific gravity (spĕ-sĭf′ĭk grâvĭ-tĭ): the measured weight of a substance compared with an equal volume of another taken as a standard.
spectrum (spĕk′trûm): the band of rainbow colors produced by decomposing light by means of a prism.
spermaceti (spŭr-mă-sĕt′ē): cetaceum; an animal wax obtained from the head of the sperm whale; used to give body to creams.
sphere (sfẽr): a ball or globular body.
spherical (sfẽr′ĭ-kâl): relating to or having the shape of a sphere.
sphenoid (sfē′noid): wedge-shaped; a bone in the cranium.
sphincter (sfĭnk′tẽr): a muscle which surrounds and closes a natural opening of the body.
spinal (spī′nâl): pertaining to the spine or vertebral column.
spinal accessory (ăk-sĕs′ŏ́-rē): eleventh cranial nerve.
spinal column (kŏl′ŭm): the backbone or vertebral column.
spinal cord (kôrd): the portion of the central nervous system contained within the spinal or vertebral canal.
spinal nerves (nûrvz): the nerves arising from the spinal cord.
spindle-shaped (spĭn′d′l-shāpt): tapering toward each end.
spine (sp n): a short process of bone; the backbone.
spiral (spī′râl): coil; winding around a center, like a watch spring.
spiral rod (rŏd): a rod upon which the hair is wound in a spiral manner for a permanent wave.
spiral winding (wĭnd′ĭng): winding the hair on a rod, like the thread of a screw, from the scalp to the ends.
spirillum (spĭ-rĭl′ûm); pl., **spirilla** (-ă): curved bacterium.
spirocheta pallida (spī-rṓ-kē′ta pălʹĭ-dă): pathogenic bacteria responsible for syphilis.
spleen (splēn): a large vascular ductless gland between the stomach and the diaphragm.
splenius (splē′nē-ûs): a muscle or a group of muscles at the side and back of the neck.
spongy (spŭn′jē): elastic; porous.
spore (spōr): a tiny bacterial body having a protective wall to withstand unfavorable conditions.
spray (sprā): to discharge liquid in the form of fine vapor.
squama (skwā′mă): an epidermic scale made up of thin, flat cells.
squamous (skwā′mûs): scaly.
stagnation (stăg-nā′shûn): lack of action; cessation of activity.

fāte, câre, ăm, finâl, ärm, ȧsk, sofă; ēve, ĕ́vent, ĕnd, recênt, evẽr; īce, ĭll; ōld, ŏ́bey, ôrb, ŏdd, cônnect, sŏft, fōod, fŏot; ūse, ûrn, ŭp, circûs

staphylococcus (stăf'ĭ-lṓ-kŏk'ûs): cocci which are grouped in clusters like a bunch of grapes; found in pustules and boils.

static electricity (stăt'ĭk ē-lĕk-trĭs'ĭ-tē): electricity produced by friction.

steamer, facial (stēm'ẽr fā'shâl): an apparatus, used in place of hot towels, for steaming the scalp or face.

steam pocket (stēm pŏk'ĕt): pertaining to permanent waving, a special folding of the permanent wave pad to make a closed steam chamber, to protect the scalp from steam burns.

stearate (stē'ă-rāt): a salt of stearic acid.

stearic acid (stê-ăr'ĭk ăs'-ĭd): a white fatty acid, occurring in solid animal fats and in some of the vegetable fats.

steatoma (stē-ă-tō'mă): a sebaceous cyst; a fatty tumor.

steatosis (stē-ă-tō'sĭs): fatty degeneration; adiposis.

sterile (stĕr'ĭl): barren; free from all living organisms.

sterility (stê-rĭl'ĭ-tē): a condition of being unfruitful; barren.

sterilization (stêr-ĭ-lī-zā'shûn): the process of making sterile; the destruction of germs.

sterilizer (stĕr'ĭ-lī-zẽr): an agent or receptacle for sterilization.

sterno (stûr'nṓ): a prefix denoting connection with the sternum (breast bone).

sterno-cleido-mastoideus (stûr″nṓ-klī-dṓ-măs'-toid'ē-ŭs): a muscle of the neck which depresses and rotates the head.

sternomastoid (stûr-nṓ-măs'toid): pertaining to the sternum and the mastoid process.

sternum (stûr'nûm): the flat bone of the breast.

stimulant (stĭm'ū-lânt): an agent that arouses organic activity.

stimulation (stĭm-ū-lā'shûn): the act arousing increasesd functional activity.

stimulus (stĭm'ū-lŭs): an agent which causes stimulation.

stomach (stŭm'ŭk): the dilated portion of the alimentary canal, in which the first process of digestion takes place.

strand (strănd): a fiber, hair or the like.

stratum (strā'tûm); pl., **strata** (-ă): layer of tissue.

stratum corneum (kôr'nḗ-ŭm): horny layer of the skin.

stratum granulosum (grăn-û-lo'sum): granular layer of the skin.

stratum lucidum (lū'sĭ-dûm): clear layer of the skin.

stratum mucosum (mū-kō'sŭm): mucous or malpighian layer of the skin.

streptococcus (strĕp-tṓ-kŏk'ûs): pus-forming bacteria that arrange in curved lines resembling a string of beads; found in erysipelas and blood poisoning.

striated (strī'āt-ĕd): marked with parallel lines or bands; striped; voluntary muscle.

stroking (strōk'ĭng): a gliding movement over a surface; to pass the finger or any instrument gently over a surface; effleurage.

stroma (strō'mă): the framework, usually of connective tissue of an organ, gland, or other structure.

Strontium sulphide (strŏn'shē-ûm sŭl'fīd): a light gray powder capable of liberating hydrogen sulphide in the presence of water; used as a depilatory.

structure (strŭk'tûr): construction; manner of building or form.

sty, stye (stī); pl., **sties, styes** (stīz): inflammation of one of the sebaceous glands of the eyelid.

styptic (stĭp'tĭk): an agent causing contraction of living tissue; used to stop bleeding; an astringent.

sub (sŭb): a prefix denoting under; below.

subcutaneous (sŭb-kŭ-tā'nē-ûs): under the skin.

subcutis (sŭb-kū'tĭs): subdermis; subcutaneous tissue; under or beneath the corium or dermis, the true skin.

fāte, câre, ăm, finâl, ärm, ȧsk, sofă; ēve, évent, ĕnd, recênt, evẽr; īce, ĭll; ōld, ṓbey, ôrb, ŏdd, cônnect, sŏft, fo͞od, fo͝ot; ūse, ûrn, ŭp, circûs

subdermis (sŭb-dûr′mĭs): subcutis or subcutaneous tissue of the skin.
subjective (sŭb-jĕk′tĭv sĭmp-tūm): sensed by the individual and not by the examiner
sublingual (sŭb-lĭn′gwăl): under the tongue
submerge (sŭb-mûrj′): sink or plunge anything under water or other fluid
submental artery (sŭb-mĕn′tăl är′tĕr-ē): supplies blood to the chin and lower lip.
subsidiary (sŭb-sĭd′ē-ā-rē): supplementary; furnishing assistance.
substance (sŭb′stâns): matter; material.
sudamen (sū-dā′mĕn); pl., **sudamina** (sū-dăm′ĭ-nă): a disorder of the sweat glands with obstruction of their ducts.
sudor (sū′dôr): sweat; perspiration.
sudoriferous ducts (dŭkts): the excretoary ducts of the sweat glands.
sudoriferous glands (glăndz): sweat glands of the skin.
sudorific (sū-dôr-ĭf′ĭk): causing or inducing perspiration.
sulcus (sŭl′kŭs): a furrow or groove.
sulfonated oil (sŭl′fûn-āt-êd oil): an organic substance prepared by reacting oils with sulphuric acid; has a slightly acid reaction and is miscible with water; used as a base in soapless shampoos.
sulphide (sŭl′fīd): a compound of sulphur with a base.
sulphur (sŭl′fûr): a chemical element whose compounds are used in bleaching and in medicine.
sulphuric acid (sŭl-fū′rĭk ăs′ĭd): oil of vitriol; colorless and nearly odorless, heavy oil, corrosive liquid; employed as a caustic.
sunburn (sŭn′bûrn): inflammation of the skin caused by excessive exposure to the sun.
sunlight (sŭn′līt): the light rays coming from the sun.
suntan (sŭn′tăn): a brownish coloring of the skin as a result of sun exposure.
super (sū′pẽr): a prefix denoting over; above; beyond.
superciliary (sū-pẽr-sĭl′ē-â-rē): pertaining to or in the región of the eyebrow.
supercilii (sū-pẽr-sĭl′ē-ī): of or pertaining to the eyebrown.
supercilium (sū′pẽr-sĭl′ē-ûm); pl., **supercilia** (-ă): the eyebrow.
superficial (sū-pẽr-fĭsh′ăl): pertaining to or being on the surface.
superficial cervical (sûr′vĭ-kăl): a cranial nerve which supplies the muscle and skin of the neck.
superfluous (sû-pûr′floo-ûs): excessive; more than is wanted or needed.
superior (sû-pē′rē-ẽr): higher; upper; better or of more value.
superior maxillary (măk′sĭ-lâ-rē): the upper jaw bone.
superioris (sû-pē-rê-ŏr′ĭs): a muscle which elevates a part of the body.
supinate (sū′pĭ-nāt): to turn the forearm and hand so that the palm faces upward.
supinator (sū′pĭ-nāt-ôr): a muscle which produces supination of the forearm.
supine (sû-pīn′): lying flat or on the back.
suppuration (sŭp-ū-rā′shŭn): the formation of pus.
supra (sū′pră): a prefix denoting on top of, above, over, beyond, besides; more than.
supraorbital (sū-pră-ôr′bĭ-tâl): above the orbit or eye.
supra-trochlear (sū-pră-trŏk′lē-ă): above the trochlea or pulley of the superior oblique muscle.
sural nerve (sū′răl nûrv): supplies the outer side and back of leg and foot.
susceptible (sû-sĕp′tĭ-b'l): capable of being influenced or easily acted on.
suspension (sû-spĕn′shŭn): a mixture of a liquid and insoluble particles which have a tendency to settle out on standing.
suture (sū′tûr): a uniting; a stitch.

fāte, câre, ăm, finâl, ärm, åsk, sofă; ēve, évent, ĕnd, recênt, evẽr; īce, ĭll; ōld, ŏbey, ôrb, ŏdd, cônnect, sŏft, food, foot; ūse, ûrn, ŭp, circûs

swirl (swûrl): formation of a wave in a diagonal direction from back to side of head.
switch (swĭch): a separate tress of hair, or of some substitute, worn by women, to increase the apparent mass of hair.
swooning (swo͞o'ĭng): fainting.
sycosis (sī-kŏ'sĭs): a chronic pustular inflammation of the hair follicles.
sycosis barbae (bär'bē): a chronic inflammation of the hair follicles of the beard; barber's itch.
sycosis, tinea (tĭn'ē-ă): parasitic ringworm of the beard; barber's itch.
symbol (sĭm'bŏl): a mark representing an atom of an element or a molecule of a radical.
sympathetic (sĭm-pă-thĕt'ĭk): relating to or exhibiting sympathy; noting the nerves in organic life.
sympathetic nervous system (nûr'vŭs sĭs'tĕm): controls the involuntary muscles which affect respiration, circulation, and digestion.
symptom (sĭmp'tûm): a change in the body or its functions which indicates disease.
symptom, objective (ŏb-jĕk'tĭv): that which can be seen, as in pimples, pustules, etc.
symptom, subjective (sŭb-jĕc'tĭv): can be felt, as in itching.
symptomatic (sĭmp-tûm-ăt'ĭk): relating to a symptom or symptoms; indicative.
symptomatica alopecia (sĭmp-tûm-ăt'ĭ-kă ăl-ō-pē'shē-ă): loss of hair from illness.
symptomatica chloasma (klō-ăz'mă): a form of chloasma accompanying disease.
syn (sĭn): a prefix denoting along with; together; at the same time.
synovia (sĭ-nō'vē-ă): a transparent viscid lubricating fluid secreted by the lining membranes of joints.
synthetic (sĭn-thĕt'ĭk): made artificially by the unin of simpler compounds or elements.
syphilis (sĭf'ĭ-lĭs): a chronic, infectious venereal disease.
system (sĭs'tĕm): a group of organs which especially contribute toward one of the more important vital functions; an assemblage of objects united by regular interdependence.
systematic (sĭs-tĕm-ăt'ĭk): proceeding according to system or regular method.
systemic (sĭs-tĕm'ĭk): pertaining to a system or to the body as a whole.
systole (sĭs'tó-lē): the period of the heart's contraction.

T

tactile (tăk'tīl): pertaining to touch.
tactile corpuscle (kôr'pŭs'l): touch nerve endings found within the skin.
tan (tăn): sunburn; pigmentation of the skin from exposure to the sun.
tannic acid (tăn'ĭk ăs'ĭd): a plant extract used as an astringent.
taper (tā'pĕr): regularly narrowed to a point.
tapering (tā'pĕr-ĭng): shortening and thinning the hair at the same time.
tapotement (tȧ-pṓt-män'): a massage movement using a short, quick slapping or tapping movement
tapping (tăp'ĭng): a massage movement; striking lightly with the partly flexed fingers.
tar (tär): a thick, semi-solid blackish brown mass, of complex composition, obtained by the destructive distillation of the wood of various species of pine.
tarsus (tär'sûs): the root of the foot or instep; the seven bones of the instep.
taut (tôt): tensely stretched; not slack.
teasing (tēz'ĭng): back combing; combing the short hair toward the scalp while the hair strand is held in a vertical position.
technic; technique (tĕk'nĭk; tĕk'nēk): manner of performance; a skill; a process.
technical (tĕk'nĭ-kâl): relating to a technic.

fāte, câre, ăm, finâl, ärm, ȧsk, sofȧ; ēve, évent, ĕnd, recênt, evẽr; īce, ĭll; ōld, óbey, ôrb, ŏdd, cônnect, sŏft, fo͞od, fo͝ot; ūse, ûrn, ŭp, circûs

tela (tē'lă): a web-like structure.
temperature (tĕm'pẽr-ă-tûr): the degree of heat or cold.
temple (tĕm'p'l): the flattened space on the side of the forehead.
temporal (tĕm'pṓ-râl): of or pertaining to the temple.
temporal bone (bōn): the bone at the side and base of the skull.
temporalis (tĕm-pṓ-ră'lĭs): the temporal muscle.
tendon (tĕn'dûn): fibrous cord or band connecting muscle with bone.
tension (tĕn'shûn): stress caused by stretching or pulling.
tepid (tĕp'ĭd): neither hot nor cold; lukewarm; about blood heat.
teres (tē'rēz): cylindrical muscles attached to the scapula and capable of moving the arm.
terminal (tûr'mĭ-nâl): of or pertaining to the end or extremity.
tertiary (tûr'shē-à-rē): third in order.
Tesla, Nikola (tĕs'lă, nĭ-kō'lă): American electrician of Hungarian birth (1857).
Tesla current (kŭr'ênt): high-frequency current.
test curl (tĕst kûrl): a sample curl, by which the correct treatment for the hair under consideration is ascertained.
testes (tĕs'tês): the male reproductive glands.
test for color (tĕst for kŭl'ẽr): to dye a strand of hair to determine the result of the color used.
test, hair dye (hâr dī): a test made upon the scalp, behind the ear, or in the bend of the arm, for predisposition to the dye agent used; a test to determine the reaction of the dye upon the sample strand, regarding both color and breakage.
tetanus (tĕt'ă-nŭs): a disease with spasmodic and continuous contraction of the muscles; lockjaw.
textometer (tĕks'tŏm'ē-tẽr): a device used to measure the elasticity and reaction of the hair to alkali solutions.
texture (tĕks'tûr): the composition or structure of a tissue or organ.
thenar (thē'när): the fleshy prominence of the palm corresponding to the base of the thumb.
theory (thē'ṓ-rē): an hypothesis; a reasoned and probable explanation.
therapeutic lamp (thĕr'ă-pū'tĭk lămp): an electrical apparatus producing any of the various rays of the spectrum; used for skin and scalp treatments.
therapeutics (thĕr-ă-pū'tĭks): branch of medical science concerned with the treatment of disease.
therapy (thĕr'ă-pē): the science and art of healing.
thermal (thûr'mâl): pertaining to heat.
thermometer (thĕr-mŏm'ḗ-tẽr): any device for measuring temperature.
thermostat (thûr'mṓ-stăt): an automatic device for regulating temperature.
thinning hair (thĭn'ĭ ng): decreasing the thickness of the hair where it is too heavy.
thoracic (thô-răs'ĭk): pertaining to the thorax.
thorax (tho'răks): the part of the body between the neck and the abdomen; the chest.
thrombocyte (thrŏm'bṓ-sīt): a blood platelet which aids in clotting.
thymol (thĭm'ŏl; -ōl): a substance extracted from oil of thyme and used as a medicine for skin and scalp diseases.
thymus (thī'mus): a ductless gland situated in the upper part of the chest.
thyroid gland (thī'roid glănd): a large ductless gland situated in the neck.
tibia (tĭb'ĭ-à): the inner bone of the leg between the knee and the ankle.
tincture (tĭnk'tûr): an alcoholic solution of a medicinal substance.
tinea (tĭn'ē-ă): a skin disease, especially ringworm.
tinea barbae (bär'bē): tinea sycosis.
tinea capitis (kăp'ĭ-tĭs): tinea tonsurans; ringworm of the scalp.

fāte, câre, ăm, finâl, ärm, àsk, sofă; ēve, évent, ĕnd, recênt, evẽr; īce, ĭll; ōld, ṓbey, ôrb, ŏdd, cônnect, sŏft, fo͞od, fo͝ot; ūse, ûrn, ŭp, circûs

tinea sycosis (sī-kō'sĭs): parasitic sycosis; ringworm of the beard; barber's itch.
tinea tonsurans (tŏn-sū'răns): tinea capitis; ringworm of the scalp.
tinea unguium (ŭn'gwē-ŭm): ringworm of the nail.
tinge (tĭnj): a degree, usually slight, of some color, addewd to something.
tint (tĭnt): to give a coloring to; as used in beauty culture, pertaining to hair dyeing; to color the hair by means of a hair dye, color rinse, or hair tint.
Tirrell burner (tĭ-rĕl'bûr'nẽr): an apparatus used to burn the hair in ash testing.
tis; sis (tĭs; sĭs): a word ending added to the name of a part to denote inflammation of that part, such as pityriasis, dermatitis.
tissue (tĭsh'ū): a collection of similar cells which perform a particular function.
tissue, connective (kŏ-nĕk'tĭv): binding and supporting tissue.
titanium dioxide (tī-tā'nē-ûm dī-ŏk'sīd): a white substance in face powder used for its covering power.
tone (tōn): healthy functioning of the body or its parts.
tong (tŏng): an instrument for lifting or holding an object.
tonic (tŏn'ĭk): increasing the strength or tone of the system.
torsade (tôr-sād): a twisted fringe of hair.
torso (tôr'sō): the trunk of the human body.
toupee (tōō-pā): a small wig used to cover the top or crown of the head.
toxemia (tŏk-sē'mē-ă): a form of blood poisoning.
toxic (tŏk'sĭk): due to, or of the nature of poison; poisonous.
toxin; toxine (tŏk'sĭn; -sēn): a poisonous substance of undetermined chemical nature, elaborated during the growth of pathogenic micro-organisms.
trachea (trā'kē-ă; tră-kē'ă): wind-pipe.
trachoma (tră-kō'mă): a contagious disease of the eyelids characterized by small granular elevations on the lids.
tragacanth (trăg'ă-kănth): a gummy exudation from the stems of Astragalus gummifier; used as a thickener and as an emulsifier.
transformation (trăns-fŏr-mā'shûn): a change in the external appearance of an object; an artificial band of hair worn over a person's own hair.
transformer(trăns-fôr'mẽr): used for the purpose of increasing or decreasing the voltage of the current used; it can only be used on an alternating current.
transmission (trăns-mĭsh'ûn): passing on by anything, often said of disease.
transmit (trăns-mĭt'): to cause to go across; to send over; dispatch.
transmitter (trăns-mĭt'ẽr): one who or that which transmits.
transparent (trăns-pâr'ênt): admitting the passage of light.
transverse (trăns-vûrs'): lying or being across or crosswise.
transverse facial (fā'shâl): an artery supplying the skin, the parotid gland and the masseter muscle.
trapezium (tră-pē'zē-ûm): the first bone of the second row of the carpus.
trapezius (tră-pē'zē-ûs): muscle that draws the head backward and sideways.
trapezoid (trăp'ē-zoid): a small bone ini the second row of the carpus.
trauma (trô'mă): a wound or injury.
treatise (trē'tĭs): a learned or scientific discourse on a subject.
tremor (trē'mor; trĕm' ŏ r): an involuntary trembling or quivering.
Treponema pallidum (trĕp- ő -nē'mă păl' ĭ -d û m): the pathogenic parasite of syphilis.
triangular (tr ī -ăn'g ū -lăr): having three angles or corners; bone of the wrist.

fāte, câre, ăm, finâl, ärm, åsk, sofă; ēve, évent, ĕnd, recênt, evẽr; īce, ĭll; ōld, ŏ́bey, ôrb, ŏdd, cônnect, sŏft, fōōd, fŏŏt; ūse, ûrn, ŭp, circûs

triangularis (trī-ăn-gū-lā′rĭs): depressor anguli oris; a muscle that pulls down corners of the mouth.
triceps (trī′sĕps): three-headed.
trichology (trĭ-kŏl′ó-jē): the science of the care of the hair.
trichonosus (trĭk-ō-nō′sûs): any disease of the hair.
trichophyton (trĭ-kŏf′ĭ-tŏn): a fungus parasite responsible for ringworm.
trichophytosis (trĭ-kŏf′ĭ-tō′sĭs): ringworm of the skin and scalp, due to growth of a fungus parasite.
trichoptilosis (trĭ-kŏp-tĭ-lō′sĭs): a splitting of the hair ends, giving them a feathery appearance.
trichorrhexis (trĭk-ô-rĕk′sĭs): brittleness of the hair.
trichosis (trĭ-kō′sĭs): abnormal growth of hair.
tricuspid (trī-kŭs′pĭd): having three points, as the right auriculo-ventricular valve of the heart.
trifacial (trī-fā′shâl): the fifth cranial nerve; trigeminus nerve.
trigeminal (trī-jĕm′ĭ-nâl): relating to the fifth cranial or trigeminus nerve.
trismus (trĭz′mûs, trĭs′-): lock jaw; usually associated with, and due to the same cause of eneral tetanus.
trochlea (trŏk′le-ă): a pulley-like process; a smooth articular surface of bone upon which another glides.
true skin (trōō skĭn): the corium.
tubercle (tū′bĕr-k′l): a rounded, solid elevation on the skin or membrane.
tuberculosis (tū-bûr′kū-lō′sĭs): an infectious disease due to a specific bacillus, characterized by the formation of tubercles, usually in the lungs.
tumor (tū′mẽr): a swelling; an abnormal enlargement; a mass of new tissue which persists and grows independently of its surrounding structures, and which has no physiological use.
turbinal; turbinate (tûr′bĭ-nâl, -nāt): a bone in the nose; turbinated body.
turbinated (tûr′bĭ-nāt-ĕd): shaped like a top; scross-shaped.
tweezers (twēz′ẽrz): a pair of small forceps to remove or extract hair.
typhoid (tī′foid): a continued acute infectious fever, with intestinal lesions and an eruption of rose-colored spots on the chest and abdomen.

U

ulcer (ŭl′sẽr): an open sore not caused by a wound.
ulna (ŭl′nă): the inner and larger bone of the forearm.
ultra (ŭl′tră): a prefix denoting beyond; on the other side; excessively.
ultra-violet (ŭl′tră-vī′ō-lĕt): invisible rays of the spectrum which are beyond the violet rays.
un (ŭn): a prefix denoting not; contrary.
unadulterated (ŭn-ă-dŭl′tẽr-āt-ĕd): pure.
unciform (ŭn′sĭ-form): hook-shaped; the bone on the inner side of the second row of the carpus.
unctuous (ŭnk′tū-ûs): greasy; oily.
undulation (ŭn-dû-lā′shûn): a wave-like movement or shape.
unguentum (ŭn-gwĕn′tûm); pl., **unguenta** (-ă): a salve or ointment.
unguis (ŭn′gwĭs); pl., **ungues** (gwēz): the nail of a finger or toe.
umguium tinea (ŭn′gĭvĕ-ŭm tĭn′é-ă): ringworm of the nails.
uni (ūn′i): a prefix denoting one; once.
unipolar (ū-nĭ-pōlăr): a term used when oone electrode of a direct current is applied to the body.

fāte, câre, ăm, finâl, ärm, ȧsk, sofă; ēve, évent, ĕnd, recênt, evẽr; īce, ĭll; ōld, ŏbey, ôrb, ŏdd, cônnect, sŏft, fōōd, fŏŏt; ūse, ûrn, ŭp, circûs

unit (ū′nĭt): a single thing or value.
United States Pharmacopeia (ū-nīt′ĕd stāts fär-mȧ-kō-pē-yä): an official book of drug and medicinal standards.
unsanitary (ŭn-săn′ĭ-tâ-rē): not sanitary; injurious to health.
urea (ū′rē-ă): a crystalline substance found in urine.
uric acid (ū′rik ăs′-ĭd): a crystalline acid contained in the urine.
uridrosis (ū-rĭ-drō′sĭs): the presence of urea in sweat.
urine (ū′rĭn): the fluid secreted by the kidneys.
urticaria (ûr-tĭ-kā′rē-ă): a skin disease in which wheals and severe itching develops; hives; nettle rash.
uterine (ū′tĕr-ĭn; -īn): pertaining to the uterus, an organ of the female mammals in which the young is contained and nourished before birth.
utilize (ū′tĭ-līz): to make useful.
uvula (ū′vū-lă): the conical projection from the posterior edge of the middle of the soft palate.

V

vaccination (văk-sĭ-nā′shŭn): inoculation with the virus of cowpox, or vaccma as a means of producing immunity against small pox.
vaccine (văk′sĭn; -sēn): any substance used for preventive inoculation.
vaccum (văk′ū-ûm): a space entirely devoid of matter; a space from which the air has been exhausted.
vagus (vā′gûs): pneumogastric nerve; tenth cranial nerve.
valence (vā′lĕns): the degree of combining power of an element or radical.
valve (vălv): a structure which temporarily closes a passage or orifice or permits flow in one direction only.
vapor (vā′pĕr): the gaseous state of a liquid or solid.
vaporization (vā-pĕr-ī-zā′shŭn): act or process of converting water into steam or a vapor.
varicose veins (văr′ĭ-cōs-vāns): swollen or knotted veins.
varicosis (văr-ĭ-kō′sĭs): a dilated or varicose state of a vein or veins.
vascular (văs′kû-lăr): supplied with small blood vessels; pertaining to a vessel for the conveyance of a fluid as blood or lymph.
vascularization (văs-kû-lăr-ī-zā′shŭn): the formation of new blood vessels in a part of the body.
vaseline (văs′ĕ́-lĭn; ēn): a trade name; petrolatum; a semi-solid greasy or oily mixture of hydrocarbons obtained from petroleum.
vaso-constrictor (văs-ṓ-kôn-strĭk′tĕr): a nerve which, when stimulated, causes narrowing of blood vessels.
vaso-dilator (văs-ṓ-dī-lā′tĕr): a nerve which, when stimulated, causes expansión of the blood vessels.
vegetable dyes (vĕj′ê-tă-b′l dīz): comprised of Egyptian henna, indigo, and camomile used as hair dyes or hair rinses.
vegetation (vĕj-ĕ́-tā′shŭn): morbid or fungus growths; of or pertaining to growths.
vehicle (vē′hĭ-k′l): a means of conveyance; a substance in which medicaments are carried into the deeper tissues.
vein; vena (vān; vē′nă): a blood vessel carrying blood toward the heart.
vena cava (kā′vă): one of the large veins which carry the blood to the right auricle of the heart.
venenata, dermatitis (vē-nĕn-ă′tă): skin inflammation produced by local action of irritating substances.
venenation (vĕn-ĕ́-nā′shŭn): the condition due to poisoning.

fāte, câre, ăm, finâl, ärm, ȧsk, sofă; ēve, ĕ́vent, ĕnd, recênt, evẽr; īce, ĭll; ōld, ŏ́bey, ôrb, ŏdd, cônnect, sŏft, fōod, fŏŏt; ūse, ûrn, ŭp, circûs

venereal (vḗ-nē′rḗ-âl): pertaining to a disease arising from illicit sexual indulgence with an infected person.

venter (věn′tẽr): belly; the abdomen.

ventilate (věn′tĭ-lāt): to renew the air in a place; to oxygenate the blood in the capillaries of the lungs.

ventral (věn′trâl): pertaining to the belly.

ventricle (věn′trĭ-k′l): a small cavity; particularly in the brain or heart.

vermin (vûr′mĭn): parasitic insects, as lice and bedbugs.

verruca (vě-roo′kă): a wart; a circumscribed hypertrophy of the papillae and epidermis.

verrucose; verrucous (věr′oo-kōs; -kûs): warty; presenting wart-like elevations.

vertebra (vûr-tê-bră); pl., **vertebrae** (brē): a bony segment of the spinal column.

vertebrate (vûr′tê-brāt): having a backbone or spinal column.

vertex (vûr′těks): the crown or top of the head.

vesicle (věs′ĭ-k′l): a small blister or sac; a small elevation on the skin.

vesicular (vḗ-sik′û-lăr): relating to or containing vesicles.

vessel (věs′l): tube or canal in which blood, lymph, or other fluid is contained and conveyed or circulated.

vibration (vī-brā′shŭn): shaking; a to and fro massage movement.

vibrator (vi′brā-tẽr): an electrically driven massage apparatus causing a swinging, shaking sensation on the body, producing stimulation.

vibrissae (vī-brĭs′à): stiff hairs in the nostrils.

vibroid (vī′broid): a vibratory movement in massage.

villus (vĭl′ŭs); pl., **villi** (-ī): minute finger-like processes covering the surface of the mucous membrane of the small intestine.

vinegar (vĭn′ḗ-gẽr): a sour liquid used as a condiment or as a preservative, formed by fermentation of dilute alcoholic liquids as wine, cider, ec.; it contains acetic acid; used as a rinse to remove soap curds from the hair.

violet-ray (vī′ō-lět rā): high-frequency; Tesla; an electric current of médium voltaje and médium amperage.

virgin hair (vûr′jĭn hâr): normal hair which has had no previous bleaching or dyeing treatments.

virulent (vĭr′oo-lênt): extremely poisonous; disease producing micro-organisms.

virus (vī′rûs): poison; the specific poison of an infectious disease.

viscera (vĭs′ẽr-ă): plural of viscus.

visceral (vĭs′ẽr-âl): pertaining to the internal organs; the heart, lungs, intestines, etc.

viscid (vĭs′ĭd): sticky or adhesive.

viscosity (vĭs-kŏs′ĭ-tē): the quality of being viscid so that a fluid flows with difficulty.

viscus (vĭs′kŭs): pl. **viscera** (vĭs′ẽr-ă): the internal organs, such as the heart, liver, intestine, etc.

vital (vī′tāl): relating to life.

vitality (vī-tāl′ĭ-tē): the principle of life; the state or quality of being vital; power of enduring or of continuing.

vitamin (vī′tâ-mĭn): one of a group of organic substances present in a very small quantity in natural foodstuffs, which are essential to normal metabolism, and the lack of which in the diet causes beriberi and other deficiency diseases.

vitiligo (vĭt-ĭ-lī′go): milky-white spots of the skin, common in Blacks.

vitriol, oil of (vĭt′rĭ-ŭl): a common name for sulphuric acid.

vocation (vô-kā′shŭn): regular employment; profession.

vogue (vōg): fashion; custom; style.

---

fāte, câre, ăm, finâl, ärm, ȧsk, sofȧ; ēve, ḗvent, ěnd, recênt, evẽr; īce, ĭll; ōld, ṓbey, ôrb, ŏdd, cônnect, sŏft, food, foot; ūse, ûrn, ŭp, circûs

vola (vō'lă): palm of the hand or the sole of the foot.
volatile (vŏl'ă-tĭl): easily evaporating; diffusing freely; not permanent.
volatilize (vōl'ă-tĭl-īz): to convert a solid or a liquid into vapor.
vitiation (vĭsh-ē-ā'shŭn): act of spoiling or injuring the substance or quality of.
volt (vōlt): the fractional unit of electromotive force.
voltage (vōl'tāj): electrical potential difference expressed in volts.
volume (vŏl'ūm): space occupied, as measured in cubic units.
voluntary (vŏl'ûn-tā-rē): under the control of the will.
vomer (vō'mẽr): the thin plate of bone between the nostrils.
vulgaris, acne (vŭl-gā'rĭs): common principle.
vulnerable (vŭl'nẽr-ă-b'l): capable of receiving injury.

W

wall plate (wôl plāt): an apparatus equipped with indicators and controlling devices to produce various currents.
wall socket (sŏk'ĕt): a wall receptacle into which may be fitted the plug of an electrical appliance.
walnut stain (wôl'nŭt stān): one of the wood extracts used as a hair coloring.
wart (wôrt): verruca; a circumscribed hypertrophy of the papillae of the corium, usually of the hand, covered by thickened epidermis.
water (wŏ'tẽr): a compound of oxygen and hydrogen.
water softener (sŏf'nẽr): certain chemicals, such as the carbonate or phosphate of sodium, used to soften hard water to permit the lathering of soap.
watt (wŏt): the electrical unit of energy.
wattage (wŏt'âj): amount of electric power expressed in watts.
wave, cold (wāv kōld): a method of permanent waving requiring the use of certain chemicals rather than heat.
wave, croquignole marcel (wāv, krō'kwĭ-nōl mär-sĕl'): a wave produced with the marcel iron, using the croquignole winding.
wave, finger (fĭn'gẽr): arranging waves into the hair, that has been wet, with fingers and comb.
wave, hair (hâr): the art of putting a wave into the hair.
wave, marcel (mär-sĕl): resembles a perfect natural wave, produced by means of heated irons.
wave, permanent (pûr'mâ-nĕnt): a wave given to the hair which is of permanent duration.
wave, push (poosh): a wave given by pushing waved hair into place.
wave, water (wô'tẽr): arranging the waves into the hair, that has been wet, with fingers and comb, and holding in place with water waving combs until dry.
weft (wĕft): an artificial section of woven hair used for practice work or as a substitute for natural hair.
weight control (wāt kŏn-trōl'): the maintenance of normal body weight by means of proper diet and exercise.
wen (wĕn): a sebaceous cyst, usually on the scalp.
wet winding (wĕt wīnd'ĭng): pertaining to permanent waving, winding the hair that has been saturated with a permanent waving solution on the permanent wave rod.
wheal (whēl): a raised ridge on the skin, usually caused by a blow, a bite of an insect, urticarial, or sting of a nettle.

fāte, câre, ăm, finâl, ärm, åsk, sofå; ēve, évent, ĕnd, recênt, evẽr; īce, ĭll; ōld, óbey, ôrb, ŏdd, cônnect, sŏft, food, foot; ūse, ûrn, ŭp, circŭs

white corpuscle (whīt kôr'pŭs-'l): leucocytes; white blood cell; cells in the blood whose function is to destroy disease germs.
whitehead (whīt'hĕd): milium.
whorl (whûrl; whôrl): a spiral turn, in general; hence a hair whorl or cowlick, a spiral turn causing a tuft of hair which goes contrary to the usual growth of the hair.
wig (wĭg): an artificial covering for the head, consisting of hair interwoven or united by a kind of network.
winding, croquignole (wīnd'ĭng krō'kwĭ-nōl): winding the hair from the hair ends towards the scalp.
winding, helical or spiral (hĕl'ĭ-kâl or spī'râl): winding the hair from the scalp to the ends.
windpipe (wĭnd'pīp): trachea.
witch hazel (wĭch hā'z'l): after shaving lotion; an extract of the bark of the hamamelis shrub, also widely used as a remedy for bruises, sprains, and other similar ailments.
wool crepe (wōol crâp): a substance used to fasten hair when winding in permanent waving.
wrapper (răp'ēr): that in which anything is enclosed or wrapped, thus in permanent waving, the pad that covers the curl during the steaming period; that in which the curl on the rod is wrapped.
wringing (rĭng'ĭng): a massage movement in which the flesh is twisted firmly against the bones in opposite directions.
wrinkle (rĭnk"l): a small ridge or a furrow.
wrist electrode (rĭst é-lĕk'trōd): an electrode connected to the wrist.

X

xanthoma (zăn-thō'mă): a skin disease characterized by the presence of yellow nodules or slightly raised plates in the skin, especially of the eyelids.
x-ray (ĕks'rā): the Roentgen rays; these rays were discovered by the German physicist Wilhelm Roentgen and were called x-rays by him.

Z

zinc (zĭnk): a white crystalline metallic element.
zinc sulphate (sŭl'fāt): a salt often employed as an astringent, both in lotios and creams.
zinc sulphocarbonate (zĭnk sŭl-fô-kär'bôn-āt): a fine white powder having the odor of carbolic acid used as an antiseptic and astringent in deodorant preparations.
zygoma (zī-gō'mă): a bone of the skull which extends along the front or side of the face, below the eye; the malar or cheek bone.
zygomatic (zī-gő-măt'ĭk): pertaining to the zygoma; pertaining to the malar or cheek bone.
zygomaticus (zī-gő-măt'ĭ-kûs): a muscle that draws the upper lip upward and outward.

---

fāte, câre, ăm, finâl, ärm, ȧsk, sofă; ēve, évent, ĕnd, recênt, evẽr; īce, ĭll; ōld, ŏbey, ôrb, ŏdd, cônnect, sŏft, fōod, fŏot; ūse, ûrn, ŭp, circŭs

www.ingramcontent.com/pod-product-compliance
Lightning Source LLC
Chambersburg PA
CBHW081814300426
44116CB00014B/2347